D1714667

AFRICAN HISTORICAL DICTIONARIES

Edited by Jon Woronoff

Historical Dictionary
of
SOMALIA

by

Margaret Castagno

African Historical Dictionaries, No. 6

The Scarecrow Press, Inc.

Metuchen, N.J.   1975

Library of Congress Cataloging in Publication Data

Castagno, Margaret, 1922-
  Historical dictionary of Somalia.

  (African historical dictionaries ; no. 6)
  Bibliography: p.
  1. Somalia--History--Dictionaries. I. Title.
II. Series.
DT401.C3   967'.73'003   75-25681
ISBN 0-8108-0830-7

To
the memory of
Alphonso A. Castagno

CONTENTS

EDITOR'S FOREWORD

There are many "gateways" to Africa, yet, judging by the consideration and expense lavished on it, Somalia would seem to be one of the most important. When doubled as a "gateway" to the Near East, its significance can hardly be exaggerated. This has been shown by the political concern and economic assistance of countries as varied as Italy and Great Britain (the former colonial rulers), the United States, and also the Soviet Union and the People's Republic of China. Indeed, with its relatively small and semi-arid territory and a modest-sized population, Somalia has perhaps received more international economic and technical assistance per capita than most developing countries. Its attraction politically for both East and West, and more recently for the Arab world, probably ranks equally high.

Still, we really know very little about this country. Even while this dictionary on Somalia was being written, Somali students were being sent to the countryside by the government to teach the population and undertake Somalia's first complete census. Thus--as in many developing countries of the world--we do not know with any great certainty how many Somalis there are in the Republic, or exactly where they live, or, with the statistical precision desirable for administrative and development purposes, their occupations and income. This is enough to show the importance of a book that gathers together much of the existing information and integrates it in such a readable fashion. It is also most welcome that Mrs. Castagno should have gone into the very rich cultural and social life of the Somali groups, as well as the intricate relations within this otherwise quite unified people. Finally, like the Somalis themselves, she has not forgotten to tell us about parts of the ethnic family living outside the frontiers of the present state.

If we glance at the list of works on Somalia in the excellent bibliography at the end of this volume, we can see that hundreds of authors and research workers from many countries have devoted their efforts to studying various aspects of Somali history. One of the leading American writers on Somalia was Dr. Alphonso A. Castagno, who was, from 1965 until his death in 1973, Director of the African Studies Center at Boston University. Professor Castagno spent some eighteen months in Somalia during 1957-1958 and made numerous shorter visits to the country--most recently in 1971 when he had the unique opportunity of interviewing the President of Somalia's Supreme Revolutionary Council, General Mohamed Siad Barre. Dr. Castagno's Somalia, published by International Conciliation in 1959, and his many articles on Somalia's political development, educational system, strategic situation, and boundary problems helped to make the country better known in the United States.

Originally, it had been expected that Dr. Castagno would co-author this dictionary with Mrs. Castagno. Regretably, not long after beginning work on the volume, he passed away. The bulk of the material found in the dictionary was therefore compiled by Mrs. Castagno. Having lived in Somalia in 1957-1958 as well and having worked as a freelance writer, editor, and book reviewer over the intervening years, she was well equipped to carry on the task of completing the book. It is due to her efforts that Scarecrow Press can publish the dictionary, which is an important contribution to those who want to know more about the history of the Horn of Africa and the Somali people.

Jon Woronoff
Series Editor

ACKNOWLEDGMENTS AND NOTES

In compiling this Historical Dictionary of Somalia, I have been fortunate to have the advice and encouragement of a number of friends. Three who are well known for their scholarly works on Somalia must be thanked by name: Dr. I. M. Lewis of the University of London, Department of Anthropology; Dr. Lee V. Cassanelli of the University of Pennsylvania, Department of History; and Dr. B. W. Andrzejewski of the University of London, School of Oriental and African Studies. Many others, including Somalis working or studying in the United States and Great Britain, have discussed various aspects of the book with me, to my great advantage, and I thank them all. Finally, I must add that the wit and good humor of my son Arthur Castagno contributed more to the completion of this book than he thinks.

In the literature, Somali words are spelled in various ways, most often based on Italian, French, or English phonetics. I have selected an English phonetic spelling, often having to choose from among several variations, and I have indicated plurals simply by adding an s. I had hoped to employ the spelling used in the official Somali-English dictionary, but was unable to obtain a copy of the dictionary.

The map has been especially prepared for this book; it includes most of the places mentioned in the Dictionary. Much to my regret, it does not show the revised regional boundaries. I do not believe that the Somali government has yet published a map showing these boundaries. The best information that I can provide on this point is included in the entry, Regional and Local Government.

Margaret Castagno

December 1, 1974

ACRONYMS

AFIS	Amministrazione fiduciaria italiana della Somalia (Italian Trusteeship Administration)
AID	(United States) Agency for International Development
BMA	British Military Administration
DC	District Commissioner
EEC	European Economic Community
GSL	Greater Somalia League
HDMS	Hizbia Dastur Mustaquil Somali (Somali Independent Constitutional Party)
IBEAC	Imperial British East Africa Company
NFD	Northern Frontier District
NUF	National United Front
OAU	Organization of African Unity
PBU	Patriotic Benefit Union
SAIS	Società Agricola Italo-Somala
SDU	Somali Democratic Union
SIPA	Somali Institute of Public Administration
SNAI	Società nazionale per l'agricoltura e l'industria (National Company for Agriculture and Industry)
SNL	Somali(land) National League
SNP	Somali National Police
SONNA	Somali National News Agency
SRC	Supreme Revolutionary Council
SYL	Somali Youth League
UN	United Nations

UNESCO   United Nations Educational, Scientific and Cultural
                Organization

USP   United Somali Party

INTRODUCTION

On July 1, 1960, two newly independent states in the Horn of Africa united to form the Somali Republic. One was the former British protectorate of Somaliland. The other was former Italian Somaliland, which had been a UN trusteeship territory since 1950. Immediately after unification, an already lively irredentist movement in three areas contiguous with the Republic took on new momentum. These were the Haud and Ogaden regions on the eastern periphery of Ethiopia (c. one million Somalis), the present North-Eastern Region of Kenya (c. 250,000 Somalis), and French Somaliland (c. 40,000 Somalis).

The Somalis who live outside the Republic are closely related to those of the Republic, and it is inevitable that they be mentioned in many entries in the Dictionary. Not only are all Somalis related ethnically, but they speak the same language, practice the same religion, follow the same occupations, and have the same political and cultural heritage. These "Somali characteristics" differentiate the Somalis of Ethiopia, Kenya, and the French Territory from other inhabitants of those lands.

For seven years after independence, the irredentist movement, supported by a strong pan-Somali policy on the part of the political parties and the governments of the Republic, dominated the international scene in the Horn of Africa. The movement in Ethiopia and the North-Eastern Region of Kenya led to sporadic armed skirmishes, a number of deaths, and much unrest. A British Commission of Inquiry in 1962-1963 documented the strength of the movement in North-Eastern Kenya. The political activities preceding the 1958 and 1967 referenda on the status of French Somaliland pointed up the separatist and pan-Somali feelings of the Somalis in that territory.

The pan-Somali issue lost some of its intensity both domestically and internationally after 1967 when Prime Minister Mohamed Haji Ibrahim Egal began to stress the need to give first priority to the Republic's internal economic and social development.   But while attention had been focused on the pan-Somali issue, a large and unwieldy government bureaucracy grew up.   New words were invented to describe corruption, nepotism, and injustice.   Musug-masug covered all kinds of political hanky-panky, wheeling and dealing, intrigue, and graft.   Afminshar (literally, "saw-mouth") was used to describe individuals who spread rumors, who badmouthed, abused, or maligned others to attain their own ends. Today afminsharism against the government is a crime.

On October 15, 1969, the President of the Republic, Abdirashid Ali Shermarke, was assassinated by a member of his bodyguard.   Apparently the assassination was an individual act, not part of a plot or conspiracy.   Then, on October 21, when it became clear that the chief candidate for the presidency was a man who would merely continue the old "politics as usual," the Army, under the leadership of General Mohamed Siad Barre, took over in a bloodless coup.   Since the "October Revolution," the government has been led by a Supreme Revolutionary Council, with General Mohamed Siad Barre as President of the Somali Democratic Republic.

The Land and Its Influence

The Republic covers about 246,000 square miles.   This makes it slightly smaller than the state of Texas and, with its three to four million inhabitants, less than half as populous as Texas.   The Republic has a long coastline, about 2,000 miles, fronting on the Gulf of Aden and the Indian Ocean.   It has no great natural harbors, but the port facilities at Berbera in the north and Kismayu in the south were expanded and modernized in the late 1960s with Soviet and American aid.

Much of the land is semidesert, with a vegetation of thornbush, acacia, and euphorbia.   In many such areas, grass springs up during the rainy seasons and provides grazing for large herds of camels, cattle, sheep, and goats.   In other areas, primarily in the flood plains and irrigated areas near the Juba and Shebelle Rivers in the Southern (former Italian) Region, millet, sesame, bananas, sugarcane, and other crops are grown.   Rainfall is light and irregular, but when it is good, two crops can be planted and harvested in a year. Scant rainfall and the absence of rivers and lakes in a large portion of the country make nomadic or seminomadic pastoralism the natural way of life for most Somalis. About 60 per cent of the population are pastoralists, an estimated 15 to 20 per cent engage in sedentary agriculture and the remainder are town dwellers.

The nomads, with their herds of single-humped camels and their flocks of sheep and goats, are constantly on the move in search of pasturage and water for their animals. They travel in small groups (rers, or extended families), and in the course of a year cover hundreds of miles. Each year during the gu, or heavy rain season, thousands of Somalis from the Republic cross over into Ethiopia to reach their traditional grazing lands in the Haud and Ogaden. They then return to their home wells and lands in the Republic during the dair, or light rain season. The movements of the pastoralists and many of their social activities are guided by weather lore experts who study the stars, the sun and moon, the winds, and other natural phenomena to predict the most propitious time for setting out on trek and the best route to follow. Cattle herders, primarily in the central section of the Southern Region, are seminomadic; their base of operations is usually their home village, centered on a well, and their movements are more restricted than those of the camel herders.

Although the Somali landscape is mostly flat, there are high mountainous areas in the Northern (former British) Region, with peaks reaching almost 8,000 feet. This maritime range, which includes the Ogo and Golis Mountains, lies behind a coastal plain, known as the Guban. The mountains are dissected by dry river beds which become fast-running streams for a short while after a heavy rain. The weather is hot throughout the year, except for brief cold spells in some of the very mountainous areas. Along the coast, the humidity is high. The temperature varies somewhat according to the direction of the monsoons, which determine the seasons.

Somalia is subject to both drought and flood. The most recent drought was in 1971. The terrible drought that struck many sub-Saharan African nations in the 1960s and 1970s had not by 1974 seriously affected Somalia. It is reported, however, that one severe dry year would place the nation in the "hunger belt."

The People: Division and Homogeneity

The typical Somali is rather tall and thin, with a rather long head and a brown complexion. But on any street in Mogadishu, the capital, a great variety of physical types may be seen. Often apparent in facial features are signs of intermixture with Arab or Negroid peoples.

Although distinctions and allegiances based on clan-group affiliation and ethnic differences are now illegal in the Republic, such distinctions are important in Somali history. The chief division of the Somali people is between the Samaal and the Saab. The Samaal clan families--the Darod, Hawiye, Isaaq, and Dir--inhabit the areas north of the Shebelle River and south of the Juba. Largely pastoralists, they constitute the great majority of the population. The Saab clan families --the Digil and Rahanweyn--are mostly agriculturalists; they occupy the riverine and interriverine areas. The Saab have intermarried with Negroid, and perhaps Galla, peoples, who apparently occupied the fertile river areas before the Somalis came. The Samaal have traditionally regarded the Saab as less pure racially, and they regard the Saab dialect as a lower form of the Somali language. Also, the Saab engage in agriculture, an occupation which the pastoral Samaal have long regarded as menial.

Intergroup warfare and feuding among clan families and subgroups--some organized as sultanates or federations-- have also been prominent in Somali history. Disputes over pasturage and water rights were the chief causes of conflict, and the disputes were usually won by the group with the greatest number of fighting men. Feuds were often long-lasting, however, and the arena of modern national politics provided a new setting in which old clan rivalries and distinctions could be carried on. Political parties sometimes broke up because some members felt they were being dominated by others who belonged to a different clan family. Government departments were sometimes said to be under the control of certain clan groups which discriminated against persons from other groups.

In addition to the Somali, small groups of people known as sab live in the Republic. In the past, they engaged in blacksmith and leather work and other handicrafts. The sab, along with small remnants of earlier Negroid populations and the descendants of former slaves, have traditionally been considered distinct racial groups. Gradually these minorities are being accepted as full Somali citizens. Today most of

them speak Somali and practice Islam, though a few continue
to speak their own language or dialect.

Despite these centrifugal aspects of Somali society, the
homogeneity of the Somalis and the similarity of the traditional cultural and political institutions found in the various groups
is remarkable. This homogeneity is attributed partly to the
common ancestry of the Saab and Samaal and partly to the
effects of Islam. The Shari'a, the body of Islamic law, was
widely accepted in Somalia long before the European colonial
powers arrived in the area. Religious leaders have long
preached the need for unity and brotherhood and have practiced this policy to a large extent in the formation of their
religious settlements and farming communities. Today, more
than 95 per cent of the inhabitants of the Somali peninsula
are Muslim.

Language and Literacy

For a people with a literacy rate estimated at about
five per cent in 1970, Somalis are notable linguists. All
speak Somali, with some dialect differences, and all appre-
ciate the highly complex form and vocabulary of classical
Somali poetry. As Muslims, all know at least some Arabic.
Further, for reasons of employment, education, or simple
communication with colonial officials, many Somalis learned
English, Italian, or French. In addition, many who live in
the coastal trading towns and some of the small groups of
non-Somali speak Swahili.

This oral linguistic wealth reflects the history of the
Republic, and partially explains the low literacy rate. Since
Somali was unwritten (until 1972), and colonial educational
institutions used English, Italian, or French, a Somali child
normally had to learn three languages before he could begin
to attain literacy: his native Somali; Arabic, the language of
his religion; and a European language. Other explanations of
the low rate of literacy come to mind, however.

One is nomadism, which involves the constant movement
of the majority of school-age children and their active employment in the economy as herders. A second explanation is interclan antagonism and feuding. Although several scripts for
the Somali language (based on Somali, Arabic, or Latin characters) were devised by Somalis over the years, none was
acceptable nationwide. Some were alleged to assert the su-

periority of the clan of the script's deviser over the other
clans.   Others were considered technically or linguistically
inadequate.

A third explanation lies in the religious conservatism
of many Somali traditional leaders who opposed the use of
any written language except Arabic, the language of the Holy
Koran.   Unfortunately, Arabic was a language foreign to all
the colonial powers which might be assumed to have been
responsible for developing an educational system during the
late 19th century and the first half of the 20th.   A final explanation is the minimal interest in educational development
taken by the colonial powers.   This neglect was reinforced
by the Somalis' disdain of Christian teachers, whether they
were associated with missionary activities or not.

As the nationalistic fervor grew during the late 1940s
and as independence became imminent in the 1950s, Somali
recognition of the problems of widespread illiteracy and the
lack of a written Somali language grew.   Although none of the
elected governments from 1956 to 1969 felt strong enough politically to choose one of the existing scripts as the official
one of the state and to impose its choice on the whole nation,
the Supreme Revolutionary Council which came to power in
the military coup of October 1969 has declared a Somali script
based on Latin characters as the nation's only official language
This official script, introduced in 1972, has largely replaced
the use of English, Italian, and Arabic in newspapers and
government documents.   The publication of textbooks in Somali is in progress, and the preparation of a basic Somali-
English dictionary has been completed.

These developments, along with the increasing numbers of Somali teachers in the school system, may raise the
literacy rate dramatically.   In 1974, in a move to improve
literacy, the government announced that all high schools
would close for one year so that their students could go out
into the interior and participate in an expanded educational
program (and conduct a national census).

A second reason for applauding the government's adoption of a Somali script is the impetus it will give to the preservation of folk literature and the recording of traditional oral
history.

Poverty and Development

Economically, Somalia is severely handicapped by a lack of mineral resources, by the semidesert nature of much of its land, and by the traditional acceptance of subsistence living by a majority of the people. Per capita income is estimated to be not more than $55 per annum.

There has been active trading with the countries of Arabia and the Persian Gulf for many centuries, but this trade did not at any time lead to a general prosperity affecting the masses of the people. Nor did it lead to the development of any large-scale economic activities. A possible exception is the increase in agricultural exports from the river areas during the second half of the 19th century. With the importation of slaves during that period, new land was opened to farming, and agriculture became highly profitable for some of the Somali clans, such as the Bimal and Geledi. But this development was interrupted by the advent of the Europeans, who halted the slave trade and eventually abolished slavery.

Mineral resources, such as uranium, iron ore, bauxite, and gypsum, are said to exist in Somalia, but they have not been fully explored and are not being exploited. Explorations for oil, though intensive, have yielded no positive findings.

The nation's economy is supported by large inpourings of foreign assistance. The Supreme Revolutionary Council has estimated this aid at $460 million from 1960 to 1969. Much aid has come, and continues to come, from the United Nations. Before the 1969 coup, foreign aid in large amounts came chiefly from Western sources, the United States, Great Britain, and Italy, especially, although the Soviet Union underwrote the development of the Somali National Army. Today most of the foreign aid comes from international agencies and Eastern-bloc countries. Italy, as the Administering Authority of the Trust Territory (the Southern Region) and as the former colonial power in that part of the Republic, contributed significantly in both money and manpower during the 1950-1960 decade, and continued its support to the independent nation.

The economic development of the Republic is certain to be slow. It is seldom discussed in very optimistic terms, but many improvements have been recorded in the last two decades. The projected development budget for 1974-1978 is

about $550 million (So. Sh. 3,863,357,000). It allocates 40
per cent to economic development (animal husbandry, agriculture, and minerals); 11 per cent to health, education,
housing, and public works; 19 per cent to industry and electricity; 25 per cent to transportation and communications;
five per cent to population and livestock censuses.

Although Somalia is regarded as a poor nation, it is
not overpopulated. The only areas of high unemployment are
the larger government centers. In a country with few large
cities, the city is a magnet for persons tired of the hard life
of the nomadic interior and the agricultural village as well as
for persons with ambition and nationalistic sentiments. It is
primarily in the Somali city that the concrete results of the
nationalist movement are visible. Not only does unemployment grow as young people migrate to the cities, but also
political awareness and discontent. The Supreme Revolutionary Council has used self-help schemes and crash programs
to reduce urban unemployment and to encourage the young
people who crowded into the cities to return to the rural
areas.

Historical Overview

Somali colonial history dates back to the late 1880s,
and includes the names of many men and clan groups who
resisted the colonial powers overtly or simply by going their
own way and being uncooperative. Some of these, such as
the sultans of the Mijerteyn and of Obbia, succeeded in maintaining their own governments until the mid-1920s. In effect their areas were under strict European control for only
25 years, a brief period in Somali history.

One leader who developed a great following, Sayyid
Mohamed Abdullah Hassan, led a 20-year jihad, or holy war,
against the Europeans and Ethiopians--from 1899 to 1920.
He was finally defeated, but not captured, by British air at-
tacks. Sayyid Mohamed Abdullah Hassan is today recognized
as an early nationalist. With his Dervishes, he interrupted
British control of the Northern Region, influenced Italian
policy in the Southern Region, resisted Ethiopian activities
which supported the British, and waged open warfare against
Somali clans who were neutral or friendly to the colonial
powers. Sayyid Mohamed Abdullah Hassan was not only a
political leader, but a learned poet and religious leader of
the Salihiya Sufi order. His aims were to oust the foreign

"infidels" and to purify Somali Islam and unite the Somalis.
Only then, he thought, could Somalis live in peace and brotherhood, without the interclan warfare that was endemic to the
traditional political system.   The two aims--political and re-
ligious--were interrelated, farsighted, and admired by later
generations of Somali nationalists.   Often, the Sayyid's movement seems to have been very costly, however, when one
reads of the terror his activities brought to many Somali
clans and of the number of Somali lives lost in the jihad,
along with some European lives.

        Somali history is much more than the 70-year period
of colonial intrusion and neglect and Somali resistance.   Our
knowledge of the precolonial period is not well documented;
it is based largely on oral tradition and on scattered written
sources that mention the Horn of Africa only in passing.
Many of the documents were written by foreign traders and
mariners or by geographers who either traveled with the
mariners or picked up their information from them.   The
Periplus of the Erythraean Sea, written about 60 A.D. by a
Greek mariner, records that the southern ports of Somalia
were controlled by Arabs and identifies Cape Guardafui as the
Cape of Spices.   The rise of Islam in the 7th century and the
migration of Arab Muslims to the African continent are directly related to the development of the Somali people as they
are known today.

        Al Yaqubi, an Arab geographer of the 9th century,
mentions the ports of Zeila and Mogadishu, their culture and
religious institutions, in The Book of the Cities.   A Moroccan
historian, Ibn Battuta, visited a number of Somali ports in
the mid-1300s and describes them as flourishing centers of
trade.

        Chinese contacts with the Somali coast are recorded
in Tuan Cheng-shih's Yu-Yang-tsa-tsu, written during the
9th century, and in the journals of Cheng-Ho, who made
three visits to the Somali coast in the early 1400s.   Records
of Portuguese activities in the area date back to the late
1400s.

        The Book of the Zengi, a medieval Arabic compila-
tion, describes the Negroid (Zengi) inhabitants of the Somali
river areas and the "Berberi," presumably the Galla and
Somali, of the more northern portions of Somalia.   Inscriptions on tombstones and mosques in Mogadishu confirm some
of the data found in this book.   Shihab ad-Din, a Muslim

chronicler of the 16th century, recorded the Adal-Ethiopian
war led by the Adal imam Ahmad Guray.

From oral sources, genealogical accounts, and linguistic analysis, some of the more distant history of the Somalis
has been reconstructed. All these tell something about the
confrontations between various groups as the Somali clan
families developed and pursued their southwestward migrations.
Legends of clan-family origins and of wise and crafty leaders,
such as Arawelo and Wiil Waal, give further insight into the
Somali past.

But these sources tell us little about the effects of the
confrontations between groups on the evolution of Somali institutions and customs. We know, for example, that by the
19th century, the chief political forum among all the Somali
groups was the shir, an open assembly of all the adult males
of a clan or lineage formally associated by a heer contract.
In the shir every man had an equal right to speak on the
matters being discussed, and after long hours or days of dis-
cussion and deliberation, the group would reach a unanimous
decision on a course of action. The shir seems to have been
a highly democratic institution. But conjectures about how and
when the institution developed lead only to further tantalizing
speculations.

Some possible sources of early Somali history have
been left unexplored for the most part. Little archaeological
work has been carried out, and many tentative explorations
have not been followed up. The cave paintings and inscriptions in the Northern Region, the thousands of pre-Islamic
tombs, the ruined towns, the stone tools and objects found
on the surface, the coins found in various places--all these
cry out for further study. Nor has there been any sustained
attempt to determine the origin and date of introduction of
various domesticated food crops and animals.

Oral history is transmitted in the stories told by old
men and women, in the repetition of poems, and in genealogical accounts. In the history of Somalia, the names of
great poets seem to be more numerous than the names of
great political leaders. Often political leaders were also
poets and every clan had poets who composed works to com-
memorate important battles and other events. The poems
were commemorative, but they were also composed to instruct the young in the clan's history and customs. No doubt
many of these historical poems have been and will be lost

because the demands of modern nationalism require that old clan enmities and proud victories be submerged. The same is true of the genealogies.

An individual's genealogy aligns him with certain groups and makes him the "traditional enemy" of other groups. Almost all Somalis use three names--their own, their father's, and their grandfather's---and it is said that they can trace back their ancestry ten, twenty, or sometimes thirty generations. When two Somalis meet, they can often trace their genealogy to a common ancestor and to a particular clan or subclan of origin. Modern nationalism demands that these clan-group distinctions be forgotten, and so another source of historical data is drying up. Fortunately, a number of early Somali writers published genealogical accounts of their clan groups.

Because of the gaps in our knowledge of the Somali people and their past, much of what is described in the Dictionary as "traditional" refers only to the customs and practices reported by Europeans who visited the area after the mid-1880s. We cannot assume that these practices were ancient and unchanging, but only that they evolved from the--possibly quite different--customs and practices of preceding ages.

The traditions reported by European writers, however, show a definite coherence in Somali development in the various regions and among the various groups. Colonialism, involving the imposition of different legal systems and reflecting the different approaches to colonial undertakings of the colonial powers, led to some disparities in the various Somali regions. But colonialism did not destroy the basic coherence that was there when the Europeans arrived. The European impact did not prevent the former British and Italian colonies from uniting successfully and integrating their pre-independence systems of government. More drastic changes than those brought about by the colonial powers are perhaps seen in the acts of post-independence governments, such as the termination of the arifa, or patron-client, system; the abolition of blood compensation and collective responsibility for certain crimes; and the elimination of chiefly titles and privileges.

Above and beyond the impact of colonialism stand the traditional Somali culture and the influence of Islam, two elements which bind all Somalis together and unite them as one people.

CHRONOLOGY

Date	Event
1st century	Earliest known written record of the Somali area in PERIPLUS OF THE ERYTHRAEAN SEA.
8th-10th centuries	First legendary ARAB ancestors of Somali CLAN FAMILIES migrate to the Somali region and introduce ISLAM.
	Founding of coastal cities, MOGADISHU, BERBERA, BRAVA, MERCA, by Arabian or Persian immigrants.
	ADAL sultanate founded, with center at ZEILA.
	Trade between interior and coast.
11th-14th centuries	Somalis begin southern and westward MIGRATIONS; Islamization of the interior continues; and Somali migrants begin ouster or conquest of GALLA and BANTU populations.
15th-16th centuries	Adal wars with ETHIOPIA; AHMAD GURAY war with Ethiopia.
	Mariners and traders from CHINA visit Somali ports in 1416, 1421.
	Intensification of Somali migrations to south and west.
	AJURAN sultanate established in middle and lower Shebelle valley.
	Ships from PORTUGAL bombard Mogadishu (1499), sack Berbera (1518), place Brava under

Portuguese protection (1503 until mid-1600s).

17th-18th centuries	Somalis occupy all of the area east of the JUBA River; migrations continue southwest.

Portuguese evicted. BENADIR COAST comes under nominal control of the Sultan of OMAN by the end of the 18th century.

19th century   Introduction of Sufi orders: AHMADIYA, DAN-DARAWIYA, QADIRIYA, RIFAIYA, SALIHIYA.

1819   Founding of religious community at BARDERA.

1820s   GREAT BRITAIN has first contacts with NORTH-ERN REGION.

1827   British sign trade treaty with Somalis at Ber-bera.

1840s   Benadir Coast comes under control of ZANZI-BAR.

Bardera wars begin.

1855   RICHARD F. BURTON'S camp attacked.   So-malis sign further treaties with Britain.

1859   Sultan of Obock signs treaty with FRANCE.

1880s   Trade between Europe, Arabia, America grows in SOUTHERN REGION.

Ethiopia announces claims to Somali territory.

1888   BRITISH EAST AFRICA COMPANY acquires leases to southern coast from Zanzibar.

1889   Britain sublets Benadir Coast north of Juba River to ITALY.

Italy signs treaties of protection with sultans of MIJERTEYN and OBBIA.

1893-1896   FILONARDI COMPANY administers Italian bases in Southern Region.

1896   Italian defeat by Ethiopia at ADOWA.

1897   Treaties between Ethiopia and France, Britain,
              and Italy regarding Somali areas.

1898-1905   BENADIR COMPANY administers Italian bases
              in Southern Region.

1899   Jihad of SAYYID MOHAMED ABDULLAH HAS-
              SAN begins.

20th century

1904   Italy establishes protectorate for Sayyid Mo-
              hamed Abdullah Hassan in NUGAL VALLEY.

1905   Italian government purchases Benadir Coast
              (Warsheikh to Brava) from Sultan of Zanzibar.

1920   Defeat of Sayyid Mohamed Abdullah Hassan by
              British and extension of British control in
              Northern Region.

1920s   Italians initiate plantation agriculture in South-
              ern Region.

1925   Italy establishes direct control over sultanate
              of Obbia.

              Britain cedes JUBALAND to Italy.

1927   Italy establishes direct control over sultanate
              of Mijerteyn.

1934   WAL WAL incident.

1935-1936   Italo-Ethiopian war.

1941   BRITISH MILITARY ADMINISTRATION takes
              over after defeat of Italy in Somalia, British
              protectorate, and Ethiopia.

1940s   Formation of political parties and growth of
              nationalism (SOMALI YOUTH LEAGUE, HIZBIA
              DIGIL-MIRIFLE SOMALI).

1948   FOUR-POWER COMMISSION visits Somalia in

January.   Question of disposition of Italian Somaliland referred to United Nations in September.

1950   TRUSTEESHIP ADMINISTRATION inaugurated in Southern Region in April.

1954   British and Ethiopians implement treaty of 1897 re boundary of Northern Region.

Municipal elections in Trust Territory.

1956   First general elections (LEGISLATIVE ASSEMBLY) in Trust Territory.   ADEN ABDULLA OSMAN (President); ABDULLAHI ISSA (Prime Minister).

1957   Establishment of LEGISLATIVE COUNCIL in Northern Region.

1958   First general elections in Northern Region (LEGISLATIVE COUNCIL).

1960   Elections in Northern Region (LEGISLATIVE ASSEMBLY).   MOHAMED HAJI IBRAHIM EGAL (Leader of Government Business).

Independence of SOMALILAND (former British Protectorate), June 26.

Independence of Trust Territory; unification of Northern and Southern Regions to form the Somali Republic, July 1.   Aden Abdulla Osman (President); ABDIRASHID ALI SHERMARKE (Prime Minister); Abdullahi Issa (Minister of Foreign Affairs); ABDIRAZAK HAJI HUSSEIN (Minister of Interior); Mohamed Haji Ibrahim Egal (Minister of Defense).

1961   Referendum on CONSTITUTION, June.

Short-lived and abortive coup in Northern Region, December.

1963-1964   IRREDENTISM leads to armed clashes with Ethiopia and guerrilla warfare in northern KENYA and in Ethiopian OGADEN.

1964   National elections.   Aden Abdulla Osman (Presi-
                dent); Abdirazak Haji Hussein (Prime Minister).

1967   Change of government.   Abdirashid Ali Sher-
                marke (President); Mohamed Haji Ibrahim Egal
                (Prime Minister).

1969   National elections, March.   Abdirashid Ali
                Shermarke (President); Mohamed Haji Ibrahim
                Egal (Prime Minister).

                Assassination of President Abdirashid Ali
                Shermarke, October 15.

                Army coup d'état, October 21.   Major General
                MOHAMED SIAD BARRE, leader of the mili-
                tary government (SUPREME REVOLUTIONARY
                COUNCIL), assumes title of President and
                changes name of the country to SOMALI DEMO-
                CRATIC REPUBLIC.

1970   SCIENTIFIC SOCIALISM proclaimed as the Re-
                public's guiding ideology.

1972   Supreme Revolutionary Council adopts a script
                with Latin characters as the sole national
                LANGUAGE.

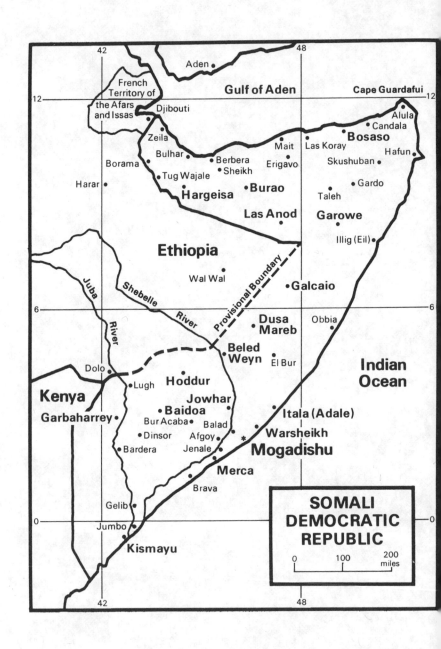

THE DICTIONARY

ABBAAN. 1) The patron in a host-client relationship or a patron-sab relationship, both of which were abolished in 1960. See ARIFA; SHEEGAT.
2) The protector of caravans or travelers as they passed through hostile areas. See CARAVAN TRADE.

ABDARAHMAN ALI ISE. Sultan of the Bimal, who in the 1930s was made a Cavaliere Ufficiale by the Italian government. In the late 1800s and early 1900s, the Bimal were extremely anti-Italian.

ABDILLAHI KARSHE. The most acclaimed modern Somali musician, a singer and composer of patriotic and popular songs. He was a civil servant in the British protectorate and a singer on Radio Hargeisa. In 1954, he formed a drama company which was soon broken up by the government because of its call for a violent response to the Anglo-Ethiopian Agreement of 1954. He is best known for his composition commemorating Patrice Lumumba, the Congolese leader who was killed in 1961.

ABDILLAHI MUUSE. A poet, born in the late 19th century, known as a wise and peace-loving man; some of his sayings have become proverbs. It is said that he could recite the entire Koran from memory.

ABDIRASHID ALI SHERMARKE (1919-1969). Second president of the Somali Republic.
Abdirashid Ali Shermarke was born at Haradera, about 300 miles northeast of Mogadishu. He was a member of a chiefly family of Obbia. He attended Koranic school and in 1932 moved to Mogadishu, where he entered elementary school. He served briefly in the Italian colonial administration, and was employed as a government clerk by the British Military Administration

1

in the Southern Region. During the trusteeship period
he attended the School of Politics and Administration
and later the Higher Institute of Law and Economics.
He then went to the University of Rome, where he grad-
uated with honors, receiving a degree in political science in 1958.

He became a member of the central committee
of the Somali Youth League in 1950, and was elected
to the Legislative Assembly in 1959, his first political
post. From 1960 to 1964 he was Prime Minister, and
President from 1967 until his death. He was considered a champion of militant Pan-Somali aspirations,
but after he became President, he modified his policy
to favor peaceful relations with neighboring countries.
On October 15, 1969, he was assassinated by a member of his bodyguard.

ABDIRAZAK HAJI HUSSEIN (b. 1924). Prime Minister from
June 1964 to 1967.

Abdirizak Haji Hussein was born near Galcaio
in the Mudugh Region. During the British Military Administration of the Southern Region, he served in the
army (1942 to 1947), and in 1950, during the Italian
trusteeship period, was imprisoned for six months for
political reasons. He joined the Somali Youth League
in 1944 and served as its president in 1955-1956. In
1959 he was elected to the National Assembly. In the
late 1950s, he was president of the Higher Institute of
Law and Economics and later was president of the University Institute. In the first government of the Republic, he served first as Minister of Interior and
later as Minister of Public Works and Communications.

During his administration as Prime Minister, the
Somali government was suspected of giving aid and support to the irredentist movements in the Ethiopian Ogaden, North-Eastern Kenya, and French Somaliland. Although Abdirazak Haji Hussein strongly favored a Greater Somalia, he persistently denied reports that the
government was actively involved. His stated policy
was to pursue the issue constitutionally, i.e., by peaceful means. He called for UN plebiscites in the Somali-
inhabited areas outside the Republic and asked the Organization of African Unity to send fact-finding commis-
sions to the areas to determine Somali desires. Neither organization acted, although the OAU passed a resolution favoring the retention of existing boundaries
throughout Africa. See IRREDENTISM.

At the time of the 1969 coup, Abdirazak Haji
Hussein was a member of Parliament. After the coup,
he was detained and held, along with other detainees,
in the presidential palace at Afgoy, until 1973. He is
now (1974) the Somali Ambassador to the United Nations.

ABDULCADIR SHEIKH SAKAWA (SHEIKH) (1871-1947). A
religious leader and one of the founders and early presi-
dents of the Somali Youth Club (later League).

ABDULLAH SHAHARI. In 1905, he served as Sayyid Mohamed Abdullah Hassan's representative in making an agreement with the Italians in which the Sayyid was given the
Nugal Valley territory. In 1908, he broke with the Sayyid and reputedly obtained letters from the head of the
Salihiya order in Mecca denouncing the Sayyid and thus
weakening the Sayyid's position.

ABDULLAH SHEIKH MAHAMMAD (SHEIKH). A religious
leader and first president of the Hizbia Digil-Mirifle
Somali, a political party formed in the mid-1940s.

ABDULLAHI ISSA MOHAMUD (b. 1922). A chief spokesman
for the Somali Youth League before the Four-Power
Commission and the United Nations in the late 1940s
and early 1950s; Prime Minister in the Trust Territory
from 1956 to 1960; and after independence a member of
the cabinet. Following the October 1969 coup, he was
held in detention until 1973. He is now (1974) the
Somali ambassador to Sweden.
    Abdullahi Issa Mohamud was born in the Mudugh
Region. In 1938 he worked as a clerk in the Italian
administration, and in 1941 went into business. He
joined the Somali Youth League in 1945, and served as
its secretary-general from 1947 to 1954.

ABDULRAHMAN KARIYEH (SHEIKH). A religious leader
who became president of the National United Front when
it was established as a political party in 1959.

ABDURRAHMAN SHEIKH NUR (SHEIKH). A poet, and formerly chief qadi of Borama in the Hargeisa Region.
In 1933, he devised the Gadabursi (Borama) script in
which he transcribed some of his own works. About
1920 he transcribed Somali into an Arabic script. Was
for some years a teacher of religion in the Education
Department of British Somaliland.

ABGAL. A clan of the Hawiye clan family; the Abgal are largely nomadic pastoralists who live near Mogadishu. The Abgal (Darandolla) played a large role in overthrowing the Muzaffar dynasty which ruled Mogadishu from about 1500 to 1625.

ABRUZZI, DUKE OF THE (d. 1933) (Luigi of Savoy). Arrived in Somalia in 1919, and in 1920 established the Società Agricola Italo-Somala on the Shebelle River at Jowhar (Villagio duca degli Abruzzi, or Villabruzzi), where he obtained land by direct contract with the Shidle clan.

ABYSSINIA see ETHIOPIA

ACACIA. The most common and most useful tree in the northern and central areas. Its roots are used in building the nomadic hut (agal); its bark is used to make mats and rope; its fruit is used for food; its trunk is used for firewood and charcoal; and its bark provides tannin for waterproofing woven fiber vessels. Certain species produce aromatic gums.

ADAL. The Adal Sultanate, formerly called the Sultanate of Ifat, developed in the 9th or 10th century, with its capital at Zeila, a center of Arab trade with the interior. The Muslim sultanate was engaged in a holy war with the Abyssinians in the 14th and 15th centuries, and the first recorded use of the word Somali dates from Ethiopian songs celebrating the defeat of the Muslims. See HAQ AD-DIN; SA'D AD-DIN.

In the 16th century, an Adal war against the Abyssinians was led by Ahmad Guray; at that time the capital of the sultanate was at Harar, in present-day Ethiopia. After some initial successes, the Muslims were again defeated and their expansion toward the west halted. See AHMAD GURAY.

ADEN. Some 20,000 Somalis live in Aden, across the Gulf from Somalia.

ADEN ABDULLA OSMAN (b. 1908). President of the Legislative Assembly of the Trusteeship Territory from 1956 to 1960, and the first President of the Somali Republic (1960-1967). On July 1, 1960, he proclaimed the independence of the Somali Republic and the unification of the former Trust Territory and the former British

Somaliland protectorate. From October 1969, the date
of the coup, until April 1973, he was detained, along
with others, at the presidential palace at Afgoy.
        Aden Abdulla Osman was born at Beled Weyn.
His father fought in the campaigns against Sayyid Mohamed Abdullah Hassan. In 1922, when the first elementary school was opened at Baidoa, he entered
school. For the next five years he continued his
schooling and worked as a domestic servant in Baidoa
and Mogadishu. From 1928 to 1933, he was a medical
assistant and chief of infirmary personnel at the De
Martino Hospital in Mogadishu. Then he served in the
government as a typist and interpreter. During the
British Military Administration of the Southern Region,
he engaged in trading, and in 1944 joined the Somali
Youth League (which he served as president in 1954,
1955, and 1958). He was named a member of the
Territorial Council in 1951 and selected Vice President
of the Council (the highest post a Somali could hold).

ADOWA. In 1896, Italian forces in Ethiopia were defeated
at this Ethiopian town. The defeat is important in
Somali history because it forced Italy, Britain, and
France, the three European powers who had an interest
in the Somali territory east of Ethiopia, to realize the
need to establish boundary lines between their areas of
influence and Ethiopia. The three powers signed
boundary agreements with Emperor Menelik II in 1897.
The agreements with Britain and Italy have been disputed by the Somalis, and a large section of the boundary between the Republic and Ethiopia is still under dispute. See BOUNDARIES; IRREDENTISM.

AFAR. Also called Danakil. A non-Somali people living
in the French Territory of the Afars and Issas, known
until 1967 as French Somaliland, or the Côte Française
des Somalis. The Afar make up slightly more than
half the population of the territory and the Somali Issa
the remainder. A sizable number of Afars also reside
in Ethiopia.

AFGOY. A center of banana production, 20 miles west of
Mogadishu, on the Webi Shebelle. The Central Agricultural Research Station and the education and liberal
arts faculties of the National University are at Afgoy.
In the 19th century, the town was an important market
center in the domain of the Sultan of Geledi.

AG.   A naturally formed hole for collecting rain water.   The
      word is used primarily in the south.

AGAL.   The transportable beehive hut of the nomads.   Flex-
      ible branches, forming the rounded skeleton of the hut,
      are tied together with cords made of root or skin.
      The skeleton is then covered with waterproof straw
      mats or formerly, among some groups, skins.   See
      GURGI.

AGE SETS.   No age-set organization exists among the Somali,
      although vestiges of age-set practices are found among
      some groups of non-Somali origin.   Circumcision and
      infibulation are individual rites, accompanied by no
      group ceremony.

AGRICULTURE.   About 12 per cent of the nation's land is
      regarded as cultivable; only about five per cent of this
      is actually under cultivation.   Most of the cultivable
      land lies in the riverine areas of the Southern Region,
      where irrigation is made possible by the flooding of the
      Juba and Shebelle Rivers and where rainfall is about 20
      inches per year.   Some dryland farming is practiced
      by pastoralists in the western part of the Northern Re-
      gion around Tug Wajale.   Subsistence agriculture,
      chiefly the production of grains, is carried on wherever
      rainfall permits.
           Market crops are, primarily, bananas, sugar-
      cane, cotton, and such grains as maize and millet.
      Sesame, rice, tobacco, kapok, peanuts, citrus fruits,
      beans, and other vegetables are grown on a small scale.
      Banana production employs about 25,000 workers and
      accounts for about 40 per cent of the foreign exchange
      earnings.   In all, 15 to 20 per cent of the total popula-
      tion of three to four million is engaged in sedentary
      agriculture.   See CONCESSION AGRICULTURE.
           Compared with livestock herding, which em-
      ploys about 60 per cent of the population, farming is
      regarded by the pastoralist as a demeaning occupation.
      The farmers have a proverb to counteract this attitude.
      The proverb says: The man who owns no spot of land
      on earth cannot claim one in heaven.
           A form of agriculture which has been carried
      on in the northeast since time immemorial, and which
      has provided a unique export crop for many centuries,
      is the collection of frankincense, myrrh, and gum ara-
      bic.

AGRICULTURE DEVELOPMENT. The Agricultural Development Corporation (formerly Agency) was established in
1966. Its chief aims are to improve agricultural practices and increase yields. Thus, it seeks to bring more
land under cultivation, promote the formation of cooperatives, aid farmers in procuring low-cost credit, and
provide technical assistance in irrigation and in the production, storing, and marketing of crops. A further
aim is to promote agricultural research and dissemi-
nate experimental findings. The Corporation embraces
the National Grain Marketing Organization and the National Organization for Agricultural Tractors, a machinery pool. See NATIONAL COMPANY FOR AGRICUL-
TURE AND INDUSTRY.

AGRICULTURE METHODS. Modern methods of irrigation
and the use of farm machinery are largely limited to
the sugar and banana plantations. Farming cooperatives
may rent government-owned tractors.
     The traditional and most common instrument
used by the individual farmer is the hoe, though some
use ox-driven plows. Under traditional methods, the
land is cleared by burning, and the ashes are left on
the soil. The earth is then dug lightly and the seed
planted. Raised platforms are constructed throughout
the cultivated plot, and guards stand on the platforms
to frighten away birds and other pests. When grain is
harvested, the leaves and stalks are fed to livestock,
the roots are left in the ground, and the grain itself is
stored in underground silos or storage pits (diyehiin or
gut), where it can be saved for long periods, even
years. See IRRIGATION; LAND TENURE; SILO.

AHMAD ABUBAKAR. A sultan of the Geledi, and a seer,
who was made a Commander of the (Italian) Order of
the Colonial Star. In the 1930s, he assisted the Italians in organizing the cooperative farming groups which
worked the plantations. It is said that the Italians con-
sulted him in 1940 about the outcome of the war in the
Horn of Africa.

AHMAD GURAY ("the left-handed") (c.1506-1543). Also referred to as Ahmed Gran, Mohamed Gragne, and Ahmed
ibn Ibrahim al-Ghazi. Some authorities give his dates
as 1488-1544, and some claim that he was a Somali of
the Darod clan family. There was, it is believed, a
Somali with the same name.

Ahmad Guray led the Muslims of the Adal Sultanate in a jihad, or holy war, against the Ethiopians and their Portuguese allies. His own army contained some Turkish and Egyptian contingents, as well as many Somalis. Using cannons, probably imported from Turkey, he succeeded in capturing sections of the Ethiopian highlands, but was eventually defeated and killed near Lake Tana. His use of Turkish and Egyptian support provided the basis for later Turkish and Egyptian claims to the area he ruled.

Ahmad Guray's jihad against Ethiopia may have precipitated the migration of some Somali groups from the Gulf of Aden hinterland toward the south. Ahmad Guray is important in Somali history because, whatever his ethnic origin, he provided the Somalis with their first national hero.

AHMAD SHIRWA BIN MUHAMMAD (SHEIKH). A follower of Sayyid Mohamed Abdullah Hassan. In 1917, Sheikh Ahmad was arrested by the Italians and found to be carrying letters from the Sayyid to the Ottoman Turks in which the Sayyid asked that he and his followers be placed under Turkish protection.

AHMADIYA. One of the major Sufi orders, or tariqas, in Somalia. See DANDARAWIYA; QADIRIYA; RIFAIYA; SALIHIYA.

The Ahmadiya was introduced into Somalia by Sheikh Ali Mayi Durogba in the mid-19th century. Its agricultural settlements (jamaha) are found in many regions of Somalia, but are most numerous in the areas near or between the Juba and Shebelle Rivers. Its members devote themselves mainly to teaching. The order is regarded as somewhat puritanical in that it opposes the use of tobacco and khat, a narcotic. The Salihiya and the Dandarawiya orders branched off from the Ahmadiya.

AJURAN. The Ajuran inhabited the Shebelle valley from the late 14th to the early 17th century and controlled the watering places, the agricultural centers, and the trade routes to the coastal cities of Merca and Mogadishu. It is not known whether they were members of the Hawiye clan family, a confederation of various clan groups, or an aristocracy growing out of Somali-Arab intermarriage. The rise of the Ajuran coincided with the migration of the Hawiye to the Shebelle area and the

arrival of new groups of Arabs to the coastal areas.
The Ajuran maintained their control by military might,
but, if not from the beginning, at least from some unknown time, they also governed according to Islamic
law.

The Ajuran were headed by an imam, a chief
who lived in the interior, and who was allied to or,
perhaps, related to the Muzaffar dynasty that ruled Mogadishu from about 1500. The Muzaffar dynasty was
overthrown by new Somali (Abgal, Darandolla) incursions in the 17th century, and the last imam of the
Ajuran was killed in battle while fighting the Somali
migrants who were then moving into the Shebelle valley
and the coastal area. The Ajuran at this point migrated southward.

Traditional history holds that the stone wells
in the Benadir interior and some of the irrigation systems in the Shebelle valley were constructed by the Ajuran.

AKIL. An Arabic word meaning "headman." From 1874 to
1884, Egypt occupied Harar and claimed jurisdiction
over the Somali coast from Zeila on the Gulf of Aden
to Ras Hafun on the Indian Ocean. To maintain liaison
with the Somalis, the Egyptians appointed Somali representatives with the title of akil. When the British assumed jurisdiction in 1884, they continued the policy of
appointing and paying akils, persons approved by the
Somali groups they represented. In the area under
Italian control, the same policy was followed, but the
stipended representatives had the title of chief or notable.

The akil or chief was supposed to explain colonial administrative policy to his people and assist in
maintaining order. The akil institution was not indigenous to the Somali system and was never a very satis-
factory solution to the need it was intended to serve.

AKIL COURTS. In the Northern Region, during the British
administration, akils, in some circumstances, held
minor courts to handle noncriminal cases. These
courts were replaced by Subordinate Courts in 1945.

ALI YUSUF (d. 1960). Sultan of Obbia from 1911 to 1925,
when he was deposed by Italian colonial forces. During the years of activity of Sayyid Mohamed Abdullah
Hassan (1899-1920), the sultans of Obbia were on the

whole hostile to the Sayyid, but in 1903, Ali Yusuf and
his father, the Sultan Yusuf Ali "Kenadid, " were briefly
arrested and exiled after being accused of cooperating
with the Sayyid.

AMARANI.   A group who live primarily at Brava, but also
at Merca, Mogadishu, and Afgoy.   Most are merchants
or sailors, speaking a Swahili dialect (Chimbalazi).
According to their traditions, the Amarani were the
first inhabitants of the Brava area.   Their ancestors
are believed to have come to the Benadir coast from
south Arabia, possibly being Israelites who left Arabia
during the early expansion of Islam and who intermarried with the local inhabitants.   See BRAVA.

AMULETS.   Small leather cases containing a paper on which
are written passages from the Koran; worn on a string
around the neck or arm to guard the wearer against
illness or other misfortune.

ANGLO-ETHIOPIAN DIPLOMACY.   After the 1896 defeat of
the Italians at Adowa by the army of the Ethiopian Emperor Menelik II, the British sought to delineate the
boundary between the British protectorate of Somaliland
and the territory under Ethiopian control.   The first
treaty was signed in 1897, and out of it a series of
other treaties or agreements arose.

ANGLO-ETHIOPIAN TREATY OF 1897.   During the 1880s,
Ethiopia announced her claim to all of the Horn of Africa and expanded a limited control to some territory
populated by Somalis.   During this period, Great Britain had signed treaties with Somali groups, guarantee-
ing them protection against Ethiopian claims.   Under
the 1897 treaty, Ethiopia gave up her claim to about
half the protectorate area, and Britain ceded to Ethiopia
the region of the Haud, a traditional Somali grazing
area.   Under the treaty, Ethiopia guaranteed orderly
government in the Haud and Somali access to it.   The
Somalis themselves were unaware that any treaty had
been signed until 1954; the treaty was not published or
the boundary marked until the early 1930s.   This treaty
is the basis of the present boundary dispute between
Ethiopia and Somalia in the Northern Region.

ANGLO-ETHIOPIAN BOUNDARY COMMISSION.   The Ethi-
opian-British Somaliland boundary agreed upon in the

1897 treaty was marked on the ground by an Anglo-Ethiopian commission between 1932 and 1934. Concrete posts were installed to mark the boundary line. Somalis protested the installation of the markers and knocked some of them down. The protest gave rise to several incidents, in which one British district commissioner lost his life. Late in 1934, the commission went to Wal Wal, where Somalis had access to wells and grazing areas. There the commission encountered an Italian armed force which had taken possession of the wells. The Wal Wal encounter led to the Italian invasion of Ethiopia and the Italo-Ethiopian war of 1935-1936. The Italians conquered Ethiopia and remained in control until defeated by the British in 1941. See WAL WAL.

ANGLO-ETHIOPIAN AGREEMENTS OF 1942 AND 1944. In 1941, the whole of the Somali-inhabited area formerly held by the Italians and Ethiopians, as well as British Somaliland, which the Italians captured for a short while, came under the British Military Administration (BMA). Ethiopian Emperor Haile Selassie, who had been in exile in Europe during the Italian occupation of Ethiopia (1935-1941), returned to Ethiopia and in 1942 and 1944 signed two agreements with Great Britain regarding the Somali-inhabited Haud and "reserved" area ceded to Ethiopia in the 1897 treaty. The "reserved" area was a strip of territory adjoining French Somaliland, through which the Djibouti-Addis Ababa railroad passes. The 1942 and 1944 agreements placed the territory under BMA control. The Ogaden territory, which lies to the south of the Haud and is contiguous with the fomer Italian colony, was also placed under the BMA, where it remained until 1948. The 1942 and 1944 agreements had specific time limitations, and were primarily for the purpose of assuring Somalis of their traditional grazing and watering rights in the war-torn area until Ethiopia could reestablish her government and guarantee these rights herself.

ANGLO-ETHIOPIAN PROTOCOL OF 1948. This agreement marked the return of the Ogaden area to Ethiopia and the withdrawal of the British Military Administration. The protocol also fixed the provisional boundary line between Ethiopia and the ex-Italian colony. This line became effective in 1950, and is the subject of the disputed boundary between Ethiopia and the Southern Region of Somalia.

ANGLO-ETHIOPIAN AGREEMENT OF 1954. The 1954 agreement merely implemented the treaty of 1897. But the
announcement of the agreement apprised the Somalis for
the first time of the 1897 treaty and set off a strong
and bitter outcry among the Somalis of the protectorate.
In response to the Somali reaction, the British offered
to buy the Haud from Ethiopia, but were turned down.
At this point, the Somalis organized the National United
Front and attempted to present the case to the International Court at The Hague. See NATIONAL UNITED
FRONT.

ANGLO-FRENCH TREATY OF 1888. The boundary between
the Somali Republic and the French Territory of the
Afars and Issas, fixed by this treaty, is the only
boundary of Somalia whose legality the Somalis recognize.

ANGLO-ITALIAN ACCORDS. With the signing in 1889 of the
Treaty of Ucciali between Italy and Ethiopia, Italy and
other European powers believed that the Ethiopian Emperor Menelik II had placed his country under Italian
protection and that Italy was responsible for Ethiopia's
external relations. On this assumption, Britain and
Italy sought to agree on their respective spheres of influence in the Horn.

ANGLO-ITALIAN PROTOCOLS OF 1891 AND 1894. These
agreements were an attempt to define the boundaries
between Italian and British areas in the Jubaland, north
of Kenya, and in the Somali-Ethiopian interior. The
1891 agreement recognized that the Somali port of Kismayu and the territory on the west bank of the Juba
River belonged to Britain, while the territory on the
east bank belonged to Italy.
      The 1894 agreement recognized the Ogaden
area as falling within the Italian sphere of influence
and the Haud as within the British. Ethiopia was not
informed of the 1894 agreement; if she had been, she
would have rejected it, because she did not accept the
interpretation of the Ucciali treaty which appeared to
give Italy the right to go forward with the 1894 agreement.
      After the Italian defeat at Adowa in 1896, the
British dealt directly with Ethiopia in the Anglo-Ethiopian treaty of 1897.

ANGLO-ITALIAN AGREEMENT OF 1925. This agreement
arose from the 1891 Anglo-Italian protocol regarding
the Jubaland, and other agreements between Britain
and Italy concerning the "spoils" of World War I. After the war, Britain assumed control of certain former
German colonies, unrelated to Somali history, and ceded
to Italy Kismayu and the Jubaland. The 1925 agreement confirmed these transfers and fixed the boundary
between the British colony of Kenya and Italian Somaliland. The boundary line was drawn through Somali-
inhabited territory, leaving some Somalis in Kenya and
adding some to the Italian colony.

ANGLO-ITALIAN-FRENCH TREATY OF 1906. Under this
agreement, Great Britain, Italy, and France agreed to
cooperate to maintain the political and territorial status
quo of Ethiopia. The Italians, however, felt that the
treaty expanded their sphere of influence and gave them
the right to respond militarily if Ethiopia threatened
their position in Somalia. See WAL WAL.

ANIMALS. Somalia is primarily a land of nomadic or seminomadic pastoralists. In 1971, the livestock population,
according to one estimate, was almost 15 million:
camels (three million), sheep (3.95 million), goats
(five million), cattle (2.85 million), and small numbers
of oxen and horses. By contrast, a 1967 estimate
placed the total number of domesticated animals at
about ten million. See HERDING; LIVESTOCK DE-
VELOPMENT.
        Somalia's wild animals are typically African--
elephant, hippopotamus, rhinoceros, buffalo, cheetah,
antelope--though some are unique to the area. Clark's
gazelle, Speke's gazelle, and the Somali wild ass are
believed to be unique to Somalia. The reticulated giraffe, found only in East Africa, is seen in the lower
Juba area. The Somali leopard is the source of the
world's most expensive fur.
        Game reserves have not been widely developed
in Somalia, and the wildlife has not been effectively
protected. Many animals formerly plentiful are now
vanishing. Some fell victim to poachers and to organizations which in the 1960s tracked them down by aircraft and truck and shipped them out alive. The ever-
increasing herds of camels, cattle, and goats and the
destruction of forests by herds and by charcoal producers have further limited the wildlife population.

ARABIC. Most, if not all, Somalis know some Arabic; it
    was one of the official national languages until 1972
    when Somali was established as the sole national lan-
    guage. During the 1950s and 1960s, some newspapers
    and newspaper columns were printed in Arabic. Be-
    ginning in 1974, New Era, a government-sponsored
    monthly review, was printed in an Arabic edition (as
    well as in English and Italian editions). Arabic is the
    language of instruction in the Koranic schools, which
    many Somali children attend from about four to six
    years of age. See LANGUAGE; LITERACY.

ARABS. It is believed that Arabs inhabited the Somali coast-
    al centers in the first century A.D. In the 7th century
    and thereafter, at the time of the Muslim wars in Ara-
    bia, Arabs came to Somalia as traders, immigrants,
    and propagators of Islam. Beginning about 1300, and
    continuing during the Muslim wars with Ethiopia, Ara-
    bian sherifs and sayyids came to the Horn in the hope
    of augmenting their wealth and religious following. Al-
    though there were probably no tribal migrations of
    Arabs to the area, individuals and small groups estab-
    lished themselves on the coast and were, in general,
    in charge of the coastal trade. They lived in close
    touch with the native inhabitants, adopted their language,
    intermarried, and in the process carried out the Is-
    lamization of the region. Al Yaqubi, an Arab geogra-
    pher of the 9th century, wrote of the trade, culture,
    and religious institutions centered in Zeila and Mogad-
    ishu.
            The eponymous ancestors of the Somalis derive
    from members of the Koreish (or Quraysh) tribe of
    Arabia, from which the Prophet Mohamed sprang.
    Little is known about early Arab immigrants, but their
    influence on the religion and social organization of the
    Somalis is clear. See CLAN FAMILIES.

ARAWELO. A legendary queen, remembered in folk tales
    for her cruelty as well as her wisdom. Her intense
    hatred of men led her to set impossible tasks for them,
    and then have them killed when they were unable to
    carry out her wishes.

ARCHAEOLOGY. Virtually no systematic excavations of
    ruined buildings have been undertaken in Somalia, al-
    though the number of ruins in evidence would seem to
    warrant investigation. See PREHISTORIC RUINS.

In August 1932, Gualtiero Benardelli spent five
days excavating the remains of a small walled town on
the coast near Meregh, about 200 miles north of Mogadishu. He suggested that the town may have been an
administrative center in Ajuran times, in the 16th
century.
      The British Institute of Archaeology and History
in East Africa conducted a two-week preliminary survey of ruins along the coast from Kismayu to Merca in
1960, but the survey was not followed up despite some
promising finds. In 1971, a team of Soviet archaeolo-
gists looked for sites in the central and northern areas,
but in 1974, had not published the results of their inquiry.

ARCHITECTURE. Arabian-style houses, with two or more
      stories and with crenellated roofs, are typical of the
      larger coastal towns. The houses are built of stucco
      and stone and are whitewashed, or sometimes pastel-
      colored. Many buildings constructed during the coloni-
      al administrations and since independence follow this
      pattern. Persian influences have also been noted in
      some of the minarets of the coast. Among the nomads,
      dwellings are the transportable beehive hut, while
      among the settled agriculturalists and in the coastal
      villages and quarters of the larger towns, the houses
      are of wattle and daub. See AGAL; ARISH; MUNDUL.

ARIFA. Strangers adopted as clients of a host clan. The
      practice of adoption was especially important in the up-
      per and lower Juba areas during the period of Somali
      migrations. After the status of arifa was abolished in
      1960, the arifa often had difficulty retaining the land
      they had been allocated by their patrons, and they of-
      ten lost the protective dia-paying, cooperative-farming,
      livestock-marketing, and watering arrangements they
      had with their patrons. Sometimes spelled harifa.
      See ABBAAN; SHEEGAT.

ARISH. Ordinary dwelling houses of several rooms found in
      the coastal towns. The arish is rectangular, with a
      broken, sloping roof thatched with palm leaves or
      grass, and with walls of slender posts covered with a
      daub of soil, ashes, and dung. Sometimes the arish
      is painted white or rose. The construction is similar
      to that of the mundul (q. v.).

ARMS. Before the use of firearms during the jihad (1899-
1920) of Sayyid Mohamed Abdullah Hassan, Somali
weapons of war consisted chiefly of knives, bows,
swords, and spears. Knives intended for war and
hunting and for daily use are double-edged, with handles
of hippo ivory. They are carried in leather cases attached to the belt. The spear, used also for protection against wild animals, has a staff of knotted wood
and an iron tip. Swords have long, narrow blades and
handles of horn, and are carried in leather cases.
Bows, little used today, are made of wood, with a
cord of camel tendon or gut. Arrows, with iron tips,
are carried in quivers of wood and leather. Shields
are round, about 12 inches in diameter, with a raised
point in the center, and are made of rhino, giraffe, or
oryx skin. They have a leather handle on the inside,
and are ornamented with incised concentric circles and
parallel lines.

      The use of poisoned arrows is recorded during
the Muslim-Ethiopian wars of the 16th century; a group
known as the El-Maya, armed with bows and poisoned
arrows, fought on the side of the Ethiopians against the
armies of Ahmad Guray. Poisoned arrows have been
prohibited since the 1930s. Poison was made from
certain roots, boiled and pounded, and kept in cattle
horns. See FIREARMS.

AROMATIC GUMS. The trees supplying aromatic gums are
concentrated in the northeast: frankincense (maidi)
comes from three species of Boswellia; myrrh (beio)
from the Commiphora; and gum arabic from the acacia.
Aromatic gums have been an important export of the
area for hundreds, perhaps thousands, of years.
Somalia supplies about 60 per cent of the world's frankincense, much of it going to Islamic countries where
it is used in religious ceremonies.

      The trees are usually regarded as the property
of the clan within whose area they grow. In the past,
the incense gatherers sold their produce to middlemen
in the coastal cities; today they are largely joined together in cooperatives made up of producers, gatherers,
and merchants. The gatherers make an incision in the
tree and return in a few days to collect the "tears"
and make a new incision. The gum is not processed in
Somalia, but sold in much the same form in which it is
collected.

      Somalis use the gums in religious and other

ceremonies. Women use them for smoke baths. Myrrh
is used in treating wounds.

ART. Although paintings and wood carvings of animal and
human forms are sometimes seen today, the Somalis,
as Muslims, have traditionally rejected the reproduction of such forms. Domestic objects of wood, such
as combs, vases, bowls and plates, spoons, water
bottles, headrests, small boxes, and mortars, are
decorated with geometric designs. Such patterns as
the undulated plait, triangles filled with crosshatchings,
the circle and dot, concentric circles, and chevrons
are common, as is the rosette. Incense burners and
charcoal burners of meerschaum are similarly decorated.

Fine gold and silver jewelry is made in a
variety of intricate designs. Ivory and hippo teeth are
used for knife handles, and leather is used for carrying cases and shields. Mats and receptacles are woven
of natural or brightly colored straw; the latter are
sometimes decorated with cowry shells. See also
AZANIA; MUSIC; POETRY.

ASKARI. Policeman.

ASTROLOGY. There is a rich oral literature concerning the
use of astrology and astronomy in connection with agriculture, livestock herding, and personal and religious
events. See DABSHID; WEATHER LORE.

AU. 1) Title for a wadad, saint, or religious devotee,
used before the individual's name.

2) In the southern agricultural areas, an au,
or magistrate of water, sometimes referred to as au
uared, may be chosen to regulate the use of uars, or
man-made ponds.

AU BARKHADLE see SHEIKH YUSUF KAWNEYN

AU HILTIR. A legendary pre-Islamic figure of Rahanweyn
origin, an important saint among the Shidle clan. According to legend, Au Hiltir gave the Shebelle River to
the Shidle because they received his body, which flew
to them after it was desecrated by the Geledi who then
lived on the river banks. Au Hiltir is said to protect
people from the crocodile. It is believed by some authorities that at some time in ancient history, the Shebelle River did change its course.

AU MAD.   Also spelled Au Mahhad.   A pre-Islamic saint of
    Rahanweyn origin who, after his death, flew from Bur
    Acaba to Badi-Addo on the Shebelle River.   Au Mad is
    the guardian of the harvest, protecting the crops from
    predatory birds.

AWES CADRIA (SHEIKH).   First president of the Somali
    Youth League.   Son of Sheikh Awes Muhammad Barawi
    (q.v.).

AXUM.   An ancient kingdom in the highlands of modern Ethi-
    opia, one of the outposts of the Roman Empire.   Axum
    accepted Christianity in the 4th century.   Zeila, a
    Somali coastal town on the Gulf of Aden, was one of
    Axum's major outlets to the sea.   Axum was at its
    height in the 5th century, had begun to disintegrate in
    the 7th, and by the 8th, its coastal areas were con-
    trolled by Muslims.   Modern Ethiopian claims to the
    Somali-inhabited areas are based on events dating back
    to the Axumite era.

AZANIA.   The term refers to the coastal strip of East Afri-
    ca from Cape Guardafui, in Somalia, to Sofala, in
    Mozambique.   It is used in early books, such as the
    Periplus of the Erythraean Sea (c. 60 AD) and Ptolemy's
    Geography (c. 400 AD).   The predominantly Arab and
    Persian culture of Azania gave rise to a distinctive art,
    called Azanian art.   In Somalia, the chief examples of
    this art are seen in the Mosque of Sheikh Abdul Aziz
    and the Mosque Fakhr ad-Din, both in Mogadishu.

AZIENDA AGRARIA GOVERNATIVA.   In 1912, this organiza-
    tion was granted concessions at Jenale on the lower
    Shebelle River for the production of bananas.   The
    plantations did not accomplish very much until the
    1930s, when the Italian government moved to improve
    working conditions, establish villages for the workers,
    and give the concessionaires incentives for increased
    production.   The plantations were unproductive during
    the war years, 1935 to 1942 and thereafter, but were
    put back into operation under a new system during the
    1950s.   These plantations, now owned by Italians and
    Somalis, provide Somalia's chief agricultural export.
    See also BANANA MONOPOLY; ROYAL BANANA MO-
    NOPOLY.

- B -

BAALI.   Natural basins where rain collects.   Traditionally,
baali belong to the group inhabiting the territory where
they are located, and all members of the group can
water their livestock at the baali freely.   Visiting
groups must obtain the consent of the owning group before taking their livestock to the baali.

BAIDOA   see   ISHA BAIDOA

BAJUNI.   A non-Somali ethnic group of about 1,000 living
primarily in the Bajuni Islands, off the coast of the
Lower Juba Region, south of Kismayu.   The Bajuni are
largely engaged in fishing and sailing.   Chinese records
of the Ming period (1368-1644) indicate that the Bajuni
traded in tortoise shell, shark fins, and sea cucumbers.
The Bajuni speak a Swahili dialect.   It is believed that
they descended from an intermixture of Arab or Persian settlers and the local population, although some
authorities note that they may also have a Melanesian
affinity.

BALOLEY.   A song of short verses, each often independent
of the others in content.   Sometimes it is didactic, to
instruct the listeners in the language, in comportment,
in controversial questions.   It is a song of the nomadic
interior, and is always sung in a recreational setting
and an entertaining manner.

BALWO.   An Arabic word meaning evil or misfortune.   In
Somalia, the modern love songs, now called heello,
were originally called balwo.   The balwo has been
described as a "miniature" because it often consists of
only one or two lines.   The form was invented in 1944
and became very popular.   It is not much used today.

BANANA EXPORTS.   Until 1962, bananas were Somalia's
chief source of foreign exchange earnings.   Since 1962,
banana exports have continued to rise, but have been
exceeded in most years by exports of livestock and
animal products.   Most of the bananas are purchased
by Italy.   After the Suez Canal was closed in 1967,
banana ships had to travel around the Cape of Good
Hope.   The opening of the enlarged deep seaport at
Kismayu, the introduction of the Poyo variety of banana
on the plantations, and the employment of better fungi-

cides and faster and better-equipped ships--all in the late 1960s--to a large extent overcame the disadvantages of the around-the-Cape journey.

BANANA MONOPOLY. During the colonial period, the Somali banana industry was an Italian state monopoly (the Royal Banana Monopoly). In 1950, at the beginning of the trusteeship period, the Italian Banana Monopoly was established, and Somali banana exports began to rise. Under the monopoly, all bananas for export were sold to Italy at high, government-supported prices, thus assuring the producers (largely Italian plantation owners) a profitable market. While the industry prospered, it probably could not have become competitive on a free market. The monopoly was dissolved in 1965, but the Italian government continued to subsidize banana production until 1969 by purchasing Somali bananas at a price above the international market price. See NATIONAL BANANA BOARD.

BANANAS. The Juba banana, a local strain of the Cavendish or Musa sinesis, was the chief variety of banana grown in Somalia until the late 1960s. Today, the Poyo variety has largely replaced the Juba. The Poyo can withstand the long period of shipment better and has, in the long run, resulted in higher yields. It is more suited to local conditions and is less easily bruised than the Juba.

BANKING. During the colonial period, banking facilities were largely limited to branch banks of British and Italian firms. In the 1950s, a Government Savings Bank was established in British Somaliland, and the Somali National Bank and the Somali Credit Bank (Credito Somalo) were created in the Trust Territory. Branches of four British and Italian banking houses that operated in the two territories before independence and during the 1960s were nationalized in 1970.

The Somali National Bank is the Republic's central bank; the Somali Savings and Credit Bank extends medium- and long-term credit, and the Somali Commercial Bank provides short-term loans.

BANTU see HABASHO; NEGROID PEOPLES

BARDERA (Tall palm). A town on the Juba River, about 150 miles inland, founded in 1819 as the site of one of

the first <u>jamaha</u> in southern Somalia. The settlement
may have been affiliated with the Qadiriya Sufi order,
although some authorities feel that its puritanical regulations point to links with the Ahmadiya. The founder
of the settlement, Sheikh Ibrahim Hassan Jebro, died
shortly after his arrival in Bardera. He was succeeded
by Ali Dure. The community outlawed the use of tobacco, abolished frivolous dancing, compelled its women
to wear the veil, and condemned the ivory trade.

In 1836, the settlement entered a militant phase,
first under Sheikh Abiker Aden Durow, then under
Sherifs Abdurahman and Ibrahim. The reformers declared a <u>jihad</u> (holy war) against the "lax" Muslims of
the region, and in 1840 sacked the coastal town of
Brava. In 1843, Bardera was besieged and destroyed
by an alliance of the Tunni of Brava and the Geledi,
whose trade in ivory and other products was interrupted
by the militant Bardera religionists. In the 1843 war--
a vivid event in Somali oral tradition--Bardera found
allies among the Bimal, old enemies of the Geledi.
Bardera was not reoccupied until the 1860s.

Throughout the late 19th century, Bardera was
governed by a series of fundamentalist Muslim sheikhs
who engaged in sporadic warfare with the Galla inhabitants of the right bank of the Juba. Bardera's leaders
also apparently condoned the attack on the ill-fated von
der Decken expedition which ascended the Juba River as
far as Bardera in 1865. The remains of the German
explorer's boat can still be seen in the rapids above
Bardera. Though never openly hostile to the Italian
colonizers who arrived in the 1890s, elements of the
Bardera community may have collaborated with the dervishes of Sayyid Mohamed Abdullah Hassan. The town
is today an important religious settlement.

BENADIR COAST. The southern coastal area from Itala
(Adale) to Kismayu. The area came under the nominal
control of the Sultan of Oman in the late 17th century.
When the seat of the sultanate was permanently shifted
to Zanzibar in 1840, the Benadir Coast fell under the
close scrutiny of the Sultan of Zanzibar, from whom
Britain and Italy acquired it in 1888-1889.

BENADIR COMPANY (1898-1905). This company, the <u>Societǎ
Anonima Commerciale Italiana del Benadir</u>, replaced the
Filonardi Company in administering the Italian-controlled
ports of the Benadir Coast, after a two-year period of

direct government control.   It, like the Filonardi Company, did little to upset the traditional Somali political and social system.   The Benadir Company was largely organized by Antonio Cecchi, an avid colonialist who initially hoped to build up agricultural concessions in the Benadir and carry on trade with the Somalis of the interior.

After Cecchi was killed in 1896, the company was headed by Ernesto Dulio. It was unable to establish any agricultural enterprises and its staff was torn by internal disputes.   The threat of Somali uprisings and Ethiopian incursions and a scandal stemming from the continuation of the slave trade and domestic slavery also contributed to the company's failure.   In 1905, the Italian government assumed direct responsibility for the Somali areas.

BENADIR COTTON.   A cotton cloth produced at Mogadishu, Brava, and Merca.   The cloth, plain or striped, in red, yellow, blue, and other colors, with a white background, is handwoven by men.   It is used locally and has been an article of export since the 14th century, if not before.

BERBERA.   (pop. c. 45, 000)   An ancient Gulf of Aden port in the Hargeisa Region.   Berbera was mentioned by Arab geographers in the 13th century.   It was sacked by the Portuguese in 1518.   By the early 1800s, and perhaps much earlier, Berbera was controlled by Somali clans of the interior, and was a major center of trade.

In 1855, after a British officer in Richard F. Burton's expedition was killed at Berbera, the British secured a trade treaty with the Somalis and established a British Resident at Berbera.   This treaty was the basis for British claims to the Somali coastal areas on the Gulf of Aden.   Berbera served as the center of British colonial operations from 1885 until the conclusion of World War II, when the government center was moved to Hargeisa.

The port of Berbera has facilities for oceangoing vessels, and is the chief export point for livestock.   It has two 4, 000-foot piers, constructed with USSR aid, plus a radio station with a 5, 000-mile range.

BERKAD.   A concrete water reservoir.   Often a village will develop around a berkad, and nomads who come there

to water their stock remain for extended periods, with
the result that the area becomes overgrazed.

BEVIN PLAN. A proposal presented in 1946 by British
    Foreign Secretary Ernest Bevin to the Allied Powers'
    Council of Foreign Ministers during its deliberations
    on the disposition of the former Italian colonies. The
    Bevin Plan would have placed the Somali-inhabited areas
    of British and Italian Somaliland (then under British
    Military Administration) under a British trusteeship.
    Bevin used the phrase "greater Somaliland" to describe
    the proposed trust territory, a phrase which later be-
    came a rallying cry for Somali nationalists. The Bevin
    Plan, which was rejected, was strongly opposed by the
    Russian delegation to the Council of Foreign Ministers;
    it was favored by some Somalis.

BIMAL. The Bimal are the largest Dir clan-family group.
    They have occupied the town of Merca and its hinter-
    land since perhaps 1690 when their traditions claim
    they overthrew the representatives of the Sultan of
    Ajuran. Predominantly pastoralists, the Bimal from
    time to time controlled the caravan trade routes to
    Merca. They also engaged (and continue to engage) in
    agriculture in the lower Shebelle area. When the im-
    portation of slaves for farming became widespread in
    the mid-1800s, the Bimal grew rich and powerful, ex-
    changing agricultural products as well as livestock and
    goods from the interior (ivory, hides, skins, horses,
    slaves) for imported goods at Merca.
        The Bimal engaged periodically in wars with
    the Geledi, their traditional rivals, who controlled the
    trade routes to Mogadishu and Brava and a great share
    of the wealth of the Shebelle farming country; the two
    clans were opponents in the Bardera wars. In this
    rivalry, the Bimal sought assistance from the Sultan
    of Zanzibar, who established a garrison at Merca in
    the 1860s--the only Zanzibari garrison on the coast at
    the time. In the recurrent Bimal-Geledi wars, the
    politically cohesive Bimal were largely successful, kill-
    ing at least two powerful Geledi sultans.
        Italian efforts to abolish slavery and engage in
    trade were strongly resisted by the Bimal, as well as
    by sections of the Geledi, both of whom depended on
    slaves to cultivate their farms and both of whom were
    engaged in the caravan trade. The Bimals' resistance
    to the Italians began in 1896. They besieged an Italian

garrison at Merca in 1904, and repeatedly ambushed
and attacked Italian-led troops. The Italian administration decided to "pacify" the area, but the "Bimal revolt," which began in 1905, was not crushed until 1908.
        In their "revolt," the Bimal gained some as-
sistance in the way of firearms from Sayyid Mohamed
Abdullah Hassan, the Salihiya leader of the jihad in the
north. Some of the Salihiya followers in the south
broke with the Sayyid in 1908 after he was denounced
by the Salihiya leader in Mecca, and the split among
the Salihiya undoubtedly worked to the advantage of the
Italians in "pacifying" the Bimal. In these battles, the
Italians appear to have received some assistance from
the Geledi sultan. See HAJI ABDI ABIKAR.

BIO. Somali word meaning water; a metaphor for prosperity.
        See also WELLS.

BIRTH RITES. Traditionally, the umbilical cord is tied with
        hairs from a camel's or cow's tail, and the animal
        from which the hairs are taken becomes the property
        of the child. The child remains in the mother's house
        one year, at which time the kalaqad ceremony takes
        place. In this ceremony, the baby boy's maternal
        uncle or the baby girl's maternal aunt places the baby
        on his or her shoulders, carries it outside the enclo-
        sure, and then returns it to the mother, who puts the
        baby in its sling on her back. After childbirth, the
        mother stays in the house for a purification period of
        40 days, during which she does not work or have con-
        jugal relations.
                The child's name is customarily given by the
        father without any particular name-giving ceremony.
        Children are members of the father's dia-paying group
        --not the mother's. For male children, a banquet is
        traditionally held, and gifts are provided to the Yibir
        (q.v.) who carries out magical rites and prepares an
        amulet, which is tied around the child's neck.
                These traditional ceremonies are most common
        among the nomadic groups. In modern times they are
        often ignored or modified.

BLOOD COMPENSATION. The Somali word is mag; the
        Arabic dia is commonly used. Homicide is the chief
        offense for which blood compensation is required under
        Islamic law. Lesser offenses include wounds and in-
        sults. Blood compensation, which involves group

responsibility for the payment and receipt of fines, usually in livestock, is now illegal. See DIA; DIA-PAY-
ING GROUPS.

BOGOR OSMAN MAHMOUD (1854-1943). Bogor is a chiefly
   title, meaning "belt"--to bind people together. Bogor
   Osman Mahmoud was a powerful sultan among the
   Mijerteyn; he is remembered for his resistance to the
   Italians. See MIJERTEYN.

BOUNDARIES. The Republic is bounded by Ethiopia and
   Kenya on the west and southwest and by the French
   Territory of the Afars and Issas on the northwest. It
   faces the Gulf of Aden and the Indian Ocean on the
   north, east, and south. The interior boundaries are
   rather arbitrarily drawn straight lines laid down during
   the colonial period, cutting through Somali-inhabited
   territory and dividing the Somali people. During the
   trusteeship period, unsuccessful efforts were made to
   define the boundary between Ethiopia and the Southern
   Region, which is now marked by the Provisional Administrative Line laid down by the British and Ethiopians in 1950. See ANGLO-ETHIOPIAN DIPLOMACY;
   ANGLO-FRENCH TREATY OF 1888; ANGLO-ITALIAN
   ACCORDS; GREATER SOMALIA; IRREDENTISM.

BRAVA. A coastal city in the South founded probably in the
   10th century by Arabs or Persians and governed at that
   time by a council of chiefs. More Arab and Persian
   immigrants came to Brava, and by the 12th or early
   13th century, Somalis from the north were moving in.
   By the 15th century, Brava rivaled Mogadishu as a
   center of trade. In 1503, Portuguese seamen captured
   vessels carrying some of the leaders of Brava and
   forced them to place the city under Portuguese protection. When the leaders repudiated the agreement in
   1506, Portuguese ships bombarded the town and looted
   it. Brava was defeated, and remained under Portuguese domination until the middle of the 17th century,
   when the Iman of Oman ousted the Portuguese. The
   city then remained under the nominal control of the
   Sultans of Oman and Zanzibar until 1888 and was the
   center of Zanzibari government for the Benadir Coast.
       In the 17th century, the Tunni Somali arrived
   in the environs of Brava. Thereafter, they and the
   descendants of the original Arab and Persian inhabitants, who had intermarried with Negroid and Somali

groups, constituted the city's permanent inhabitants.   In
1840, the city was attacked by the tariqa of Bardera,
which found allies among the Bimal.   In rebuffing this
attack, the Tunni allied themselves with the Geledi, who
ruled the hinterland beyond the port.   Brava was something of a pawn in the later Bimal-Geledi wars, and in
1871 appealed to the Sultan of Zanzibar for protection.
In 1875, Egyptian warships appeared at Brava.   They
withdrew a year later, under pressure from the British,
and the Zanzibari increased their force and built a wall
around the city.

In 1888, the Imperial British East Africa Company obtained from the Sultan of Zanzibar a 50-year
concession to Brava and the other Benadir ports.
Great Britain transferred this concession to Italy in
1889.   Brava was administered by the Filonardi Company (1893-1896) and the Benadir Company (1898-1905).
In 1905, the Italian government purchased the Benadir
ports north of the Juba River from the Sultan of Zanzibar and placed them under direct government control.

From its earliest history, Brava was an important center of trade, particularly for livestock and
ivory exports, and was at one time the most important
Benadir port.   The merchants of Brava served as
middlemen between Arabian, European, and American
merchants (mid-1800s) and the peoples of the interior.
When the caravan routes became disrupted, when there
was a drought, or when the livestock of the area were
struck by disease, Brava suffered.   All these factors
as well as the abolition of slavery and the development
of other ports more suitable for ocean-going vessels
combined in the late 19th and early 20th centuries to
undermine the city's prosperity and led to its decline.

BRIDE WEALTH   see   MARRIAGE

BRITISH EAST INDIA COMPANY.   This company, seeking to
use the harbor of Obock (in the present French Territory of the Afars and Issas), concluded treaties with the
Sultan of Tajura in 1840 and acquired two small islands
from him.   In 1827, the company had signed commercial treaties with Somali sultans and sheikhs on the
Gulf of Aden coast.

BRITISH MILITARY ADMINISTRATION (BMA).   In 1941,
after the Italians were defeated by the British in Ethiopia and in the Somali areas, the British Military

Administration was established. It governed British
Somaliland and the Haud and "reserved" area (until
1948, when it was replaced by a civilian government),
the former Italian colony (until 1950), and the Somali-
inhabited Ogaden area of Ethiopia (until 1949).

After World War II, the BMA attempted to
modernize the government and court system in the
former Italian colony. It established a number of new
schools for boys and girls, opened schools for nurses
and teachers, permitted the formation of political
parties, organized the Somalia gendarmerie, and set
up a police school. It encouraged the plantations to
renew their production, and during this period, the
former colony became almost self-sufficient in food.

Also in the British protectorate of Somaliland,
the BMA moved to modernize. It established Subordinate Courts; set up local advisory councils to discuss
such economic problems as water shortages, food
scarcities, and unemployment, and, in 1946, inaugurated a Protectorate Advisory Council consisting of
Somali delegates from each district.

BRITISH SOMALILAND. On June 26, 1960, the British
    Somaliland protectorate became the independent state of
    Somaliland. On July 1, 1960, it amalgamated with the
    newly independent state of Somalia, the former Italian
    colony and United Nations Trust Territory, to form the
    Somali Republic. Within the Republic, the former pro-
    tectorate is referred to as the Northern Region.

        Early British interest in the area was related
    to the need to keep open the interior trade routes to
    Berbera, Zeila, and other ports which supplied the
    British colony of Aden with supplies of fresh meat.
    After the Egyptians evacuated the ports in 1884, Bri-
    tain signed trade and protection treaties with several
    Somali clans. Later treaties established the protecto-
    rate in 1887, with Berbera as the center of govern-
    ment.

        From 1899 to 1920, the protectorate govern-
    ment was concerned primarily with its continuing con-
    flict with Sayyid Mohamed Abdullah Hassan. After the
    defeat of the Sayyid in 1920, the government became
    more secure, but it did little to interfere in the So-
    mali way of life. During the 1920s, some pastoralists
    in the western part of the protectorate began to grow
    millet, and by the 1930s cultivation and pastoralism
    were both important activities in the western districts.

Elsewhere, nomadic pastoralism remained the dominant activity.

Each of the six government districts was headed by a British District Commissioner (DC), whose contact with the people was primarily through akils and stipended chiefs. The DC acted as magistrate and had under his control the illalo, or local police.

The protectorate was overrun by the Italian army in 1940, but was retaken by the British in 1941 and placed under the British Military Administration until 1948, when civilian government was restored. In the meantime, the center of government was moved from Berbera to Hargeisa. After 1948, some progress was made in providing education, improving agricultural and veterinary services, and extending local government participation to the Somalis.

In 1954, Britain signed a new agreement with Ethiopia, implementing the 1897 boundary treaty. The British withdrew from the Haud and "reserved" area, except for the retention of a British liaison officer, who was to be a link between the protectorate government and the British-protected Somalis who grazed their livestock in the Haud several months of the year. The announcement of this agreement, and the first public announcement of the 1897 treaty, aroused bitterness and resentment among the Somalis, who believed that their territory was being given away. The British in the area were embarrassed; many felt that their government had betrayed the Somalis. A British offer to buy the grazing area was declined by Ethiopia.

Somalis began to organize, hoping to retrieve the Haud and demanding independence. They received independence in 1960. With regard to the grazing grounds, Ethiopia--after initially refusing--decided to continue to allow Somali pastoralists to cross the boundary and use the Haud as they have been doing for hundreds of years.

BUR ACABA. An inland town, about 100 miles northwest of Mogadishu. In 1968, a United Nations survey team reported uranium and other mineral deposits near Bur Acaba.

Historically, Bur Acaba has been an important religious center for certain Rahanweyn clans which arrived in the interriver area in the 17th century. It appears to have been a center for the propagation of Islam in the southern interior. About 1700, the legen-

dary Haran Medare prophesied that a great Muslim
teacher would come to the area. The prophecy was
fulfilled in the person of Sheikh Mumin Abdullahi (q.v.),
whose tomb near Bur Acaba is today a scene of pilgrimage.

BURAAMBUR. Poems composed by and for women. Sometimes the chanting of the poems, sung solo by women,
is accompanied by drums, tambourines, handclapping,
and stepping. Every stanza ends with a chorus of
trills. The buraambur is lighter and less stylized than
the gabay (q.v.). The subject may be a wedding, the
death of a loved one, the excellence of a friend, or
other important and serious matters. Although there
are many buraambur, the names of their composers
are on the whole unknown, or at least unrecorded. See
also GEERAAR; JIIFTO; MANSO; POETRY; SONGS.

BURTON, RICHARD F. (1821-1890). In 1854, the British
explorer and writer traveled from Zeila to Harar, then
an independent Muslim principality. Burton's book describing this journey, First Footsteps in East Africa,
is of great historical interest. Preparing to embark
on a new expedition in 1855, Burton was at Berbera,
where his camp was attacked by Somalis; a British officer in his party was killed, and Burton received a
sword wound. The Habr Awal clan of the Isaaq clan
family acknowledged responsibility for the attack, paid
the British $15,000 in compensation, and signed a
trade treaty which allowed the British to establish a
Resident at Berbera.

- C -

CAMEL CONSTABULARY. Organized by the British in 1912
to maintain order in the interior of the protectorate.
Under Richard Corfield, it carried out punitive operations against Sayyid Mohamed Abdullah Hassan and
other armed dissidents. It was ambushed in 1913 and
Corfield and most of the 150-member force were killed.
It was re-formed and continued to combat the dervishes
until 1920.

CAMELS (geel). Of the several breeds of camels in Somalia,
all are of the Arabian type, with one large hump. The
camel is the most prized possession of the nomadic

pastoralist, next to the horse, and camel herds may range from 10 or fewer to many thousands. Camels are praised in poems and are sung to by the camel herders at night and while on trek and at the wells.

The camel is both a sign of wealth and a source of food, providing milk and, on special occasions, meat. Its skin is used for leather. Although never ridden, the camel is used to carry loads, such as the materials for the nomadic hut (agal). Traditionally the camel is a unit of value in paying bride wealth (mahar) and blood compensation (dia). Camels are an important item in the export trade.

Camels bear the brand of the lineage group, while sheep and goats carry that of the individual owner. Camels are herded by unmarried males between the ages of about seven and twenty. The boys caring for a herd of camels are usually brothers or cousins. During the rainy season of gu, when the grass is full of moisture, the Somali camel can go without water for perhaps two months. In the dry seasons, it must be watered every two or three weeks. See GEELHER; HERDING.

The grazing camels are mostly breeding females; male camels and unproductive females are sold. Some males are fattened for slaughter on festive or religious occasions, are used for carrying burdens, and a few are retained for breeding.

A boy in the nomadic family is given a female camel at birth and at other times as a gift. Thus, his herd begins with the "navel-knot," or first, camel, and grows as she and others that he receives as gifts breed.

CAPE GUARDAFUI. The easternmost tip of the Horn of Africa, marking the entry to the Gulf of Aden from the Indian Ocean. The cape was historically a signal of danger for small ships buffeted by the monsoons. The Italians raised a lighthouse on it in 1922.

CARAVAN TRADE. Produce from the interior to the coastal cities has been carried by caravans of 15 to 20 or more camels since time immemorial. The caravans passed through the territory of many, often hostile, clans, and their safety depended, at each stage, on the protection of a local abbaan.

CATTLE. Somali cattle are largely of the Zebu variety,

with a hump on the back.   They are a major item in
the export trade.   Cattle herding is carried on primarily in the Southern Region.   Cattle provide milk, meat,
butter, and leather.   Oxen are used for plowing, but
not as pack animals, except in areas where there are
no camels.
       Since cattle are more vulnerable to the semi-
desert conditions of the country than camels, cattle
herding is practiced in the better-watered areas, often
in conjunction with agriculture.   Somali cattle herders
often had as their clients the farmers who lived in the
Juba and Shebelle river areas.   See ARIFA; HERDING;
MEAT PROCESSING.

CECCHI, ANTONIO (d. 1896).   Italian consul at Zanzibar in
    1896, an explorer who made several journeys into the
    little-known interior of northeast Africa, and an ardent
    colonialist.   Cecchi was one of the chief organizers of
    the Benadir Company, which in 1898 took over adminis-
    tration of the areas formerly administered by the Filo-
    nardi Company.
       In the fall of 1896, Cecchi led an expedition to
    explore the Shebelle River area and to meet Osman
    Ahmed, Sultan of the Geledi.   The expedition was am-
    bushed, and Cecchi and 13 other Italians were killed.
    In 1897, the Italians avenged the attack by sending an
    armed expedition against the Geledi and other clans.
    An investigation later determined that the ambushers
    were not operating on orders from the Geledi sultan,
    but were instigated by a former Arab employee of the
    Filonardi Company, discontent over his discharge by
    the Benadir Company.

CENSORSHIP.   No official board of censorship existed in
    Somalia prior to the 1969 coup, but most of the media
    of communication were government-owned, and radio
    and newspaper comments normally represented the of-
    ficial point of view.   A few private newspapers and
    journals were published intermittently, some of them
    highly critical of the government.   Immediately after
    the October 1969 coup, a Board of Censorship was es-
    tablished in the new Ministry of Information and Na-
    tional Guidance.   Its function is to tailor books, plays,
    pictures, radio programs, films, publications, etc. so
    as to convey the right ideas and prevent the dissemina-
    tion of unsuitable material from abroad and within.

CENSUS. No scientifically based census has been undertaken,
and all statistics on population are estimates. While
government estimates of population in 1971 were set at
4.5 million, other estimates were as low as three million. In 1974, high school students were released from
school for a year to conduct a national census. See
also POPULATION.

CHADAR. A legendary figure, an immortal person, usually
disguised as an old beggar, who bestows good fortune
on those who are kind to him. It is believed that Chadar has no bone in his right thumb. This has led to
the handshake where not only the palm, but also the
thumb, is grasped.

CHIEFS. Traditionally, chiefs were regarded as first among
equals. Even though there might be a chiefly family
from which leaders were chosen, the individual had to
be elected or approved by the entire clan assembly
(shir). The colonial governments paid stipends to the
chiefs, and this practice was continued by the Republic.
     Since the 1969 coup, the title of chief or elder
(soldaan, bogor, ugas, gerad, malak, akil, etc.) has
been abolished, and that of peacekeeper (nabaddon) substituted. Former chiefs continue to draw their stipends, but no longer represent their clans. They are
primarily engaged as officers of self-help schemes, in
which they collect funds for the schemes and collabo-
rate with the police or army groups in charge of the
self-help operations. They attend orientation seminars
at which they study the charters of the government, the
principles of scientific socialism, and other subjects
important to their particular area.

CHINA. Chinese records of contact with the Somali coast go
back to the 9th century. Chinese coins of the Tang
(618-960) and Sung (960-1279) dynasties and pieces of
pottery of the Sung period have been found at Mogadishu
and Brava. Records of the Ming dynasty (1368-1644) indicate that the Chinese navigator Cheng-Ho visited Mogadishu, Brava, and other ports in 1416 and 1421.
These records describe the coastal cities as flourishing
centers of commerce. They seem to indicate that am-
bassadors from the cities visited China.
     It is not definitely known whether these early
contacts actually occurred or whether the records were
based on evidence that Chinese mariners and geographers

obtained from Arab traders and seamen with whom the
Chinese dealt.   It is conjectured that the Chinese coins
and pottery might have been brought to Somalia by
Arabs who obtained them at other trading centers.
These doubts do not preclude the possibility that direct
Chinese contacts with Somalia did occur, however.   After the mid-1400s, Chinese seapower became more restricted, and Portuguese mariners began to dominate
the Indian Ocean sea lanes.

     Since independence, the Republic has received
loans, grants, and technical assistance from the
People's Republic of China.   Trade agreements have
been signed, Somali students have studied in the People's
Republic of China, and, on a broader basis, it has
played a role in promoting Afro-Asian solidarity.

CIRCUMCISION.   Boys are circumcised between the ages of
six and ten.   An uncircumcized male is considered un-
clean (haram), and cannot marry a Somali woman.
Circumcision is traditionally performed by a Midgan
(q.v.), and is usually an individual, not a group, rite.
See also INFIBULATION.

CIVIL SERVICE.   An independent Civil Service Commission
was established under the 1960 Constitution, and a
commission to regulate appointments and promotions
was established in 1962 to assure impartial arrangements in the Northern and Southern Regions.   Entrance
to the civil service was based on competitive exams
and scholastic ratings.   Civil servants could not hold
office in political parties or run for political office.
But, because of the strength of clan kinship ties, which
led many civil servants to deal with their own clansmen on a preferential basis, the civil service did not
develop as an impartial, neutral institution.

     After the 1969 coup, civil service officials
were given a three-month orientation course to acquaint
them with the new government's aims and were required
to spend a period working on crash development programs.   Students are assured of work in government
service and are required to attend a four-month orientation program upon graduation.   The government introduced a new and generous pension system for civil servants in 1970, passed a law prohibiting high-ranking
officials from buying or constructing private buildings,
and required them to take an oath to serve the country
and its people honestly and without corruption.

CLAN FAMILIES.   There are six important Somali clan
families.   Four of these--the Darod, Dir, Hawiye, and
Isaaq--make up the Samaal (sometimes spelled Somal)
division of the Somali people, while the other two clan
families--the Digil and Rahanweyn--make up the Saab
division.   The Samaal clan families have a nomadic
pastoral tradition; the Saab have a sedentary tradition
of cultivating or landownership, although many also own
cattle.   See SAAB; SAMAAL.   Also see SAB.
   The Saab and Samaal are grouped together at a
high genealogical level, where the two ancestors in the
total Somali genealogy are traced back to common
Arabian origins and linked to the lineage of the Prophet
Mohamed.   In times past, the Saab were considered inferior by the Samaal for several reasons: their ethnic
heterogeneity, which includes intermixture with Negroid
and probably Galla peoples; their "more lowly" genealogical antecedents; and their association with agriculture rather than pastoralism, which the Samaal regard
as the most noble occupation.

CLAN-FAMILY SEGMENTATION.   In the traditional nomadic
social structure, the clan family was too large, too
widely scattered, and too unwieldy to act as a single
political unit.   Within each clan family, smaller units
were able to act; the largest such unit was the clan
and the smallest was the rer.   In between the clan,
which may have thousands of members, and the rer,
which may consist of as few as five families, are
other groupings which, especially among the nomadic
pastoralists, would often act together under formal
agreements (heer), to wage war, pay or receive blood
compensation, and engage in other cooperative activities.
   In the sedentary agricultural areas of the
northwest and around the rivers, political groups were
more usually related to village organization than to
clan-family units.   And in the oldest cities and towns,
local clans, unrelated to the large clan families,
existed.

CLITORIDECTOMY   see   INFIBULATION

CONCESSION AGRICULTURE.   In 1908, some of the lands
along the Shebelle River were set aside by the colonial
government for an expected influx of Italian farmers.
The lands had previously been farmed by the clients

and slaves of Somali clans who, after the abolition of
slavery, returned to a life of nomadic or seminomadic
pastoralism. Few Italian farmers came, and most of
the early concessions failed; the concessionaires did
not understand the nature of the soil and climate, and
they were unable to secure an adequate supply of farm
workers, except through a system of forced labor.
        A highly successful venture in the production
of sugarcane was initiated in 1920 by the Duke of
Abruzzi--the Società Agricola Italo-Somala (SAIS)--at
Jowhar. The Somali government in 1963 purchased a
one-half ownership in SAIS and formed the National
Company for Agriculture and Industry (SNAI). After the
1969 coup, the company was completely nationalized.
        Banana plantations had become the chief form
of concession agriculture by the 1930s, and from 1932
to the mid-1960s bananas were the country's chief export. Banana plantations were established at Jenale
and other villages on the Shebelle River. The Supreme
Revolutionary Council established a National Banana
Board in 1970 to regulate and control the industry, but
it has not nationalized the plantations, which are now
owned by Italians and Somalis.

CONFERENZA see SOMALIA CONFERENCE

CONSTITUTION. When the state of Somaliland (the present
    Northern Region) became independent on June 26, 1960,
    its constitution established a four-member Council of
    Ministers and a Legislative Assembly of 33 elected
    members.   Five days later, Somaliland and the newly
    independent trust territory (the present Southern Region)
    united to form the Somali Republic; their legislatures
    combined to form the National Assembly.   At that time,
    the constitution of the trust territory, written and de-
    bated during the preceding three years, became the
    constitution of the entire nation.   It was ratified in a
    national referendum in June 1961.   In this referendum,
    the constitution was not approved in the Northern Re-
    gion (where some groups boycotted the referendum),
    but it was overwhelmingly approved in the South, and
    so carried.
        The constitution included a bill of rights not
    subject to amendment.   It provided for a democratic
    state, with a president (head of state) elected by the
    National Assembly; a prime minister (head of govern-
    ment) named by the president; an independent judiciary;

and a unicameral National Assembly of 123 deputies elected for five years. The constitution provided a system of checks and balances to ensure that no one branch of government would gain dominance over another, and it provided that ex-presidents would become deputies in the National Assembly for life.

After the coup in 1969, the constitution was suspended. Even before the coup, President Abdirashid Ali Shermarke had called on constitutional experts to examine the constitution and suggest revisions, especially in connection with election malpractices.

CONSULTATIVE COMMISSION FOR INTEGRATION (LEGISLATION). After unification in 1960, this commission was established. Its purpose was to ensure the smooth integration of the Northern and Southern Regions. The two regions, having had different pre-independence colonial governments, had disparate legal and educational systems, election rules, taxation and customs regulations; they had separate budgets, civil service systems, currencies, police forces, etc. The commission was headed by Paolo Contini, a United Nations expert, and had members from Somalia, Great Britain, and Italy. When it finished its work in 1964, it was renamed the Consultative Commission for Legislation, and was headed by a Somali, Michael Mariano.

CORPO ZAPTIÉ. An armed force established in the Italian colony in 1923. It was composed of about 800 Somali, Eritrean, and Arab troops led by Italian Carabiniere officers, and was employed to dis-arm the nomadic population. Later it included policemen (askari) recruited from local clans. During the Italo-Ethiopian war (1935-1936), the Corpo Zaptié contained about 6,000 Somalis. In all, about 40,000 Somalis took part in that war, many of them porters and laborers.

CÔTE FRANÇAISE DES SOMALIS see FRENCH TERRITORY OF THE AFARS AND ISSAS

COTTON. Cotton of the Sakellaridis variety is grown largely in the irrigated areas of the lower Juba River; some is grown on the plantations of the National Company for Agriculture and Industry at Jowhar, where some cottonseed oil is also produced. Cotton was the chief export crop of the Italian colony in the 1920s, but was surpassed by bananas in the 1930s. Although wild cotton

may have grown in Somalia in the distant past, it is
believed that cotton for the urban weaving industry was
imported prior to the mid-1800s. By the late 1800s,
cotton grown in Somalia supplied the local weavers.
See BENADIR COTTON.

COUNCIL OF ELDERS. 1) In 1957, this largely advisory
body replaced the Protectorate Advisory Council in
British Somaliland; it constituted a kind of "Upper
House."
          2) The phrase is also used in a general sense.
See, for example, COURTS.

COUPS D'ETAT. An attempted coup in the north in 1961
was quickly aborted. The only successful coup d'état
in the Republic, the "October Revolution," took place
on October 21, 1969. Suspected counter-coups were
squashed in 1971 and 1974 and their alleged leaders
either executed or imprisoned.

COURTS. Courts in the traditional society consisted of
councils of elders and specialists in customary law
known as wayel and akhyar. See also DIA-PAYING
GROUP.
          The constitution (suspended in 1969) provided
for five levels of courts: (1) qadi courts which deal
with family and personal matters under Islamic and
customary law; (2) district courts which deal with civil
and criminal cases; (3) regional courts with civil and
criminal sections (also dealing with military justice in
Mogadishu and Hargeisa); (4) high courts of assize, with
appellate sections for civil, criminal, and military
cases; and (5) a supreme court, the final court of appeal.
          The Supreme Revolutionary Council (SRC) as-
sumed all judicial as well as executive and legislative
powers at the time of the October 1969 coup. The
SRC suspended the Supreme Court, but reopened it in
December 1969. The new government also established
a National Security Court to rule on cases involving
persons accused of attempting to destroy the independence, unity, and security of the state. On the whole,
the court structure remains very much the same as
before the coup.

CREDITO SOMALO   see   SOMALI CREDIT BANK

CROCE DEL SUD HOTEL. The Hotel of the Southern Cross
    in Mogadishu is a landmark and popular meeting place,
    with its sidewalk cafe. The hotel is the oldest modern
    hotel in the city. It was constructed to accommodate
    the entourage accompanying the Italian King Victor
    Emanual III on his visit to Somalia in the summer of
    1934.

CURRENCY. Chinese coins of the period 618 to 1279 have
    been found in the sand along the southern coast. A
    collection of over 7, 000 coins dating from the 13th to
    the 16th century, minted in Mogadishu, apparently,
    under 23 different rulers, indicates that the city in that
    period had its own currency. Egyptian silver coins of
    the late 1300s have been found in the Adal towns of the
    Northern Region. The Maria Theresa, or Levantine,
    thaler, originally an Austrian coin issued for trade pur-
    poses after 1780, was used widely in the Somali ports
    until 1910. It was the currency in which the colonial
    powers paid for their concessions and protectorates on
    the Somali coast.
        The Italians introduced an Italian rupee, which
    was used for a while in their area; later the Italian
    lira was used. In British Somaliland, the British East
    African and Indian rupees were used, and later the
    East African shilling. The dollar was used to some
    extent in international trade after the 1850s, though
    American and European traders sometimes paid for
    their purchases in silver or gold.
        During the Trusteeship period, the somalo was
    introduced in the Southern Region; somalos were con-
    verted into the Somali shilling in 1962. The East Af-
    rican shilling which had been used in the Northern Re-
    gion was exchanged for Somali shillings and ceased to
    be legal tender in the Republic in 1961. The Somali
    shilling exchanged at about seven shillings to the dollar
    in 1975 and was not easily convertible outside Somalia.
        Until the late 1900s, purchases in the interior
    were based almost exclusively on barter arrangements.
    The tob, a 14-yard length of cotton cloth, was the
    standard of exchange for large transactions. Glass
    beads and tobacco were used for smaller purchases.
    Traders often bartered cloth for livestock, and then
    exchanged the livestock for ivory, which they exported.

CUSTOMARY LAW see HEER; TESTUR

- D -

DABSHID.   The Somali seasonal new year (the night of the
        fire).   Also called neirus.
                The Gregorian calendar is used by the govern-
        ment and by the townspeople, but the life of the pas-
        toralists and agriculturalists is traditionally based on
        the lunar and solar calendars, with specific dates de-
        termined by astrologers and weather lore experts.   Ac-
        cording to the date of dabshid, usually one of the first
        four days of August, the expert foretells the rains, the
        winds, the time of foaling, the dates of feasts, fasts,
        pilgrimages, and so on.
                Traditionally, the dabshid celebration begins at
        dusk on the last night of the old year.   A small fire is
        lit in front of the house, and old and young gather
        around.   All members of the family, including children
        and grandparents, leap over the fire a number of times,
        each according to his age.   It is a happy and lively
        festival and is celebrated throughout the Republic.

DAGAHTUR MONUMENT.   Dagahtur means "throwing stones."
        In 1948, in Mogadishu, at the time of the visit of the
        Four Power Commission of the Allied Powers' Council
        of Foreign Ministers, a politically motivated riot oc-
        curred in which 17 Somalis and 51 Italians were killed.
        In 1970, the Dagahtur Monument was constructed on the
        site, which was formerly marked by a column of stones.
        The monument is dedicated to the nation's heroes.

DAIR.   The light rainy season from September or October
        to December, when there is a lull between the mon-
        soons.   During dair, the nomads concentrate near their
        home wells.   Among the agriculturalists, early dair is
        the season of the first harvest and the sowing of the
        second crop; it is traditionally the season of marriage
        among the cultivators.

DALAD.   The founding stock among the Digil-Rahanweyn
        clan families.   The term mindihay (knife-bearer) is al-
        so used to designate this clan segment, as is the word
        urad.   Traditionally the dalad initiated all joint clan
        activities, such as the rainmaking ceremony (roobdoon)
        and the ritual slaughtering of livestock used in religious
        ceremonies.   The dalad represent the unity of the clan
        despite its political subdivisions and ethnic heterogene-
        ity.

DANCES.   Traditionally, dances are performed on many religious and civil occasions, on feast days, on the kill-
ing of a lion, and at other times.   Among the Somalis,
dancing is accompanied by handclapping and singing,
and sometimes by drums; the Negroid groups use drums
and tambourines, and some groups of non-Somali origin
use masks.
        Among the nomads particularly, where marriage
is exogamous, dances in which both men and women
take part are performed by the young men of one clan
segment and the young women of another.   Seldom if
ever do men and women of the same group dance together.   During the dances, men sing improvised praise
songs and jests, often in metaphoric language, and the
women reply.   Sometimes the men dance with their
spears and shields.

DANDARAWIYA.   A small tariqa, a branch of the Ahmadiya,
with a few agricultural settlements in the north.   The
Dandarawiya is more puritanical in its religious ob-
servances than the Ahmadiya, Qadariya, Rifaiya, or
Salihiya.

DARDOWN.   A sab group engaged primarily in weaving.
Traditionally they lived among the Hawiye in the Mudugh
Region.

DAROD.   One of the four Samaal clan families.   The Darod
is the most numerous and the most widely dispersed of
the clan families.   Within the Republic, the Darod number over 1.5 million; they occupy the Bari and Nugal
Regions and parts of the Mudugh, Tug Dheer, Sanaag,
and Lower Juba Regions.   Outside the Republic, they
are found in the Ogaden and Harar regions of Ethiopia
and in the North-Eastern Region of Kenya.   Those in
the trans-Juba and in Kenya are primarily cattle herders, while the others are camel herders.   Most engage
in some form of agriculture wherever cultivation is
possible.
        Genealogically, the Darod are believed to have
descended from Darod, an immigrant from Arabia in
the 10th or 11th century, who married a daughter of
the ancestor of the Dir clan family.   Other traditions
regarding the origin of the Darod exist.   See SHEIKH
JABARTI IBN ISMAIL.

DARWISH.   The Somali word for "dervish." 1) A dervish is a

person who lives in a religious settlement or jamaha.
In Somalia, "Sufi" and "dervish" are synonymous.

2) Darwish also has a special meaning in the
Somali area. The word was used to designate the followers of Sayyid Mohamed Abdullah Hassan. The Sayyid called his followers "darwish" to signify a brotherhood which transcended clan-family affiliations. Most
of his early followers were members of the Salihiya
tariqa, but as the movement grew, it embraced persons from perhaps all the tariqas and clan families.
Some of these were religious devotees in the sense
described in 1), but most were not.

DEATH RITES. Funeral rites are dictated by Islamic religious practices. Incense burners are lit under the
bed on which the corpse lies; burial is held promptly
after the body is washed and shrouded. Before burial,
and again on the seventh day, a funeral feast is celebrated by the wadad.
The grave is dug in an east-west direction,
and the body is placed so that the head faces Mecca.
Burial is accompanied by prayers. After the grave is
covered, it is outlined by a circle of stones, or if
stones are not available, the grave is covered with
branches. Slabs of stone or wood are placed at the
head and foot of the grave, and if the deceased is a
woman, a third slab is placed in the center. In some
areas, shrubs are planted on the grave.
Only widows wear signs of mourning--a white
head scarf in place of the usual colored one. Traditionally, the widow remains in a period of purification
for four months during which she does not go out of
the house or annoint herself with butter or remarry.
In earlier times, the widow of a man killed in battle
shaved her head.

DEG-DER (long ear). Deg-Der is a character in many Somali folktales, a kind of bogey man (or woman).

DEMOCRACY. The traditional Somali society has been described as democratic, almost to the point of anarchy,
with every adult male having equal voice in the shir,
or clan assembly. It has been said that "every Somali
is a sultan." Elders, not only old men but also younger ones who were seen as wise, acted as arbitrators,
conciliators, and decision makers. The power of chiefs
was personal, not institutionalized, and depended on the

charisma and leadership qualities of the individual.
    Among the nomads, there was no tradition of
hierarchical government. Among the sedentary agriculturalists, some elements of hierarchy did develop,
owing to the year-round attachment of people to one
place and the necessity of cooperative work on the
farms.
    In the traditional system, women and members
of the sab groups were excluded from the shir assemblies; arifa, or clients, might participate in an advisory
capacity. Under the modern system of government,
women and former sab members are legally equal to
Somali men and are entitled to all the rights and privileges traditionally and constitutionally accorded to Somali men.
    Differentiation within the adult male population
was traditionally made on a secular-religious basis,
with every Somali male being either a warrior (waran-
leh) or a religious (wadad).
    The relative absence of "great men" in Somali
history is directly related to the democratic system of
rule, in which power was exercised not by one strong
leader but by council meetings in which decisions were
taken by unanimous vote after every voice had been
heard.

DERVISH see DARWISH

DESERT LOCUST CONTROL ORGANIZATION OF EAST AF-
    RICA see LOCUST CONTROL

DESHEK. A natural basin which retains the river flood
    waters. Desheks may cover 2,000 to 5,000 acres and
    may remain flooded from two weeks to several months.
    When the flood recedes, the farmers plant their crops;
    the time of planting and the yield vary according to the
    extent of flooding and the time of recession.

DHOW. An ocean-going sailing vessel; some have engines
    today.

DHOW TRADE. Trade between the Somali coast and Arabia,
    India, and the Persian Gulf has been carried on by
    dhow for many centuries. Much of the coastwise ship-
    ping is today done by dhow. The dhow trade is season-
    al, depending on the monsoons. The northeast mon-
    soon, coming from the Arabian deserts, blows from

October to April; during this period dhows from the
east make their way down the Somali coast. With the
southwest monsoon, from April to September, the sailing vessels head toward the eastern Gulf of Aden ports,
and the Somali coastal towns that depend on the dhow
trade are inactive and relatively deserted.
     In 1965, about 60 per cent of the ships at
Somali ports were dhows and over 50 per cent of the
passengers arrived and left on dhows. These vessels
carried only seven per cent of the cargo of Somali
ports, however.

DIA. The compensation (often referred to as blood compen-
     sation) paid by a group when one of its members was
     found guilty of homicide or such lesser crimes as in-
     sult and injury. Compensation was traditionally made
     in livestock, or perhaps, in more recent times, par-
     tially in money. In the distant past, it is believed
     that payment may have been made in nubile women.
     Dia (Arabic), or mag (Somali), was paid by the group
     of the offender to the group of the victim; dia payment
     and receipt was thus a group responsibility and right.
     Dia, or blood compensation, is today illegal, and group
     responsibility for homicide has been replaced by indi-
     vidual responsibility.

DIA-PAYING GROUP. Traditionally, every Somali belonged
     to a dia-paying group. Children automatically belonged
     to their father's group; married women remained mem-
     bers of their own fathers' groups. In 1964, it was es-
     timated that over 1, 000 dia-paying groups existed in
     the Republic. Among the nomads, the dia-paying group
     was an alliance of lineages which acted as a unit in
     their dealings with members of other dia-paying groups.
     Among the agriculturalists, dia-paying groups were
     more often based on village of residence (or a group
     of villages). If a person was killed or injured by a
     member of a rival group, the elders of the two groups
     would meet to discuss the matter and arrange the pay-
     ment of compensation. Payment and receipt of com-
     pensation was a group, not an individual, responsibility.
          Among the nomads, the dia-paying groups
     ranged from 200 or 300 males to 5, 000. Among the
     sedentary farmers, dia-paying groups included whole vil-
     lages or groups of villages and ranged from perhaps
     5, 000 to 100, 000 men. The groups were concerned not
     only with the security of people and livestock, but also

with land and water rights. See DIA.

Warfare or combat between dia-paying groups
which resulted in death was traditionally compensated
by payment of 100 camels for a man (50 for a woman).
Settlement of compensation restored peace, while non-
settlement led to feuds and further intergroup warfare.
The obligations of dia-paying groups were traditionally
set forth in formal heer agreements, often written.
The agreements were subject to revision, and the membership of the groups, especially among the nomads,
changed frequently. During the colonial period, the
written agreements or treaties were filed with the District Commissioners or Residents.

DIGIL. One of the two Saab clan families. The Digil live
in the Southern Region, mainly between the two rivers
and on both sides of the Juba. Their number is estimated at 100, 000. Most of the Digil are agriculturalists,
although some also herd cattle and, to a lesser extent,
camels. Genealogically, the Digil are believed to be
the descendants of Saab, the brother, perhaps, of Samaal.

DIR. Believed to be the oldest of the four Samaal clan
families. By the 10th century, ancestors of the Dir
occupied land along the coast of the Gulf of Aden.
Within the Republic, the Dir are widely dispersed,
some (the Gadabursi) living in the northwestern part
of the Northern Region, some (the Bimal) in the area
between Mogadishu and Merca, and a few among other
groups in the riverine areas and in the trans-Juba.
The Issa clan in the French Territory of the Afars
and Issas is believed to belong to the Dir clan family;
other Dir live in Ethiopia. Most of the Dir in the
Northern Region are camel herders; those in the
Southern Region are primarily cattle herders; some are
farmers.

The Dir are believed to be descendants of an
Arab who migrated to the northern Somali shore. In
the genealogy of the Somali clan families, the daughters
of the Dir ancestor are said to have married immigrant
Arabs and thus given rise to the Isaaq and Darod clan
families.

DISTRICT COMMISSIONER (DC). Outlying units of government were in the colonial period administered by District Commissioners (called Residents in the Italian

area). This title and office was continued during the
trusteeship period in the Southern Region, and was also
continued by the Republic. See DISTRICT COUNCIL.
See also REGIONAL AND LOCAL GOVERNMENT.

DISTRICT COUNCIL. Established in the Southern Region in
1939, but without clearly defined powers. Councils
were composed of local clan leaders and operated under
the District Commissioner (or Resident). In 1946, the
British Military Administration (BMA) created District
as well as Provincial Advisory Councils whose chief
functions were to discuss local economic problems and
serve as a liaison between the people and the BMA
officers.
        During the trusteeship period, district councils
were composed of chiefs and notables, elected in clan
assemblies, and representatives of local political parties.
Their function was to aid the District Commissioner
(DC), the representative of the central government in
the district, and the DC was required to consult with
the council on local matters. The councils, especially
in the nomadic areas where the members were widely
scattered, were not very effective, but they did help to
minimize hostilities among the nomadic groups and to
settle disputes. See also MUNICIPAL COUNCIL.
        Under the Supreme Revolutionary Council, the
district councils are designated District Revolutionary
Councils.

DIVORCE. Among the Somali, permanent marriage is not
necessarily expected by either men or women, and the
divorce rate is said to be high. Traditionally, only the
man takes the initiative in divorce. If he is impotent
or diseased, however, the wife may appeal to the qadi,
or judge, for divorce. If the woman has committed a
grave offense or insists on divorce when the husband
does not want it, she may have to forfeit her bride
wealth (mahar). See MARRIAGE.
        The laws regulating divorce have been altered
in recent years so that men can no longer divorce their
wives simply by repeating three times the divorce form-
ula, "I divorce you, " as they could in the past. When
there is a divorce, the father traditionally has custody
of the children, although they usually stay with the
mother throughout early childhood, and in the case of
girls, until puberty.

DJIBOUTI (pop. c. 50,000). The capital and chief port of the French Territory of the Afars and Issas.

DJIBOUTI-ADDIS ABABA RAILROAD. The only railroad in the Horn of Africa. It is 486 miles long. It was begun in 1897 and completed in 1917 after many delays and interruptions. It lies wholly within Ethiopia and the French Territory of the Afars and Issas.

DOI. The large plain between the Juba and Shebelle Rivers; it is unfit for cultivation, but provides fine pasturage. It is sometimes called geel-geel (literally, many camels). Many of the pastoralists in the doi are attached to farming villages near the rivers, the farms being cultivated by hired workers, or in former days by slaves or clients.

Though the doi is now inhabited mainly by Digil, Rahanweyn, and some Hawiye, it was successively inhabited by various groups of Somalis during the southward migrations. The Digil may have entered the area in the 10th century, according to some authorities; the Rahanweyn, according to their traditions, entered the doi in the late 1500s. The Hawiye began drifting southward about 1300. The Bimal (Dir clan family), now in the zone between Mogadishu and Merca, probably passed through the doi in the 1500s. Darod groups passed through in the 1800s and moved on to the trans-Juba area.

DOUH. A dry watercourse which, after a heavy rain, may become a fast-moving stream. Also called tug or nulla.

DRYLAND FARMING. Wherever annual rainfall is at least 12 inches--in some places in the northwest and in some other areas, but chiefly between the two rivers--grain and other crops are grown. See AGRICULTURE.

DUBAT. A Somali word meaning an irregular fighter (not a regular member of a more or less permanent armed force) who was employed by the colonial governments to take part in the "pacification" expeditions.

DURRA. A variety of sorghum. See MILLET.

DWELLINGS see AGAL; ARCHITECTURE; ARISH; GURGI; MUNDUL

- E -

EDUCATION.   Traditionally, formal education in Somalia
means religious education.   Four- to six-year-old
children in the nomadic and agricultural hamlets are
taught the principles of Islam.   Teachers are wadads
or advanced Koranic students who travel from place to
place, teaching and performing religious services.
Such schools are called her schools, her being the
word for the religious teacher.   Boys, and some girls,
whose parents wish them to receive further religious
education attend schools run by a tariqa where they
study math and learn to read and write Arabic.   The
most dedicated students may then enroll in an Islamic
institute.

    Some Koranic schools received small grants
from the colonial governments, but in large part, the
her schools, often operating only intermittently, were
supported by the groups they served.   On the whole,
schools run by Christian missionaries during the colonial period were rejected by the Somalis because of
their suspicion of non-Islamic teaching.   Some boys
who completed five years of mission school, however,
were sent by the colonial authorities to Islamic schools
in the Sudan for further instruction.

    It is said that in the Northern Region, Western-
style formal education was begun in the interval between
the two world wars by Mohamoud Ahmed Ali, a government clerk.   He asked the British administrator for financial help, and after some delay, was given £19 to
start a school for Somali boys.   In 1949, Mohamoud
Ahmed Ali was appointed inspector of schools in British
Somaliland.   Another educator, Haji Ismail Farrah,
opened a school for girls in Burao.   A similar development took place in the Southern Region, pioneered by
Jama Bilal Mohamed, who opened a private school in
Mogadishu in 1936.   Twelve Catholic mission elementary
schools were established in the larger southern towns
in the 1920s and 1930s; they were attended by Italians
as well as some Somalis.

    Beginning in the mid-1940s, or slightly earlier,
the Somali Youth League was instrumental in improving
education in the Southern Region.   It held classes in
many major towns, introduced English instruction in the
south, and adopted a secular approach to Western-style
education, which Somalis could more easily accept than
the mission approach.

During the 1950s, the Trusteeship Administration in the south, with the aid of a UNESCO team, launched a unified educational system designed to prepare the territory for independence. Attempts were made to provide basic education for adults and children, not only in the towns, but also in the nomadic interior. Under the program, a teacher training institute was established, and a number of vocational training institutions (agriculture, fishing, commerce, carpentry, construction, mechanics, electronics, etc.) were set up. Most of the teachers at this time were Italian, although the Egyptian government established several schools in the trust territory, with Egyptian teachers and with instruction in Arabic.

The School of Politics and Administration, later converted into the School of Public Finance and Commerce, was organized for persons with some experience in government, politics, or commerce. This was an upper-level secondary school, and its graduates received 18-month scholarships to study in Italy. A Higher Institute of Law and Economics was inaugurated in 1954 to provide a two-year diploma course. It was associated with the University of Rome and later (1960) became the University Institute of Somalia. Similarly in the Northern Region, education was improved in the 1950s, especially after the middle of the decade when it became apparent that the protectorate was headed for independence.

After independence, all these institutions were continued, and additional elementary and secondary schools were established. Education up to the intermediate level was made compulsory in 1974. The National University, established in the early 1970s, grew out of the University Institute. Located in Mogadishu, but with branches at Afgoy, it is a degree-granting institution, with instruction in law and economics, liberal arts, general science, veterinary medicine, mathematics, engineering, agriculture, and education. A four-year medical faculty was established in 1972. See also LANGUAGE.

EGYPT. It is believed that ancient Egyptian contact with the Somali coast dates back to perhaps 3700 BC, and continued until about 350 BC. Some authorities believe that the people of the two areas at that time were racially related and that they maintained cultural and commercial ties both by overland travel and by sea.

In 1869-70, Egypt, under Ottoman Turkish rule, made a first attempt to gain control over the Somali Gulf of Aden ports, which were under the general control of Turkey, but governed by local chiefs or sultans. Between 1874 and 1876, Egypt sent expeditions to the coast and established a garrison at Harar, a city on the interior trade routes. In 1877, Egypt and Britain signed a treaty in which Britain recognized Egypt's occupation of the entire northern coastal area. Great Britain was primarily interested in keeping the ports open, because her colony at Aden depended on supplies from the Somali interior. Egypt improved the ports, built lighthouses, and constructed some watering places. In 1875, Egypt tried to extend her dominion to the southern ports. Egyptian ships appeared at Brava in that year, but withdrew in 1876. In 1879, Egyptian seamen attempted to sail up the Juba River.

When Egypt was forced to withdraw from the northern area in 1884, because of a revolt in the Sudan, where her troops were needed, Britain occupied the northern coastal towns and signed treaties of protection with the Somali clans on the Gulf of Aden coast.

During the trusteeship period in the Southern Region, an Egyptian member served on the United Nations Advisory Council in Mogadishu. In 1957, the delegate who was then in Mogadishu, Mohammed Kamal Eddine Saleh, was assassinated by a Somali; the murder did not, apparently, have any political implications.

Egypt has granted Somalia credits for development projects since the 1960s, and has operated schools in Somalia as well as granting scholarship aid to Somali students in Cairo.

EL. A well, excavated in the rocks or earth, as distinguished from other kinds of watering places, such as uars and ballis (q.v.). Wells are normally the property of the clan group occupying the territory where they are located. If there are many wells in one area, they are divided among the clan subgroups. Some wells are privately owned.

Traditionally, the right to use wells varies from group to group. Among the Hawiye, a person who digs a well in a region where there are other wells may restrict the well to his own use; if there are no commonly owned wells in the vicinity, he cannot keep his fellow clansmen from using his well, but he may require them to pay for the water they take.

Among the Darod, the owner of a privately dug well cannot deny his fellow clansmen free use of it, no matter where it is located. Among the Rahanweyn, wells are communal property and are usually divided among the rers, or subgroups. With the chief's permission, a person may excavate a private well where communal wells already exist; his fellow clansmen may use the well, but they must pay him--in money, milk, butter, or grain.

EL BUR. A town in the Galguduud Region, the center of meerschaum production and craftsmanship. In 1925, El Bur was the scene of an anti-Italian uprising led by Omar Samantar (q.v.).

ELMI "BONDERII" (c. 1908-1941). A Somali poet who composed gabay (q.v.). The poet's last name is not known; bowndheri or boderii, as it is sometimes written, is believed to be a corruption of the word "boundary." The poet is said to have died of love, and the story of his unrequited love is known to all Somalis. His use of the gabay form to discuss the subject of love was an innovation.

ETHIOPIA. Contiguous with Somalia along the disputed western boundary. Ethiopia has long laid claim to the Somali areas, and at times, even in recent decades, Ethiopian-Somali conflicts over the boundary have ended in battle. See AXUM; IRREDENTISM.

In the 15th and 16th centuries, the Ethiopians, with the aid of the Portuguese in the 16th century, invaded the territory belonging to the Adal Muslim sultanate in the north. This action along with the Galla-Ethiopian wars of the same period halted Somali expansion to the west. See ADAL; AHMAD GURAY.

Menelik II, formerly King of the region of Shoa, became Emperor of Ethiopia in 1889. Under his rule, the Ethiopian empire was consolidated under one central government, and attempts were made to expand into territories which the European powers were seeking to colonize. These included the Somali-inhabited areas adjacent to and embracing the present Republic. See ANGLO-ETHIOPIAN DIPLOMACY; FRANCO-ETHIOPIAN AGREEMENTS OF 1897; ITALO-ETHIOPIAN ACCORDS.

The Somalis living in Ethiopia today number at least 1 million; they occupy about one-fifth of the nation

(territory contiguous with Somalia in Ethiopia's Harar
and Sidamo Provinces). In addition to those Somalis
who live permanently in Ethiopia, thousands of Somali
nomads from the Republic spend several months of
each year in the Ogaden and Haud regions of Ethiopia,
their traditional grazing grounds during the rainy season.

     Although a few Somalis have from time to time
been appointed to serve in the Ethiopian Parliament
and a few have held other high-ranking positions, it is
believed that the great majority of Somalis living in
Ethiopia would prefer to unite with the Republic. During the trusteeship period, and during the first seven
years of independence, the political parties and the
government of Somalia strongly advocated the extension
of the Republic to include the Somali-inhabited areas
of Ethiopia (as well as such areas in northeast Kenya and
the French Territory of the Afars and Issas). The
Somali Constitution of 1960 incorporated this policy, but
designated the use of peaceful means only to accomplish
it. Between 1960 and 1964, armed clashes along the
provisional Ethiopian-Somali border were not infrequent.

     In the Northern Region, one of the chief moti-
vations behind the demand for independence in the
middle and late 1950s was the 1954 Anglo-Ethiopian
agreement which transferred the Haud and "reserved"
area to Ethiopian rule. See GREATER SOMALIA; IR-
REDENTISM.

ETHNIC BALANCE. After the 1959 general elections, the
    Somali government in the trust territory instituted a
    policy of balancing the weight of ethnic (i.e., clan-
    family) groups within the cabinet and other appointive
    offices. To a large extent, the policy was continued
    in the Republic throughout the next ten years. Theo-
    retically, it was a continuation of the traditional politi-
    cal system, in which the ability to conciliate competi-
    tive forces was one of the chief requirements for lead-
    ership.

     The policy was criticized by persons and
groups who had little power in government, and was
equated with corruption, nepotism, and tribalism. In
particular, critics claimed that the policy prohibited
the government from dealing with tribalism and from
devising a modern tax structure that would enable it to
handle urgent social and economic problems. Some
claimed that ethnic balance in government encouraged

clan competition and thus undermined attempts to eliminate tribalism.   See TRADITIONALISM; TRIBALISM.

EUROPEAN ECONOMIC COMMUNITY (EEC).   Somalia is an
associate member of the EEC by virtue of the Southern
Region's status as a former trust territory of an EEC
member.   Somalia's chief export to the EEC market is
bananas.   The Republic has received assistance from
the EEC in the funding of a hospital; in the construction of roads, watering facilities, and a telecommuni-
cation system; in the control of animal diseases; in the
development of a grapefruit plantation; and in the funding of other projects, such as the construction of the
new university.

EXPORTS.   The major exports of the Republic are bananas,
canned meat and fish, raw hides and skins, livestock,
and aromatic gums.   The last three items have been
the area's chief exports for many centuries.   Bananas
became an important export during the 1930s.   The
total value of exports is estimated to be about $30
million per year.
         In the late 1960s, the government chartered a
ship, in competition with carriers from other nations,
to ensure that livestock exported on hoof would not be
overcrowded.   It is reported that as a result the mor-
tality rate of such exports dropped from ten per cent
to 0.03 per cent.   In 1968, over 1.25 million sheep
and goats, 17,000 camels, and 37,000 head of cattle
were exported from Berbera, the point of export of
most livestock.   The opening of the new harbor at
Berbera in 1968 ensured that shipping could be carried
on with no gap between monsoons.
         To offset the effect of the 1967 closing of the
Suez Canal on the shipment of bananas, the government
engaged faster, better refrigerated ships to carry its
bananas to Europe.   As a consequence, the trip around
the Cape of Good Hope was only two days longer than
the old Suez route.   The opening of the deep seaport
at Kismayu in 1968 and the use of improved packaging
and better fungicides also helped to reduce wastage in
transit.

- F -

FAKHR DIN DYNASTY.   A hereditary sultanate established

in Mogadishu sometime during the 13th century to replace the loose federation of Arab and Persian immigrants who had governed the city since its founding in
the 9th or 10th century. Ibn Battuta, a Moroccan mariner, visited Mogadishu in 1331 and described the city
as the capital of a prosperous commercial sultanate,
ruled by a sultan of Somali origin who spoke "Maqdishi"
but also knew Arabic. The founder of the sultanate
was Abu Bakr b. Fakhr ad-Din. The sultanate was
replaced by the Muzaffar dynasty about 1500.

FARAH NUR (1858-1928). A poet, philosopher, and war
leader of the Arap in their successful efforts to free
themselves of Aidagalla domination (both groups are sub-
clans of the Isaaq clan family). He is known for his
poetic accounts of the anticolonial jihad of Sayyid Mohamed Abdullah Hassan and for his gabays on Somali
traditions.

FEUDS see INTERGROUP WARFARE

FIBER PRODUCTS. Heavy woven fiber mats are used to
cover the nomadic hut and to protect the back of the
pack camels. Finer ones are used as mattresses and
carpets. Some are made entirely of straw or leaves;
some are straw combined with colored cloth or thread.
Woven watertight vessels (dhiil) are used for carrying
milk and water. Wicker bags and baskets fill other
domestic needs; some are made of dyed straw woven
in geometric patterns, and some are decorated with
cowrie shells.

FILONARDI COMPANY. From 1893 to 1896, this company,
organized by Vincenzo Filonardi, administered the
Italian Benadir territories under lease to the Italian
government by the Sultan of Zanzibar. The main purpose of the company was to carry on a profitable trade,
and so the company made little attempt to colonize or
change the traditional political or social system. The
Treaty of Ucciali (1889) between Italy and Ethiopia was
in dispute during this period, and the Ethiopians were
beginning to lay claim to areas with which Filonardi
was attempting to build up trade relations. The Italian
defeat at Adowa in 1896 led to an upsurge of anti-
imperialistic sentiment in Italy, and Filonardi's request
for garrisons to protect his agents was disapproved by
the home government. In 1896, the company failed and

was, after a time, replaced by the Benadir Company. Although the Filonardi Company was not financially successful, its relations with the Somalis--except for one serious confrontation at Merca--were peaceful; it established Italian Residents at Mogadishu, Merca, Brava, and Lugh, and trading stations at Itala (Adale), Jumbo, and Warsheikh, all situated along the coast. The company had scant influence beyond the coastal districts.

FILONARDI, VINCENZO. Besides heading the Filonardi Company, Vincenzo Filonardi was the Italian consul at Zanzibar in the late 1880s. In 1889, he concluded treaties with two Somali sultans in the northeast and thus created two Italian protectorates, which remained under the administration of the Italian consul at Aden until 1908. See MIJERTEYN; OBBIA.

FIREARMS. In the Somali conquest of the Horn of Africa, the chief weapons of the Somali were the spear and shield. Bows and arrows were also used, and it is believed that they may have employed a few matchlock guns during and after the 16th century. During the 1880s, about the only firearms in Somalia were a few rifles presented to chiefs by European explorers. These were largely items of prestige and were not used as weapons. Beginning in the 1890s, Djibouti in French Somaliland became the center of the arms trade supplying the Ethiopian Emperor Menelik II. Some of these firearms found their way into Somalia, but it was not until the jihad (1899-1920) of Sayyid Mohamed Abdullah Hassan that firearms in significant quantities were used by Somalis. After the Sayyid's defeat, firearms were common.

The introduction of firearms into the territory upset the traditional balance of power among the various clan segments. No longer was the relative strength of the clans based primarily upon numbers. The first Fascist governor of the Italian colony, de Vecchi (1923-1928), sought to use the Corpo Zaptié to dis-arm the populations of the Benadir, Obbia, and Mijerteyn interior, a policy which led to the rebellions of Haji Hassan Barsane, Hersi Bogor, and Omar Samantar. Under the British Military Administration, after World War II, efforts were made to retrieve the rifles that had fallen into Somali hands during and after the war.

In 1970, the Supreme Revolutionary Council

issued regulations requiring that all firearms be turned
in to the government except those kept by nomads, dip-
lomats, tourists on temporary visits, foreigners working in remote areas, governors, and district and regional commissioners.

FISH PROCESSING. During the 1950s, the Kandala and Habo
companies, both private but assisted by public grants,
were established to produce canned tuna and fish flour.
In the 1960s, an American company built a cold storage
and canning plant at Alula, in the Bari Region on the
Gulf of Aden coast, but it failed because the quantity
of tuna caught was not sufficient. A private company
owned by a Somali was opened in 1968, with a concession area of about 200 miles of coast between Brava
and the Kenyan border. This company bought lobsters
from local fishermen and flew them to the company's
cold storage plant where they were prepared for export.
A state-owned tuna-processing plant at Las Koray, a
coastal town in the Sanaag Region, was built with aid
from the USSR and opened in 1970.

FISHING. Somalis traditionally dislike fish and disdain
people who eat fish. Some of the people living along
the rivers and southern coast do eat fish, and some of
them, for example the Bajuni, have a long tradition of
fishing. The Bajuni have developed a special method
of catching turtles; a trained sucker fish attached to a
line clamps onto the turtle's shell. The fisherman
reels in both turtle and sucker fish, and after remov-
ing the turtle, repeats the process. The shells of
both turtles and tortoises are sold. The meat is not
eaten.
          North of Hafun, in the Bari Region, ambergris
is swept up on the beaches along the Indian Ocean
coast. There the villagers, who have hereditary beach
rights, collect the ambergris and sell it to Arab traders. South of Hafun, villagers collect pelagic fish swept
up on the shores, dry it in the sun, and sell it.
          On the eastern coast of the Bari Region, deep-
sea shark fishing is an old industry. Sharks were traditionally caught in a net and killed by blows with a
harpoon. The pieces of meat were salted, exposed to
the sun, and then taken to Lamu and Zanzibar for sale.
The tail and fins were dried and sent to Bombay. See
FISH PROCESSING.

FLAG. The Somali flag is light blue with a five-pointed white star in the center. It was first flown in 1954 in the Southern Region. The five points represent the five areas in which pre-independence Somali peoples lived: the Trusteeship Territory, British Somaliland, French Somaliland, the Ethiopian area contiguous with the Republic, and the present North-Eastern Region of Kenya.

FOOD. While European and Oriental-style food is popular in restaurants in the coastal towns, traditional Somali dishes are generally preferred. Meat is not a staple in the diet; it is greatly liked, but is eaten most frequently during the dry seasons when camels and cattle produce little milk. Otherwise, meat is eaten mainly on festive or ritual occasions. It is either boiled or cut into small slices and cooked in butter (ghee) with aromatic herbs. It may be dried in the sun, cut into strips, and conserved in a vase of honey, from which it is taken to be cooked.

Millet, rice, and corn are staples. Millet is boiled in water to make a porridge. It may also be mixed with water or milk and made into cakes which are cooked over hot coals; sometimes it is boiled with beans. Grains of millet may be cooked in butter. Corn is boiled in water or parched. Beans and squash are boiled or cooked with butter. In the south, coffee beans are fried in butter and served with sugar or honey as a delicacy.

In the northeast, and wherever it is found, a fruit called geeb-yeeb is eaten; dates, which also grow in the northeast, are a popular item in the diet. In some areas, the fruit of the dum palm is used for making flour.

Milk, especially camel milk, is a staple in the Somali diet; when it is plentiful, it may be the sole food of camel herders for months on end. All Somalis drink tea (shah), which is made by boiling tea leaves in water with cinnamon sticks, cloves, and cardamom, with plenty of sugar, and with milk added.

FORCED LABOR. Although many farm laborers worked voluntarily, the success of the plantations of the early Italian settlers and concessionaires was made possible only by the use of forced labor. The forced laborers were paid (slightly less than voluntary workers) and were provided certain health and other benefits, but

they did not work on the plantations willingly. On the
whole, Somali agriculturalists preferred to work their
own farms only, and pastoralists regarded agricultural
work as demeaning. The early colonial literature
abounds with discussions of the "labor shortage" in the
colonies.

FOREIGN AID. Before independence, Great Britain in the
Northern Region and Italy in the Southern were the
chief sources of the external aid needed to balance the
budget and provide for development expenditure. From
1954 to 1960, the United States and Italy provided the
bulk of the $14 million in money and technical as-
sistance required to carry out the Seven-Year Development Plans in the Trust Territory.
    After independence the need for external aid
did not diminish, and the sources of foreign aid were
widely expanded. Italy remained the chief source, with
large amounts also coming from the US, the United
Nations, Great Britain, the EEC, the Soviet bloc, the
United Arab Republic, and the Federal Republic of Germany.
    Between 1954 and 1970, Somalia received from
the US over $49 million in grants and over $19 million
in loans, a total of $69.8 million. US aid was cut off
in 1969 when ships flying the Somali flag were spotted
trading with North Vietnam, although projects then
underway were continued. Between 1959 and 1967,
grants and loans from the USSR totaled $65.7 million.
USSR aid continues, going primarily for development
projects and military assistance. Aid from Great
Britain was halted from 1963 to 1968, a period when
diplomatic relations between the two nations were brok-
en off. In recent years, substantial aid, primarily in
the construction of roads and wells and in experimental
agricultural projects, has been received from the
People's Republic of China.
    It is reported that during the decade of the 1960s
Somalia received more foreign aid per capita than any
other developing country.

FOUR-POWER COMMISSION. Composed of representatives
of the US, USSR, Great Britain, and France. The
commission was appointed by the Allied Powers' Council of Foreign Ministers after World War II to determine the disposition of the former Italian colonies. It
visited Mogadishu in 1948 to try to ascertain the wishes

of the Somalis. The Somalis uniformly expressed their desire for self-government, but were not in agreement on the length of time needed to prepare for independence and on the nation or nations which would be most acceptable to govern them in the interim.

The British had put forward the Bevin Plan, which some Somalis favored. The Italians living in the area and pro-Italian Somalis (organized in a group called the Somalia Conference) wanted Italy to be the interim governor. Others, including the Somali Youth League, preferred a United Nations authority, while the Hizbia Digil-Mirifle Somali favored a four-power arrangement. The Four-Power Commission was unable to agree upon what to do, and so decided to turn the unresolved question over to the United Nations General Assembly. See UNITED NATIONS.

FRANCO-ETHIOPIAN AGREEMENTS OF 1897. In three agreements, France and Ethiopia established the boundary between the French Somaliland colony and Ethiopia and arrived at other political and economic accords. Under the boundary agreement, France ceded to Ethiopia a considerable portion of territory formerly regarded as part of French Somaliland. In return, France received assurances of increased Ethiopian trade through Djibouti, and vague promises of Ethiopian assistance for French occupation of the west bank of the White Nile.

FRANCO-ITALIAN AGREEMENT OF 1935. In this agreement between Mussolini, Italy's Fascist leader, and Pierre Laval, France's premier, France agreed to cede to Italy a part of French Somaliland and to sell Italy shares in the Djibouti-Addis Ababa railroad. After Italy's defeat in the Horn in 1941, the agreement was invalidated.

FRANKINCENSE see AROMATIC GUMS

FRENCH SOMALILAND see FRENCH TERRITORY OF THE AFARS AND ISSAS

FRENCH TERRITORY OF THE AFARS AND ISSAS. Since 1967 the name of the French overseas territory formerly called the Côte Français des Somalis, or French Somaliland. The territory covers about 8,800 square miles and has a population of about 95,000, approxi-

mately 45 per cent of whom are Issa and the remainder
Afar and Arab. The Issa are a clan of the Somali Dir
clan family. The Territory's major economic asset is the
port of Djibouti, which lies at the juncture of the Red Sea
and the Gulf of Aden.

It is believed that Arab immigrants came to
this coast as early as the 3rd century BC. Islamic
missionaries arrived in the 9th century or before and
formed Muslim states, the most important being Adal.
From the 13th to the early 17th centuries, the Muslim
states waged war with Ethiopia, which is believed to
have had some control over the area prior to the 9th
century. The Issa arrived after the Afar, perhaps in
the 9th or 10th century; they drove the Afar from the
southern area, fought with the Ethiopians to acquire
grazing lands, and were firmly established in the southern part of the territory by the 17th century.

French explorers visited the Red Sea in the
1830s and 1840s; in 1859, France signed trade treaties
with local Afar and Issa leaders, and in 1862 purchased the port of Obock on the Gulf of Tajura. A
French governor of Obock was appointed in 1884, and
in 1885 France extended her control, via treaties with
local leaders, to the northern shore of the Gulf of Tajura and to Djibouti in the south. The French government center was moved from Obock to Djibouti in 1892.
France signed boundary agreements with Great Britain
in 1888 and with Ethiopia in 1897. See ANGLO-FRENCH
TREATY OF 1888; FRANCO-ETHIOPIAN AGREEMENTS
OF 1897.

While Sayyid Mohamed Abdullah Hassan was
engaging Italy and Great Britain in the other Somali
territories, the French territory was relatively quiet,
and the French were strengthening their ties with Ethiopia and constructing the Djibouti-Addis Ababa railroad.
The railroad led to the growth and prosperity of the
port of Djibouti, where about half of the territory's
population resides.

The post-World War II wave of nationalism
that swept the Somali areas to the south had little effect on French Somaliland. The French had developed
Djibouti and established a salt factory, and the colony
was the most prosperous of all the Somali territories.
French policies hardly touched the life of the people
outside the port. A Representative Council, with most
of its members appointed by the French governor of
the territory, was established in 1945; a Somali repre-

sentative was appointed to the Council of the French Republic; and an Afar was appointed to the French Union Assembly. The territory also had an elected deputy in the French National Assembly.

The French loi cadre, applied in 1956, brought some important governmental reforms. In 1957 an elected Territorial Assembly, with responsibility for internal affairs was established. In 1958, a referendum was held, with voting extended to adult males, in which the territory voted to remain a French territory. The Territorial Assembly then voted to maintain the status of an overseas territory within the French Community.

Small political parties which had been organized in the mid-1950s disintegrated after the reforms were made, but by the mid-1960s local politicians were again organizing. In 1966 when the French President Charles de Gaulle visited the territory, tensions regarding the future of the area were so high that he was unable to make a planned public speech. Riots flared and a number of lives were lost. A second referendum was held in 1967, and again the territory opted to remain within the French Community, although it was alleged that the vote was "rigged."

The referenda of 1958 and 1967 aroused hopes among the Somalis of the neighboring areas that the French territory would become independent and perhaps unite with the Republic. The referenda aroused fear in Ethiopia that the territory would opt for independence and perhaps cut off Ethiopia's important outlet to the sea via the Djibouti-Addis Ababa railroad. Ethiopian troops massed near the border, and Haile Selassie announced that French Somaliland was an integral part of Ethiopia. Some observers feared that the situation would lead to a military confrontation between Ethiopia and the Republic. But the vote to remain with France tended, on both occasions, to ease international tensions.

After the 1967 referendum, a new statute renamed the Territorial Assembly "the Chamber of Deputies," and changed the name of the territory itself. French President G. Pompidou visited the Territory in January 1973. He was warmly received, and promised the Territory increased economic aid.

It appears that the referenda, although settling France's status in the territory, did not touch the real preferences of the local inhabitants. Observers believe

that the Afar and the Issa would probably both prefer
independence, but perhaps not in a single state, since
they are not natural allies, do not intermarry, and
have a tradition of enmity.

FUTA.   The traditional wrap-around sarong-like garment
worn by males and females.   Also called maro, or tob
(an Arabic word).

- G -

GABAY.   Poems about serious or important matters, often
political or religious.   Gabays are usually chanted solo
by men to a slow, simple, and dignified melody, with
the end notes of each line sustained.   They are not
traditionally accompanied by music or handclapping.
Gabays are generally between 30 and 150 lines, though
some are much longer.   Each line contains 14 to 18
syllables.   Sometimes the word gabay is used to refer
to poetry in general.   See POETRY; SONGS.   See also
BURAAMBUR, GEERAAR, JIIFTO, MANSO.

GADABURSI SCRIPT.   This Somali script, also called the
"Borama script," was devised about 1933 by Sheikh
Abdurahaman Sheikh Nuur.   It was never seriously
considered for use in the nation as a whole, but it was
used by Sheikh Abdurahaman for writing his own poetry.
The Gadabursi are a northern clan of the Dir clan
family.

GALCAIO.   A town in the Mudugh Region, northwest of the
port of Obbia and about 40 miles from the Ethiopia
border.   Galcaio is a site of permanent wells in the
Mudugh oasis.   It was also the site of a major Somali-
Galla battle in the distant past; the word signifies
"where the Galla were driven away."

GALLA.   A people linguistically and culturally related to the
Somali.   They are primarily animist or Muslim in religion, and today live predominantly in northeast Kenya
and in Ethiopia.   Older historical interpretations assume that the Galla inhabited large parts of the Horn
before the Somali migrations westward and southward
(from the 10th to the 19th centuries) pushed them into
their present areas.   Recent linguistic and documentary
evidence has cast some doubt on this view and has sug-

Ganane

gested that both Galla and Somali may have expanded outward from the Lake Abbaya area of southwest Ethiopia. In any case, small groups of Galla, known as akiso, today live in the Northern Region of the Republic.

So-called "Galla graves" in the Northern Region are now thought to be galo graves (that is, in Somali, the graves of "foreigners"), but not necessarily Galla--a confusion that arose among European writers because of the similarity of the words galo and Galla. See MIGRATIONS.

GANANE. The town of Lugh, about 10 miles from the provisional boundary with Ethiopia, on the Juba River. An important center of trade in the past and the seat of a Somali sultanate.

GARESA. 1) A stone building of more than one floor, either the palace of a sultan or a fortification. The structure is of Arab origin.

2) The building in Mogadishu in which the National Museum is housed. It was constructed in the 1870s by the Sultan of Zanzibar as a fortress and residence for the Zanzibari governor. The Garesa, or National, Museum, an impressive white, stone and stucco building, with a crenellated roof, was used by the colonial government as an office building until 1934 when the museum was installed. It contains a wealth of ethnographic materials and many books, although it is said that about half of the contents were destroyed or removed during the 1940s, following the ouster of the Italians and the takeover by the British Military Administration.

GEEL. Camel. Also spelled ghel.

GEELHER. A camp of young herdsmen and their camels. The boys and young unmarried men, whose families are residing elsewhere in a gurgi, or nomadic hamlet, live a difficult life in the open pastures, moving long distances in search of water and pasturage for their herds. They have no huts; at night they place the camels in a zariba, an enclosure made of thornbush branches. They live largely on camel's milk. The membership of the camp is constantly changing as herdsmen with their camels separate and join other groups, but always the groups are closely related by kinship ties. See HERDING.

GEERAAR. A chanted poem on a serious subject, sung solo
    by men, and not ordinarily accompanied by music or
    handclapping. The chant is faster than that of the
    gabay (q. v.), and the average line is shorter. Tradi-
    tionally the main subject of the geeraar was war and
    conflict, and the chant was often used to raise the
    morale of the warriors and ridicule their opponents.
    See POETRY; SONGS.

GELEDI. The Geledi are a clan of the Rahanweyn clan
    family. It is believed that they entered the Shebelle
    River area from a western direction, arrived in the
    territory held by the Ajuran (q. v.) in the 17th century,
    and eventually drove the Ajuran out of the Afgoy area.
    They are cattle herders, but their wealth in earlier
    times was also based on trade and on agriculture prac-
    ticed by clients and slaves. The Geledi controlled the
    caravan routes from the interior to Mogadishu and
    Brava and charged a transit duty on the river crossings
    at Afgoy and other locations. During the 19th century,
    when Darod clans migrated into the area, the Geledi
    and Helai led an alliance of Digil and Rahanweyn clans
    against the Darod and forced them to move on toward
    the south.
        The first Geledi leader to bear the title of
    "sultan" was probably Sheikh Ibrahim Adeer; his grand-
    son Yusuf Mohamed was addressed by that title by the
    Sultan of Zanzibar in the 1840s. The Geledi controlled
    the Shangani quarter of Mogadishu; the elders of the
    Hamarweyn quarter of the city, feeling vulnerable to
    the power of the Geledi, asked the Sultan of Zanzibar
    to appoint a governor in Mogadishu, which he did in
    1843. The governor so named remained in that posi-
    tion for only a few years; he was, it is believed, a
    Somali.
        The Geledi chiefly family (from the Gobron lin-
    eage) possessed not only political power, but also
    magico-religious powers which helped the Geledi to win
    battles and shore up their political authority. Control
    over their subjects was ensured by the threat of puni-
    tive raids.
        By the middle of the 19th century, the Geledi
    were the most powerful group in the Benadir. Though
    they lived in the interior, they controlled Mogadishu
    and Brava, as well as the hinterland of these cities.
    Their chief enemies were the Bimal, who controlled
    Merca and its hinterland; the enmity of the two clans

centered on economic rivalry. In 1840, when the leaders of the religious settlement at Bardera (q.v.) attacked Brava, the ensuing war was largely between the
Bimal and Geledi and their respective allies. In a war
with the Bimal in 1848, the Geledi Sultan Yusuf Mohamed was killed, but his brother and his son, Sultan
Ahmed Yusuf, continued to lead the Geledi and their
allies. In another war with the Bimal, in 1878, Sultan
Ahmed Yusuf was killed; he was succeeded by his son
Osman Ahmed. The new sultan was not able to hold
the Geledi alliance together, and the Italian attempt to
eliminate slavery and assume control of the export
trade gradually undermined Geledi power. See also
AHMAD ABUBAKAR.

GENEALOGY. A Somali's genealogy is not only a historical
account of his ancestors, but also a statement of his
political and social position in Somali society. The
most populous clan family, the Darod, traces its genealogy back some thirty generations. The genealogy of
a clan family may go back to the lineage of the Prophet
Mohamed, and the early ancestors may have Arabic
names; the more recent and probably more historically
accurate entries in the genealogy have Somali names.
Among many groups, genealogies include the names of
Somali saints or sheikhs.
        The historical validity of the early part of the
genealogy may be doubted, but its social and political
value is great. Traditionally one of the duties of the
Somali mother was to teach her children their paternal
genealogy. The elimination of tribalism--an aim shared
by the Supreme Revolutionary Council, earlier governments and political parties, as well as many religious
leaders--requires that Somalis place much less empha-
sis on genealogy than in the past. Efforts by the Supreme Revolutionary Council in this direction have been
widely publicized. See TRIBALISM.

GERAD. A chiefly title among the Darod.

GERAD JAMA FARAH. A chief of the Dolbahanta clan of
the Darod clan family who went into voluntary exile in
Mogadishu from 1952 to 1958 because of a conflict with
the administration of the British protectorate. His son,
Ali Gerad Jama, was a leader of the National United
Front, which protested the Anglo-Ethiopian Agreement
of 1954, and was Minister of Education in the first republic government.

GERAD MAHAMUD ALI SHIRRE (d. 1960). A leader of the
Warsangeli clan (Darod) who in 1908 threw in his lot
with the Dervishes and encouraged his followers to attack colonial installations in the northeast sector of the
British protectorate.

GHANA. President Aden Abdulla Osman met in Accra with
the Ghanaian president Kwame Nkrumah in October
1961. The communique issued after their meeting
seemed to indicate Nkrumah's support of Somali irredentist claims, but was primarily an expression of
Nkrumah's Pan-Africanist goals. At meetings of the
Organization of African Unity at Dar es Salaam and
Lagos in 1964, Ghana supported a Somali request for
international observers along the Somali-Ethiopian border. After Nkrumah was ousted from Ghana in 1966,
Somalia did not immediately recognize the new government. See IRREDENTISM; PAN-AFRICANISM; PAN-
SOMALISM.

GHEE. Clarified butter made from cow or goat milk. A
staple in the Somali diet.

GOATS. Goats and sheep are usually herded together by
girls or women. Goats in the Northern Region are
mostly short-haired and white; those in the south are
more varied in color. The skin of one indigenous
breed, the degier, is used in the manufacture of fine
gloves in European importing countries. The Somali
goat is an important source of food, providing meat,
milk, and butter. The large flocks of goats are a
major cause of overgrazing in parts of the Republic.

GOBAWEYN. A small group of Negroid hunters and cultivators in the Juba River area near Lugh (Ganane).

GOGLE. A rural armed constabulary organized in the
Italian colony in 1914. By 1930, it had about 500 men.
The gogle in the Southern Region were similar to the
illalo in British Somaliland. See POLICE.

GOLIS MOUNTAINS. In the north central area of the Republic. Mountain peaks reach an altitude of almost
8,000 feet.

GOSHA. On the lower Juba River, the site of an agricultural federation of freedmen from Brava, established

in the late 1880s.   The settlement was led by Nassib
Bunde (q.v.) until 1906 when it was placed under the
jurisdiction of the Italian Resident at Jumbo.   See
WA-GOSHA.

GOVERNORS (COLONIAL).   1) British Somaliland:

1884-1888   Frederick M. Hunter (Resident/Political
            Agent)
1889-1893   Edward V. Stace (Resident/Political Agent)
1893-1896   Charles W. H. Sealy (Resident/Political
            Agent)
1896-1897   William B. Ferris (Resident/Political Agent)
1897-1898   James H. Sadler (Resident/Political Agent)
1898-1901   James H. Sadler (Consul General)
1902-1905   Eric J. E. Swayne (Consul General)
1905-1910   Harry E. S. Cordeaux (Administrator)
1910-1911   William H. Manning (Administrator)
1911-1914   Horace A. Byatt (Administrator)
1914-1919   Geoffrey F. Archer (Commissioner)
1919-1922   Geoffrey F. Archer (Governor)
1922-1926   Gerald H. Summers (Governor)
1926-1932   Harold B. Kittermaster (Governor)
1932-1939   Arthur S. Lawrance (Governor)
1939-1941   Vincent G. Glenday (Governor)
1941-1943   Arthur R. Chater (Governor)
1943-1948   Gerald T. Fisher (Governor)
1948-1954   Gerald Reece (Governor)
1954-1959   Theodore O. Pike (Governor)
1959-1960   Douglas B. Hall (Governor)

            2) Italian Somaliland: From 1888 to 1893,
there was no central administrator.   From 1893 to
1896, the Filonardi Company, and from 1898 to 1905,
the Benadir Company administered the area.   From
1896 to 1898, there was a period of direct control, with
Vincenzo Filonardi, Ernesto Dulio, and Giorgio Sorrentino serving as Royal Commissioners.

1905-1906   Luigi Mercatelli (Royal Commissioner Gene-
            ral)
1906   Alessandro Sapelli (Acting Vice-Commission-
            er General)
1906-1907   Giovanni Cerrina-Feroni (Acting Governor)
1907-1908   Tommaso Carletti (Royal Civil Commissioner)
1908   Tommaso Carletti (Governor)
1908-1910   Gino Macchioro (Acting Governor)

1910-1916 Giacomo De Martino (Governor)
1916-1920 Giovanni Cerrina-Feroni (Governor)
1920-1923 Carlo Riveri (Governor)
1923-1928 Cesare Maria DeVecchi di Val Cismon
           (Governor)
1928-1931 Guido Corni (Governor)
1931-1935 Maurizio Rava (Governor)
1935-1936 Rodolfo Graziani (Governor)
1936-1937 Ruggero Santini (Governor)
1937-1940 Francesco Saverio Caroselli (Governor)
1940   Gustavo Pesenti (Governor)
1940-1941 Carlo De Simone (Governor)
1941   Reginald H. Smith (British Military Admin-
           istration Governor)
1941-1943 William E. H. Scupham (BMA Governor)
1943-1948 Denis Henry Wickham (BMA Governor)
1948   Eric A. V. de Candole (BMA Governor)
1948-1950 Geoffrey M. Gamble (BMA Governor)

          3) United Nations Trusteeship Territory under
Italian Administration:

1950-1953 Giovanni Fornari (Administrator)
1953-1955 Enrico Martino (Administrator)
1955-1958 Enrico Anzilotti (Administrator)
1958-1960 Mario di Stefani (Administrator)

GREAT BRITAIN. The Northern Region of the Republic was
    a British protectorate from about 1884 until it received
    its independence on June 26, 1960. In the treaties of
    protection signed with Great Britain, the Somali clans
    of the northern areas granted Britain the right to estab-
    lish Residencies in the port cities, but conceded no
    rights to Somali territory. The chief purpose of the
    treaties, as far as the Somalis were concerned, was to
    ensure the clans' independence and to preserve order.
    Nevertheless, British control over the interior grew,
    sparked to a great extent by the activities of Sayyid Mo-
    hamed Abdullah Hassan from 1899 to 1920. For a
    brief period in 1940-41, the Italians gained control of
    the British protectorate. Then, from 1941 to 1948, the
    area was governed by the British Military Administration.
    After 1948, civilian authorities governed the area. On
    July 1, 1960, the independent state of Somaliland united
    with the ex-United Nations Trust Territory to form the
    Somali Republic. See ANGLO-ETHIOPIAN DIPLOMACY;
    ANGLO-FRENCH TREATY OF 1888; ANGLO-ITALIAN

ACCORDS; BRITISH EAST INDIA COMPANY; BRITISH
MILITARY ADMINISTRATION; BRITISH SOMALILAND.
In 1888, the Imperial British East Africa Company (IBEAC) acquired from the Sultan of Zanzibar a
50-year lease to the Benadir coastal area, including
the port of Mogadishu. The following year, the company sublet the area north of the Juba River to Italy.
This left the trans-Juba, including the port of Kismayu,
in British hands; it came directly under the British
government in 1895 when the IBEAC was dissolved.
The boundary between the British and Italian areas was
defined in the Anglo-Italian Protocols of 1891 and 1894.
A World War I treaty between Italy and Great Britain,
in which Britain proposed to transfer the Jubaland area
to Italy if Britain enlarged her African territory by ac-
quisition of German holdings, was implemented in the
Anglo-Italian Agreement of 1925.
After Somalia's independence in 1960, the
British continued to supply the Republic about $3 mil-
lion annually in economic assistance. Under a lease,
Britain maintained the British Broadcasting Corporation
Middle Eastern Service relay station at Berbera, and
by agreement British planes had overflight and landing
rights in the Republic. In 1963, in a dispute over
Britain's policy regarding the Somali-inhabited area of
Kenya, the Republic broke diplomatic relations with
Great Britain. British aid was cut off, the BBC relay
station was closed and dismantled, and overflight and
landing rights were discontinued. Relations between
the two countries were not resumed until 1968. See
IRREDENTISM; KENYA; PAN-SOMALISM.

GREATER SOMALIA. The phrase "Greater Somalia" was
used by Italian Fascist colonial officials to describe
their dream that the Italian colony, enlarged to include
a part of Ethiopia, would be prosperous and would provide a home for Italian immigrants. A similar phrase
was later used by Ernest Bevin in proposing the Bevin
Plan (q.v.) for post-World War II Somalia.
Before independence came to Somalia, all the
political parties, especially those in the south, had as
one of their aims the establishment of a Greater So-
malia--a Somali nation-state to include all the Somali-
inhabited areas in the Horn of Africa. The five points
of the star in the Somali flag are said to represent the
five Somali-inhabited areas. See IRREDENTISM; PAN-
SOMALISM.

GREATER SOMALIA LEAGUE (GSL). A political party
    formed in 1958 and led by Haji Mohamed Hussein, a
    former president of the Somali Youth League (1948-52
    and 1957-58). The GSL was strongly Pan-Somali and
    Pan-Arab. It attracted a number of Somali Youth
    League (SYL) members and leaders. In 1962, the GSL
    joined with several other parties to form the Somali
    Democratic Union (SDU). Still under Haji Mohamed
    Hussein's leadership, it took part in the 1964 and 1969
    general elections, but never gained sufficient strength
    to effectively oppose the SYL. The SDU called for con-
    fiscation of foreign-owned plantations and the establish-
    ment of collective farms. It opposed Somali participa-
    tion in the European Economic Community.

GU. The major rainy season, lasting from middle or late
    March to May or June (varying somewhat from region
    to region). Gu is the time of the first sowing among
    the agriculturalists. It is the season when grazing is
    best, and the nomads move out to their most distant
    pastures. If the rainfall is good, they may be able to
    stay away from their home wells from gu until dair,
    the light rain season, which begins in late September.
    Traditionally, gu is the season of courtship among the
    pastoralists. It is a joyful season for everyone.
    Grass springs up almost overnight and water is plenti-
    ful.

GUBAN (Burned). The Guban area along the Gulf of Aden
    coast is an arid, sandy maritime plain, about 60 miles
    wide at its deepest point, and only a few hundred feet
    wide at its narrowest. During the hot dry season of
    jilal, from about December to March, many of the no-
    mads who have been out with their herds and flocks
    return to their home wells in the valleys beyond the
    Guban where they may also find pasturage that has re-
    vived during their stay in the interior.

GURGI. A nomadic hamlet of a few closely related families
    of the same dia-paying group. The family consists of
    a man and wife, or wives, and their small children
    and unmarried daughters. The family lives in a trans-
    portable house (agal)--or in more than one if two or
    more wives are present. Sheep, goats, a few pack
    camels, and perhaps a few milk camels are kept in the
    hamlet.
            The group making up a gurgi changes from

time to time as men move their families and belongings
from one hamlet to another, always, however, with
members of the same dia-paying group.   Men who have
wives in more than one hamlet divide their time equally
between them.

The word rer may also be applied to a hamlet,
but strictly speaking, rer refers to the social unit of
the hamlet, while gurgi refers to the physical structure
of huts and thornbush fences.

- H -

HABASHO.   Negroid, perhaps former Bantu-speaking, groups
who own land along the rivers.   The land is acknowledged as belonging to the habasho, who in the distant
past defended it against Somali migrants into the area.
The habasho are regarded as having skill in magic;
they are Muslim and many are heads of agricultural
tariqa settlements.

HAGA.   The season when the southwest monsoon is blowing,
from June or July to September.   Haga follows gu and
precedes dair, the seasons of heavy and light rain.
Haga is a dry season, but there is usually some rain
in the southern coastal areas and in the high altitudes
of the Golis Mountains.   During haga, the nomads usually concentrate near their home wells.   Among the
agriculturalists, it is the growing season for the first
sowing.

HAILE SELASSIE (1892-1975).   Emperor of Ethiopia from 1930
to 1974, when he was deposed by a military takeover.
From 1916 to 1930, he was regent, following the de-
position of Lij Yasu, the grandson of Menelik II.   Under Haile Selassie, Ethiopia from time to time expressed claims not only to Somali-inhabited areas now
within Ethiopian borders, but also to areas now within
the Republic and the French Territory of the Afars and
Issas.   See ETHIOPIA; IRREDENTISM.

HAJI.   A religious title which indicates that the person has
made the pilgrimage to Mecca; at least one such pilgrimage is considered a requirement for all faithful
Muslims.   The feminine is Hajia.

HAJI ABDI ABIKAR (c. 1849-1921).   A Bimal political leader

and head of a Salihiya tariqa in the Merca area. During the Bimal resistance to the Italians in the early 1900s, Haji Abdi Abikar was active in securing firearms from the followers of Sayyid Mohamed Abdullah Hassan to use in the resistance.

HAJI FARAH OMAR (1864-1948). During the 1910s, Haji Farah Omar was a civil servant in British Somaliland. He became an officer in the armed forces and in the 1920s was exiled to Aden after agitating for social and political reforms. In Aden, he founded the Somali Islamic Association and publicized Somali grievances by writing letters to the newspapers in Aden, by writing to members of Parliament in London, and by sending a petition to Queen Elizabeth II. He returned to the protectorate as an old man and died in Hargeisa. He is today regarded as a national hero, a man who, like Mahatma Gandhi in India, sought change by peaceful means.

HAJI HASSAN BARSANE. A leader of the pastoral Galjal (Hawiye), who live near the Shebelle River above Balad. He opposed the forces of Sayyid Mohamed Abdullah Hassan; he then turned against the Italians in 1924 when they attempted to dis-arm the Galjal. The Fascist government decided to make the Galjal resistance an example, bringing in machine guns and artillery to quell the rebellion.

HAJI ISMAIL FARRAH (d. 1956). A Somali who was educated in Aden and who spent most of his life as a teacher in the British protectorate of Somaliland. He taught at the military school at Burao, in the Northern Region, and founded the first Somali school for girls, also at Burao. On his retirement, he was awarded a Robe of Honor by the protectorate government and given a special pension.

HAJI SHERMARKE ALI SALIH. Also referred to as Ali Sharmakay. A Somali who was governor of Zeila from 1840 to 1855, when it was under the Ottoman Empire. After being deposed as governor, he lived in Aden. Earlier he had worked on British ships; in 1825 he protected the crew of the British ship Mary Ann during an attack by Somalis at Berbera. In 1840 he acted as an interpreter for the British East India Company in treaty negotiations with the Sultan of Tajura.

HAMARWEYN. An ancient quarter of Mogadishu. Some of
the buildings now standing date back to the 13th century.
It is a densely populated quarter, with narrow streets
and lanes. The mosque Fakhr ad-Din and that of
Sheikh Abdul Aziz are located in Hamarweyn, as are
the National Museum, Indian and Somali goldsmith
shops, and the outdoor work areas of the Benadir cotton weavers.

HAQ AD-DIN. The Muslim, perhaps Somali, ruler of Adal,
a sultanate whose center was at Zeila. Haq ad-Din
led a holy war against the Coptic Christians of Ethiopia
in the 14th century. At first successful, the Muslim
forces of Haq ad-Din were later defeated, and Zeila
was occupied, for a time, by the Ethiopians. See
SA'D AD-DIN.

HARAR (pop. c. 65,000). An ancient commercial and religious center in the Haud area of Ethiopia. Harar lies
along the trade route between the Ethiopian highlands
and the northern Somali coastal cities. About 1,000
Somalis live in the vicinity of Harar.

HARBORS. The Somali coastline is about 2,000 miles long,
but it has no good natural harbors. The Somalis are
not a seagoing people, although for many years they
have worked on foreign merchant ships as interpreters,
stewards, stevedores, stokers, etc. All the larger
coastal towns were apparently founded by immigrant
peoples, primarily Arabs and Persians, who maintained
trade links with their countries of origin and were the
middlemen in the trade between the Somali interior and
foreign shippers. The ports of Berbera and Kismayu
(q.v.) were modernized and enlarged in the 1960s, and
that at Mogadishu (q.v.) underwent extensive improvement in the early 1970s. Also see BRAVA; DHOW
TRADE; MERCA.

HARGEISA (Little Harar). Hargeisa, a city of about 55,000,
was founded by Sheikh Madar, the leader of a Qadiriya
settlement. It is on a caravan trade route from the interior to the northern port cities. In the 1890s, it
was described as having a few hundred huts, surrounded
by gardens and enclosed by a high fence. It became
the government center of the British Somaliland protectorate in 1942, and most of its growth has taken
place since that time. It is the chief inland city of
the Hargeisa Region.

HASSAN SHEIKH ABDULLAH.   A brother of Sayyid Mohamed
    Abdullah Hassan.   In the mid-1960s, he was one of the
    leaders of the Somali irredentist movement in the Oga-
    den.   See IRREDENTISM; OGADENIA.

HAUD.   The word means "south," and the area referred to
    as the Haud lies partly in the Republic and partly in
    Ethiopia.   The Haud is a plateau region south of Har-
    geisa.   In the south, it adjoins the Ogaden plains, and
    on the west, reaches toward Harar.   It covers about
    25,000 square miles.
            The Haud is a major wet-season grazing area
    for the herds of nomadic Somali pastoralists, but it
    contains very few permanent wells and is little used
    in the dry seasons.   Ant and termite hills, some 30
    feet high, abound in some areas.   It is estimated that
    300,000 Somalis of the Northern Region, with their
    herds of camels, sheep, and goats, enter the Haud in
    the gu, or rainy season, and remain as long as there
    is pasturage, sometimes five or six months.   Some
    then go further south to the Ogaden where there are
    wells, and mix with their kinsmen who live in that
    area.   Similarly, Somalis from the Mudugh and Gal-
    guduud Regions of the Republic move into the Haud dur-
    ing the wet season.
            Agreements permitting the Somalis free access
    to these traditional grazing grounds were worked out
    between Britain and Ethiopia in 1897 and later.   See
    ANGLO-ETHIOPIAN DIPLOMACY; NURO.

HAWA OSMAN "TAKO."   A Somali girl killed in January
    1948 in the riots that accompanied the visit of the
    Four-Power Commission to Mogadishu.   It is said that
    she was killed by an arrow.   She is today regarded as
    a national heroine, and a monument to her was erected
    in 1971 in front of the Somali National Theater in Mo-
    gadishu.   See also DAGHATUR MONUMENT.

HAWIYE.   One of the four Samaal clan families.   Within the
    Republic, the Hawiye are believed to number close to
    750,000.   They occupy primarily the Galguduud Region,
    the Hiran Region, and parts of the Central and Lower
    Shebelle and Lower Juba Regions.   Outside the Repub-
    lic, they are found in the North-Eastern Region of
    Kenya and in Ethiopia.   Most of the Hawiye are no-
    madic pastoralists; some also have agricultural hold-
    ings along the Shebelle River farmed by Negroid groups.

The Hawiye in the Lower Juba and in northeast Kenya
are primarily cattle herders, while those in the other
areas have camels. The Hawiye are believed to have
descended from Irrir, an ancestor of the Dir clan family.

HEADREST. Wooden headrests are common among the
Hawiye and Rahanweyn in southern Somalia; they are
not generally used among other groups.

HEELLO. A modern type of love song or poem, introduced
in the mid-1940s. It is often regarded as trivial by
traditionalists, and most heello are short-lived. The
word has no meaning; it is a word-sound, usually
chanted before the poem itself is sung. The heello is
usually sung before an audience which joins in the
chorus or claps; it may be accompanied by lute, tambourine, guitar, or flute.
        Originally the heello was called balwo, an
Arabic word meaning evil or misfortune. A poem by
a pious Somali religious leader, who was tired of lis-
tening to heello, contains the line, "As the holy tradition says, they (the balwo) are the snares of the devil."

HEER. The word heer refers to compacts, contracts, or
treaties. A heer contract often concerns collective defense or political agreements. In this sense, heer refers to a body of explicit rights and duties which are
binding on all members of the participating groups. It
is said that heer encourages virtuous action by individuals and by the group as a whole, discourages un-
just and immoral acts, and helps the weak and needy.
A Somali proverb says: A clan with a sound system
of heer has no poor members.
        Modern Somali governments have abolished heer
contracts that assume collective responsibility for murder and other individual crimes. It is claimed that collective responsibility for such crimes encourages tribal
divisiveness and feuds. The Supreme Revolutionary
Council has imprisoned some who ignored the government's rulings on heer, charging them with fostering
tribalism (q.v.). See DIA; DIA-PAYING GROUPS.

HEES. A modern song influenced by European or Euro-
peanized Arabic music. The hees usually deals with
current topics, mainly politics. The word means
"song."

HELAI. The Helai (sometimes spelled Elai) are today the
    most numerous of the Rahanweyn clans. They arrived
    in the interriverine area in the 17th century and forced
    the Galla then inhabiting the Bur Acaba district to move
    out. During the 19th century they were allied with the
    Geledi and other Rahanweyn and Digil groups in oppos-
    ing Darod migrants to the Shebelle River area. The
    Helai are of two main groups: those of Bur Acaba,
    who are agriculturalists, but also have camels and
    cattle; and those of Isha Baidoa, a confederation of
    Negroid groups who apparently intermarried with the
    Rahanweyn Helai and accepted their religion and lan-
    guage. The Helai of Baidoa have as their titular head
    a descendant of Sheikh Mumin (q.v.).

HER SCHOOL. A school led by an Islamic religious teach-
    er (her), often operated only temporarily or intermit-
    tently. In such schools, often called "Koranic schools,"
    children memorize passages from the Koran and learn
    the basic principles of Islam. They may also study
    arithmetic and reading and writing in Arabic.

HERDING. It is estimated that some 60 per cent of the So-
    mali population are nomadic or seminomadic pastor-
    alists. The percentage was much higher in the past,
    and even today, in some areas, it is close to 80. The
    pastoralists regard herding--especially the herding of
    camels--as a noble occupation.
        Sporadic rainfall and the scarcity of permanent
    wells make nomadism the natural way of life in much
    of the Republic. Customary laws regulate the use of
    pastures and watering places. In areas where several
    clan groups mingle, nonobservance of these laws may
    give rise to intergroup warfare.
        Cattle and camels are herded by boys and un-
    married men, and goats and sheep by girls and women.
    Cattle are the most delicate animals found in Somalia.
    They must be watered every four days, yet must be
    kept away from the river areas where the tsetse fly
    prevails. The greatest herds of cattle are found in
    the interriverine area. The cattle herders live in
    fixed villages, surrounded by grazing areas which may
    extend to a distance equal to a three- to four-hour
    march from the village. Through intermarriage and
    sheegat arrangements, these herders are associated
    with the farmers in the river areas, and they augment
    their diet by exchanging animal products for grain and

other farm products. Cattle herders usually also have
some camels, sheep, and goats.

Camels can go 30 days without water, and
sheep and goats more than 15. Camels and goats are
much more destructive of vegetation than cattle, and
thus their grazing areas must be more extensive.
These factors both permit and require the system of
nomadic pastoralism that so many Somalis follow.
See RANGE MANAGEMENT.

In the rainy season, nomadic groups, composed
of one or several families, leave their home wells and
travel, perhaps hundreds of miles, to their traditional
grazing grounds. The women set up their huts within
an easy distance of the wells, and keep with them the
sheep and goats and perhaps a few milk and burden
camels. The young men and boys take the camels to
more distant areas. See GEELHER; GURGI.

Economically, camel herders are much more
self-sufficient in meeting their everyday needs than
cattle herders. Neither group slaughters its animals
for food except in an emergency or to provide for some
festive occasion. Since cattle are more dependent on
water, they are not as good milk producers as camels
during the dry seasons. Thus the cattle herders and
the cultivating groups in the tsetse-infested riverine
areas depend on each other and have developed a system of product exchange. The camel herders, on the
other hand, live on camel milk alone for long periods.
During the dry seasons, when the camel herders are
concentrated near their home wells and when their
milk camels are not producing, they may trade hides
and skins or animals for tea, sugar, rice, and dates.

Market centers--sometimes with only one shop
--spring up wherever there are permanent wells and
where people congregate for substantial periods of time.
If the wells should go dry or the people leave, the market moves too. Normally the traders or shopowners
are of the same lineage as the camel herders. Some
have their home base in a larger town, and simply
move some of their goods into the interior, using burden camels or, in more recent times, trucks.

HERSI BOGOR. Son of the Mijerteyn sultan Bogor Osman
Mahmoud. Hersi Bogor led his people in the final
battles between the Mijerteyn and the Italians; they had
some successes, but were defeated in 1927, and the
Mijerteyn sultanate, which had been an Italian protec-

torate since 1889, became part of the Italian colony.
See MIJERTEYN.

HERSI GUSHAN. A military commander under Ali Yusuf,
the Sultan of Obbia during the period 1911-1925. He
led the sultan's forces in their last-ditch battles against
the Italians in 1925. The sultanate of Obbia, which had
been an Italian protectorate since 1889, was then placed
under the administration of the Italian colony. See
OBBIA.

HIDES AND SKINS. Raw hides and skins are a major export.
The hide of the Somali sheep, unshorn, is a principal
export in the Northern Region. The skin of the degier
goat is sold on the world market for glove production.
The Somali leopard skin is said to be the world's most
expensive fur. Camel and cattle skins are used for
manufacturing sandals, belts, pocketbooks, and bags for
domestic use, and are also exported. Rhinoceros hide
was traditionally used for making round shields, the
major defensive weapon of the Somalis.

HIGHWAYS. The climate, with heavy rains and long dry
seasons, and the nature of the soil make road main-
tenance a continuing and costly problem. Also, the
low level of automobile ownership has made highway
construction a matter of fairly low priority, especially
in the interior. In 1967, the total road network was
estimated at 8,000 miles; approximately 500 miles
were considered all-weather roads. The construction
of hard-surfaced roads has been stepped up in recent
years. A highway from Berbera to Hargeisa was completed in the early 1970s, and a road from Beled Weyn
(Hiran Region) to Burao (Tug Dheer Region) is under
construction. Both are projects of the People's Republic of China. Other roads have been constructed by
self-help groups.

HIZBIA DASTUR MUSTAQUIL SOMALI (HDMS). This political party was founded in the early 1940s. It was first
called the Patriotic Benefit Union (PBU). In 1947, the
PBU was reorganized as the Hizbia Digil-Mirifle Somali. Its membership came mainly from the Saab clan
families. In 1958, when legislation was passed prohibiting political parties from having clan names in
their titles, the HDMS became the Hizbia Dastur Mustaquil Somali (Somali Independent Constitutional Party).

        The PBU and the Hizbia Digil-Mirifle Somali
had some Arab and Negroid members and received
some financial support from Italian colonists. For a
while the HDMS favored an Italian-administered trusteeship, but at the time of the visit of the Four-Power
Commission in 1948, it proposed a 30-year trusteeship period under a four-power administration. The
aims of the HDMS were national, even though its membership was largely clan-particularistic. During the
trusteeship period, the HDMS began to fear that the
Republic, and the Saab clan families especially, would
be dominated by the Samaal groups. The party thus
proposed that the constitution, which was then being
written, establish a system of strong regional autonomy.
The proposal received little support elsewhere and was
abandoned.
        Although the HDMS never gained the national
following achieved by the Somali Youth League, it remained the chief opposition party, and a number of its
leaders held ministerial posts. After the 1969 coup,
all political parties were abolished.

HIZBIA DIGIL-MIRIFLE SOMALI see HIZBIA DASTUR
    MUSTAQUIL SOMALI

HORN OF AFRICA. That part of Africa which embraces the
    Somali-inhabited areas: The Republic and parts of
    Ethiopia, Kenya, and the French Territory of the Afars
    and Issas. The Horn lies at the crossroads of Africa
    and the Arab world.

HUNTING. No Somali group lives exclusively by hunting.
    It is practiced largely by Negroid and other non-Somali
    groups. Some of the Saab Somalis engage in seasonal
    hunting, apparently a result of their close association
    with non-Somali hunting groups, or perhaps, because
    these Saab groups have absorbed earlier hunting popu-
    lations. Hunting is practiced primarily to obtain ivory,
    skins, and ostrich feathers, rather than meat, although
    meat may be important during the dry seasons.
        Traditionally, the northern Midgan caught os-
    triches, using fruit baited with a substance that made
    the ostrich dizzy and easy to catch. The hunters
    would remove the plumes and then set the ostrich free.
    The Yibir, also a northern sab group, practice hunting.
    The Wa-Boni, living in the backlands of Merca and in
    the trans-Juba, are a hunting group, which also prac-

tices fishing and agriculture; some of them use dogs
for hunting.   The Wa-Ribi are a hunting and cultivating
group living between Bardera and Lugh; and the Gobaweyn are hunters and cultivators living around Lugh.
        Although firearms and arrows are used in hunt-
ing, traps and semitraps are more common, in conjunction with spears and clubs.   The hunters may beat
the bush, chasing the animals into a semicircular net
held by other members of the hunting party.   When the
animals enter, the hunters close in with the net and
then stun the animals with clubs.   In some areas, a
trap may be made by placing a net over a hole dug in
the ground, covering it with branches.

- I -

IGAL SHIDAD.   Many folk stories center on a character
named Igal Shidad, a notorious coward.   He never
traveled at night because on one occasion he was
frightened by a tree, which in the darkness looked like
a ferocious beast.

ILLALO.   During the colonial period, a rural armed constabulary in British Somaliland, similar to the gogle in
the south.   See POLICE.

IMAM.   A religious teacher.   The title is also used for a
chief who has religious powers.   Ahmad Guray, the
leader in the war against Ethiopia in the 16th century,
bore this title, as did some of the Ajuran and Abgal
leaders.

IMPORTS.   The chief imports are rice, wheat, tea, tobacco,
tools, vehicles, tractors, fertilizers, and pharmaceuti-
cal and petroleum products.   The total value of imports is estimated at $50 million annually.   Because
of the chronic trade imbalance, the Somali governments
have always encouraged import substitution, the use of
domestic products rather than imported ones.   One of
the prime economic goals of the Supreme Revolutionary
Council is to reduce imports by increasing domestic
agricultural production.

INCENSE   see   AROMATIC GUMS

INDIANS.   There is evidence that Indians, as well as Arabs,

Persians, and Chinese, participated in the trade of the
Somali coast in the medieval period. Indians, in much
smaller numbers than Arabs, settled in some of the
coastal cities and engaged in commerce and trade.
The estimated population of Indians and Pakistanis in
Somalia is 1,000. Some are goldsmiths; many are
shopowners.

INDUSTRY. Livestock and agriculture are the chief bases
for industrial development. Fishing is of potential importance. Mineral deposits have not so far been exploited, and explorations for petroleum have proved
negative.

Before independence, the sugar factory at
Jowhar, in the Central Shebelle Region, was the major
industrial undertaking, although there were small fish-
and meat-processing plants, an electricity plant, tanneries, an ice plant, some soap- and oil-producing
plants, sawmills, carpentries, banana-crate factories,
and salt works. Some of these industries have been
expanded and a few new ones, such as the cotton textile and milk plants near Mogadishu, have been added.

Hindrances to industrial development include
the small domestic market, the low level of population
concentration, poor transportation and communication
systems, lack of a tradition of entrepreneurship, and
lack of financial resources. Poor planning, as at an
American-built fish-processing plant at Alula, has led
to a number of disappointing projects.

INFIBULATION. Clitoridectomy and infibulation are a common and traditional practice. They are performed,
traditionally by a Midgan woman, when the girl is between seven and 12, in the presence of the girl's
mother and female relatives. The period of convalescence is from seven to 14 days. Traditionally, the
girl is then clean in the Muslim sense (halal), and is
eligible for marriage. See CIRCUMCISION.

INTEGRATION see CONSULTATIVE COMMISSION FOR
INTEGRATION (LEGISLATION)

INTERGROUP WARFARE. Wars between clan groups in the
traditional society usually resulted from the abduction
of a woman or girl, livestock or caravan raids, and
disputes over water and pasturage. Such warfare was
discussed and unanimously approved by the entire

participating group (in the shir) before it was initiated,
because the group bore the responsibility for the payment or receipt of collective fines resulting from in-
juries or deaths sustained in the war. See DIA; DIA-
PAYING GROUP. The traditional machinery for re-
storing peace was a meeting of the elders of the groups
involved and the assessment of collective fines in livestock against the group responsible for the incidents
that brought on the war.

     In their attempts to establish laws of individual
responsibility, the colonial governments, though seldom
successful in maintaining a permanent peace, tended to
upset the traditional balance of power and to erode the
authority of the clan elders. At the same time, however, they were able to reduce the number and severity
of outbreaks. The Supreme Revolutionary Council has
taken decisive steps to eliminate intergroup feuds and
to abolish the principle of collective responsibility for
offenses.

     Historically, economic rivalry and religious
fanaticism have also been occasions for intergroup
wars. See BARDERA; BIMAL; GELEDI; SAYYID MO-
HAMED ABDULLAH HASSAN.

IRONWORK. This kind of work is traditionally done by the
    Tumal, mainly in the major coastal towns. They man-
    ufacture spears, knives, axes, awls, and other tools.
    Another blacksmith group is the Kalmashuba.

IRREDENTISM. Somalia is the only new African state where
    irredentism is an important issue. About one-third of
    the Somalis in the Horn of Africa live outside the Re-
    public. Irredentist sentiment is strongest in Ethiopia,
    where about one million Somalis live, and in the North-
    Eastern Region of Kenya, which has about 250,000
    Somalis. The movement in the French Territory of the
    Afars and Issas is more separatist than irredentist.
     Italian colonial policy, at least during the
    Fascist era, was to encourage Somali irredentism
    against the Ethiopians, and to exploit the traditional
    Muslim-Coptic antagonism in order to bolster Italian
    imperialistic ambitions. During the British Military
    Administration, 1941 to 1950, the idea of Somali politi-
    cal unity was encouraged, particularly in the Bevin
    Plan, and was expressed in the charters of the politi-
    cal parties that organized during that period. After
    independence, the desire of the Somalis living outside

the Republic to unite with Somalia was supported by
the political parties and by Somali government policy,
and was incorporated in the provisions of the 1960
Constitution.

The irredentist movements in Ethiopia and Kenya led to warfare along the Ethiopian border in 1963
and 1964 and to a number of clashes in the North-
Eastern Region of Kenya. Though the desire for unification of these areas with the Republic has not abated,
direct action toward that end was minimal from 1967
to 1975, largely as the result of more conciliatory
government policies. See ABDIRASHID ALI SHER-
MARKE; GREATER SOMALIA; ORGANIZATION OF
AFRICAN UNITY; PAN-AFRICANISM; PAN-SOMALISM.

IRRIGATION. Agricultural development depends largely on
bringing additional cultivable land under irrigation.
Modern irrigation was first put into widescale use at
Jowhar on the sugarcane plantation developed by the
Duke of Abruzzi in the early 1920s. Slightly later,
the banana and grapefruit planters at Jenale, Afgoy,
and Avai constructed irrigation facilities. In the late
1920s, irrigated cotton plantations were developed on
the Juba River.

Traditionally, Somali farmers also used irrigation procedures, relying mainly on water collected
in man-made ponds (uars) or in the flood plains
(desheks) of the rivers, though most of their agriculture outside the flood plains depended on normal rainfall. The wealth of such historically powerful clans
as the Ajuran, Geledi, and Bimal derived no doubt in
part from their use of riverside irrigation. See also
AGRICULTURE METHODS.

ISAAQ. One of the four Samaal clan families. The Isaaq
number perhaps 600,000. They live primarily in the
Tug Dheer, Sanaag, and Hargeisa Regions of the north.
Some also live in the Ethiopian Haud. Practically all
are camel herders. According to their genealogy, the
Isaaq derive from an immigrant Arab, Isaaq ibn Ahmed,
who married two daughters of Magadle (probably a Dir
Somali) and also an Abyssinian woman. Isaaq clans
trace their ancestry back to one of these three unions.
Sheikh Isaaq ibn Ahmed is believed to have arrived in
the Horn of Africa in the 12th or 13th century.

ISHA BAIDOA. Isha means "eye." Isha Baidoa is the name

often used for Baidoa, the chief town in the Bai
Region. According to legend, a shepherd noticed one
day that birds were going down, one at a time, to a
cavity in a rock. He examined the rock and saw that
some water was imprisoned in a little "eye." He
cracked the rock open and the water gushed forth,
producing the waterfall and springs seen today at Baidoa.

ISLAM. The religion of practically all Somalis, and the official state religion. Freedom of religion was
guaranteed under the constitution, and all religions are
tolerated, but proselytizing by non-Muslims is illegal.
Islam is seen as a unifying force in Somalia, not only
in religious matters, but in political action as well.
In addition to Islamic practices, some pre-Islamic religious customs are observed, such as seasonal prayers
for rain, blessings of the livestock, and prayers in
time of disaster.

Somalis have been Muslim since the time their
religion was first recorded in the 13th century. According to one legend, in the mid-700s, during the
battles among the Muslims of Arabia, many took refuge
in parts of Africa. It is said that one Mohamed Abdurahman Hambali of Yemen came to the Horn of Africa with a few followers. He preached Islam to the
Galla, many of whom converted. According to one
tradition, he married a Galla woman and had two sons,
Saab and Samaal. After his death, the sons separated
and continued to preach. The followers of Samaal established themselves along the sea coast, and eventually gave their name to the Somali peninsula. The followers of Saab went into the interior and intermarried
with Negroid and Galla groups.

This early migration of Arabs was followed by
others. In the 9th century, according to legend, Darod
Ismail (Sheikh Jabarti ibn Ismail) came from the Persian Gulf to the Somali coast near Alula. He met Dir
Egil, a nephew of Samaal, who gave him his daughter
Dahira in marriage. Another migration from the Persian Gulf in the 10th century led to the settlement of
Mogadishu, Merca, and Brava. Mogi Mohamed Bahari,
of Shiraz, was the chief of these immigrants, according to one tradition, and under him Mogadishu became
a center of commerce and Koranic study.

The Islamization of the interior was undoubtedly a slow process, but this legend of its beginning is

probably quite accurate. The spread of Islam is associated with the Somali migrations (q. v.). The Muslim
religious revival of the 19th century saw the establishment of the first tariqa in the Somali interior, at Bardera, and the spread of the other tariqas later in the
century. The jihad of Sayyid Mohamed Abdullah Hassan
was also a manifestation of the religious revival.

ISMAA'IIL MIRE (c. 1884-1950). A distant relative and ad-
visor of Sayyid Mohamed Abdullah Hassan. Ismaa'iil
Mire led an important Dervish attack against the British
in 1913. He composed a history of Somalia and its
people in poetic form.

ISSA. A clan of the Dir clan family. The Issa live primarily in the northwest part of the Northern Region of
the Republic, in the southeast portion of the French
Territory of the Afars and Issas, and near Harar in
Ethiopia. The Issa in the French Territory number
about 40, 000, while those in the Republic number about
65, 000. They are primarily camel herders.

ISTUNKA. A "stick fight" festival held annually at Afgoy on
the Shebelle River, a mock battle between groups of
young men from opposite banks of the river. It is believed that the festival derives from an ancient battle
over which group would have the use of the river's
water during the dry season. It is also said that the
festival was originally an exercise to train the young
men in fighting so that they could defeat the forces of
a tyrannical sultan who had invaded the area. When
the sultan struck, he was defeated and his village destroyed. The festival is a three-day affair held at the
time of dabshid, the seasonal new year. It has become
an attraction for tourists from other parts of the Republic. The istunka used to be a very bloody undertaking, with many men being wounded, but it has become less violent in recent decades.

ITALIAN SOMALILAND. In 1950, the area formerly known
as Italian Somaliland became a United Nations trusteeship territory, with Italy as the administering authority.
The territory became independent on July 1, 1960, and
amalgamated with the independent state of Somaliland
(the former British protectorate) to form the Republic
of Somalia.
        In 1889, Italy sublet the southern Benadir ports

from the Imperial British East Africa Company, which
had leased them from the Sultan of Zanzibar. In the
same year, treaties of protection were signed with the
northern sultanates of the Mijerteyn and Obbia. In
1905, the Italian government purchased the coastal area
from Warsheikh to Brava from the Sultan of Zanzibar
and began to govern it as a colony, gradually expanding
into the interior. In 1925, by agreement with the
British, Italy added the trans-Juba area to the colony.
About the same time, the Italians began their occupation of the Mijerteyn and Obbia sultanates.

By 1927, the colony extended from the present
Kenyan border to the boundary with British Somaliland
in the north. Inland, the boundary with Ethiopia had
been discussed in 1897 during the peace negotiations between Ethiopia and Italy, following Italy's defeat at
Adowa, and again in the Italo-Ethiopian Agreement of
1908. The boundary was never marked on the ground,
and the Italians continued to push inland, partly to
counteract Ethiopian intrusions. This activity culminated in the Wal Wal incident in 1934, which was the
first step in the Italo-Ethiopian war of 1935-1936. See
ITALO-ETHIOPIAN AGREEMENTS OF 1897 and 1908;
WAL WAL.

The chief motives behind the Italian occupation
of Somalia were the desire for trade and the desire to
establish an outlet for Italy's overcrowded population.
Large numbers of Italians were migrating to the Ameri-
cas, and the Italian government hoped to stop this loss
by setting up Italian farming communities in Africa.
The reports of some explorers described the Somaliland area as a good prospect for farm settlements,
while others were more realistic and hence less en-
couraging.

In the early years of the colony, Italian efforts
were geared toward eliminating slavery and reaping a
profit on the interior trade. These aims disrupted the
economic life of the Somalis and resulted in a long
period of conflict with the Bimal, Geledi, Digil, Mijerteyn, and Obbia peoples, as well as others. The Italians gave stipends to cooperative Somali chiefs and in
some instances returned fugitive slaves on the condi-
tion that they be treated as hired workers. With the
advent of Mussolini and the Fascist government in the
early 1920s, the possibility of agricultural concessions,
rather than settlements of Italian farmers, received
more attention. The concessions, sometimes using a

complement of forced labor, established sugar, banana,
grapefruit, and cotton plantations.

In the 1920s and early 1930s, the Italians established the plantations; did a great deal of work on
roads; improved the ports of Mogadishu, Brava, and
Merca, where most of the bananas were loaded for export; constructed many new buildings and streets in
Mogadishu, which was the seat of the central government; and built a railroad (destroyed during the British
Military Administration of 1941-1950) connecting Mogadishu with Afgoy and Villagio Duca degli Abruzzi (Jowhar). They constructed an electricity plant in Mogadishu,
founded two leprosariums, built a large hospital in
Mogadishu and smaller ones in other towns, and established centers for studying and treating animal diseases
and for experimental work in agriculture. They established a few Western-type schools, built mosques, and
subsidized some Koranic schools, constructed wells,
and built irrigation dikes. In spite of this seemingly
impressive list of accomplishments, the colonial period
did little to improve the quality of life of the Somali
people or to advance them toward self-government.

The colony was divided into seven administrative regions, with 33 districts, each presided over by
an Italian Resident. A police force with about 1,500
Somalis and 85 Italian officers was formed in 1911;
and a rural armed force, the gogle, was formed in
1914. The Corpo Zaptié, composed of 800 Somali,
Eritrean, and Arab troops led by Italian Carabiniere
officers, was organized in 1923 to dis-arm the nomads.
Later, it used askari recruited from local clans. Responsibility for law enforcement was held by the Residents, who, along with qadis in some centers, acted as
judges.

In 1935 the colony was used as the launching
point for the war against Ethiopia, which lasted until
1936. It may be that in the minds of some Italian colonial officials Somalia was never more than a stepping-
stone to the anticipated future conquest of Ethiopia, a
conquest temporarily stymied at Adowa in 1896. Italy
held Ethiopia as part of Italian East Africa from 1936
until 1941 and also controlled British Somaliland for a
short period. The British Military Administration replaced the Italians in Somalia in 1941. See ITALIAN
TRUSTEESHIP ADMINISTRATION.

ITALIAN TRUSTEESHIP ADMINISTRATION (AFIS). After the

United Nations General Assembly acted to place Italy
in charge of the Trust Territory of Somalia, AFIS
(Amministrazione fiduciaria italiana della Somalia) was
organized in April 1950. The trusteeship agreement
required that AFIS establish political institutions; expand educational, social, and economic institutions;
guarantee freedom of speech, press, and petition; and
assure independence in ten years. An Advisory Council, composed of a committee of UN members and sta-
tioned in Mogadishu, was to be kept informed on all
matters and was to make recommendations to the administering authority. In addition regular UN visiting
missions reported their findings to the UN Trusteeship
Council.

     The first two years of the administration were
marked by distrust on the part of Somalis, especially
the political parties, the result, perhaps, of overly
aggressive tactics by AFIS. When the Somalis saw
that the requirements of the trusteeship agreement
were being carried out and that their cooperation was
necessary for its success, more amicable relations developed. During the last eight years of the trusteeship, trained Somalis gradually took over practically
all government posts, and in 1956 the appointed Territorial Council was transformed into a 70-man elected
legislature with full statutory powers over domestic
legislation, subject to AFIS veto. The new body was
elected in territory-wide elections and was designated
the Legislative Assembly. The number of legislators
was increased to 90 in 1959. Two kinds of local government bodies were established: District Councils
in the rural areas and Municipal Councils in the
towns and villages. By 1956, all were headed by
Somalis.

     Independence came on July 1, 1960, five
months before the date stipulated in the trusteeship
agreement.

ITALO-ETHIOPIAN AGREEMENTS OF 1897 AND 1908. In
    1897, Italy and Ethiopia began negotiations to define the
    boundary between Italian Somaliland and Ethiopia. They
    agreed upon a boundary, marked it on two maps, but
    did not put the agreement into writing. The maps dis-
    appeared and have never been found. Italy reported
    that the agreed boundary lay about 180 miles inland
    and approximately parallel to the Indian Ocean coast.
    Ethiopia claimed that the boundary was much nearer

the coast.

In an attempt to settle the dispute, the parties entered into a second agreement in 1908. At this time, Italy paid Ethiopia three million lire for an area of about 50,000 square miles lying between Dolo on the Juba River and a point on the Shebelle about 50 miles north of Beled Weyn. Still no precise line for the remainder of the boundary was established. In 1911, an Italian-Ethiopian Boundary Commission was appointed to mark the boundary on the ground, but it was unsuccessful because of the vagueness of the 1897 and 1908 agreements. These agreements described the boundary largely in terms of the location of clan groups. Since many of the clans were nomadic or in the process of shifting their location via migration, the agreements, one of them unwritten and the maps defining it lost, were at best ambiguous. Today these agreements are, along with the Anglo-Ethiopian treaty of 1897, the basis for the disputed Somali-Ethiopian boundary.

ITALO-ETHIOPIAN BOUNDARY COMMISSION (1911) see ITALO-ETHIOPIAN AGREEMENTS OF 1897 AND 1908

ITALO-ETHIOPIAN TREATY OF FRIENDSHIP AND COMMERCE OF 1928. Under this agreement Italy and Ethiopia agreed to submit any disputes between them to an international body for arbitration and conciliation. It dealt with possible disputes concerning not only Somalia, but other Italian colonies as well. The Wal Wal incident in 1934 was an occasion on which the treaty might have been implemented, but after some initial efforts arbitration was abandoned because it could not be decided whether Wal Wal was in Italian or Ethiopian territory. Soon afterward, Italy, under Mussolini, invaded Ethiopia, and this step was the beginning of the 1935-1936 war.

ITALO-ETHIOPIAN WAR. During this war, Somalia was a major landing area for Italian troops. Somalis, as individuals and as clan groups, fought on both sides. About 60,000 Somalis served in the Italian military and supporting forces, many later nationalist leaders among them. One of those who sided with Ethiopia and whose activities are recorded was Omar Samantar (q.v.). After Ethiopia was conquered by the Italians, in 1936, the Ogaden was united with Somalia to form a single administrative unit. See BRITISH MILITARY ADMINISTRATION.

- J -

JALLE. A Somali word meaning, roughly, comrade, brother,
    or fellow-countryman. During 1971, the Supreme Rev-
    olutionary Council began using jalle as a title for its
    members and encouraged all Somalis to call one another
    jalle.

JAMA BILAL MOHAMED (c. 1885-1960). Also called
    Ma'alin Jama Bilaal. An educator, religious teacher,
    and patriot who was born and educated in Aden. As a
    young man he served as secretary to the Mijerteyn
    sultan Bogor Osman Mahmoud, and was taken prisoner
    by the Italians in 1927 when the Mijerteyn were sub-
    dued. After he was freed, he engaged in commercial
    activities, and in 1935 moved to Mogadishu, where he
    was again imprisoned for his nationalist activities.
    After his release, in 1936, he opened a school in
    Mogadishu and devoted himself to teaching. In 1950,
    under the trusteeship administration, he was named in-
    spector of elementary schools. He was given the Croce
    di Cavaliere and a medal of honor by the Italian gov-
    ernment in 1954.

JAMAHA. A tariqa community whose members engage in
    agriculture and, often, teaching. Each jamaha, follow-
    ing one or another of the Sufi orders, has its own
    leader (sheikh or kalifa) and is usually centered on a
    mosque or the tomb of the jamaha founder. The com-
    munities are training centers for wadads.
        In the nomadic regions, the jamaha leaders
    may maintain their clan connections, and the livestock
    belonging to jamaha members may be herded by their
    kinship group; sometimes men in the jamaha take jobs
    in the towns while their families cultivate the jamaha
    fields. In the agricultural regions of the south, the
    jamaha are usually outside the lineage structure. Often
    they consist of persons from many different clans or
    lineage groups.
        The formation of the jamaha was part of the
    Muslim revival of the 19th century. The first Somali
    jamaha was founded at Bardera in 1819. By 1950,
    there were over 90 jamaha in the Southern Region,
    with a total membership of about 35,000. Most of
    these were in the Bakool, Gado, and Bai Regions or
    along the mid and lower Shebelle. The number in
    other regions was small because the nature of the soil

in these areas did not as a rule encourage the development of agricultural settlements.

JENALE. A village on the Webi Shebelle near Merca. Jenale was the site of an Italian agricultural experimental
station in 1910. An irrigation project was initiated
there in the 1920s, and grapefruit and banana concessions were developed, following the pattern devised by
the Duke of Abruzzi at Jowhar: There were farm laborers' villages, in which the families were alloted
land and provided seed, health services, and a salary
in return for working on the concessions. At times,
forced labor was recruited. Most of the plantations
fell into ruin between 1941 and 1950, but some were
revitalized during the 1950s. By the 1960s, bananas
from the Jenale plantations were a chief item in the
export trade.

JIHAD. A religious or "holy" war.

JIIFTO. A chanted poem about serious or important matters.
The jiifto, sung solo by men, is not accompanied by
music or handclapping. The chant is usually quicker
than that of the gabay (q.v.), and the average line has
fewer syllables. See also BURAAMBUR; GEERAAR;
MANSO; POETRY; SONGS.

JILAL. The hot, dry, dusty season of the northeast monsoon, lasting from December to March or April. It is
the harshest season for both herders and farmers.
The nomads may begin to move out during the jilal,
but if they find the pastures dried up, they return to
their home wells. For farmers, it is the time of the
second harvest. See also DAIR; GU; HAGA.

JOWARI see MILLET

JOWHAR. Somali name for Villagio duca degli Abruzzi, administrative center of the Central Shebelle Region.
See SOCIETÀ AGRICOLA ITALO-SOMALA.

JUBA RIVER. One of the two major Somali rivers. It
rises in Ethiopia and empties into the Indian Ocean at
Kismayu. It is navigable to a few miles beyond Bardera. The water of the Juba is always fresh, and its
flow seldom fails. It reaches floodtide from March to
May (during the gu season of heavy rains) and from

October to December (the dair season of light rains).
Prior to 1925, the Juba River marked the boundary between Italian Somaliland and the British-held trans-Juba
area.   See ANGLO-ITALIAN AGREEMENT OF 1925;
JUBALAND.

JUBALAND.   The trans-Juba area, from the Juba's west
bank to the Kenyan border, was transferred to Italy by
Great Britain in 1925.   For one year, the area was
called the Jubaland Province and was administered as
a separate Italian colony.   Afterward, it was governed
as an integral part of Italian Somaliland.

- K -

KENYA.   Southwest of the Somali Republic, in the North-
Eastern Region of Kenya, live approximately 300, 000
Somalis.   They are largely Darod and Hawiye pastoralists whose forebears migrated there between 1865 and
1910.   The British government in Kenya halted the Somali migrations at the Tana River in 1910, and the
point beyond which Somalis could not pass came to be
known as the "Somali line."
          During the colonial period, the Northern Fron-
tier District (NFD), as the region was called prior to
its division in the 1960s, was always treated different-
ly from the other Kenyan areas.   The Somalis and
other inhabitants of the NFD were regarded as more
intractable than other Kenyan groups, and the land itself was barren, compared with the rich farming lands
to the west.   Ordinances in 1908, 1926, and 1934 defined the NFD as a "special district."   The movements
of the inhabitants were restricted, and the progressive
techniques of government, education, and economic development applied in the rest of Kenya were not extended to the NFD.   These government policies widened
the social and cultural gap between the inhabitants of
the NFD and other Kenyans.   Political parties were
banned in the area until 1960, and not until 1959 were
the Somalis represented in the Kenyan Legislative Council.
          By 1960, Somali pressure in the NFD to unite
with the Somali Republic became organized, and the
Somalis in Kenya asked that a UN plebiscite be held to
determine their future.   Great Britain offered instead
to send a commission to the NFD before Kenyan inde-

pendence to determine the desires of the inhabitants.
The Somalis in the NFD as well as those in the Republic welcomed this offer and expected that the North-
Eastern Region would soon be united with the Republic.
        The Commission made its inquiry in 1962 and
found that an overwhelming majority of the Somalis in
Kenya did wish to be united with the Republic. Despite
this finding, Great Britain stated that nothing could be
done to implement it until after Kenya became independent.   The Somali government regarded this decision
as an act of bad faith, and broke off diplomatic relations with Great Britain in 1963.   The Kenyan leader
Jomo Kenyatta announced that the Somali-inhabited area
would never be allowed to secede from Kenya.
        From 1963 to 1965, a number of armed
clashes took place between Kenyan authorities and Somalis living in the North-Eastern Region, and a number of deaths occurred.   With the changes of government in the Somali Republic since 1967, and with the
mediation of other African governments, the Republic
has given less overt support to the irredentist movement in Kenya (as well as in Ethiopia); has eliminated
radio propaganda that might encourage Somalis outside
the Republic to rebel; and has adopted a policy of
friendship with its neighbors.   The irredentist movement in the NFD is not dead, however, and future activities in the area remain a question.

KHAT.   Catha edulis, or celastrus edulis, a narcotic plant
        grown in the Ethiopian district of Harar, in Kenya, and
        in parts of the Northern Region of Somalia.   The green
        fresh leaves are chewed for their stimulating effect.
        A small amount produces a pleasant insomnia; a larger
        amount, a slight intoxication.   Although the Salihiya
        order forbids the use of khat, the other Sufi orders
        permit its use.   It is often considered an aid to the
        religious during the long hours of prayer and medita-
        tion.   The use of khat is regarded as harmful by the
        government and its sale is frowned upon.   The price
        is very high and constitutes a drain on the meager in-
        come of many families.   It is used chiefly by men.

KISMAYU (pop. c. 18,000).   Like Mogadishu, Brava, and
        Merca, the town of Kismayu, near the mouth of the
        Juba River, was founded in the 9th or 10th century by
        immigrant Arabs and Persians.   The history of Kis-
        mayu is not so well documented as that of the other

ports. It too was an object of Portuguese interest in
the 16th and early 17th centuries, and later fell under
the suzerainty of the sultans of Oman and Zanzibar,
where it nominally remained until the British entered
the area in 1888.   For a brief period in 1875-1876,
Egypt laid claim to Kismayu, along with Brava.   For
an even briefer period in 1889-1890, the German Witu
Company claimed Kismayu.   The Imperial British East
Africa Company (IBEAC) acquired the coastal area
from the Sultan of Zanzibar in 1888, and in 1889
leased the area north of the Juba to Italy.   The trans-
Juba area, including Kismayu, came directly under the
British government in 1895 after the IBEAC was dissolved.   In 1925, the trans-Juba was ceded to Italy.
        Kismayu is the largest city in the Lower Juba
Region and is the region's administrative center.   It is
a coastal town, with buildings in the Arab-Portuguese
style.   During the 1960s, the archaic harbor built during the colonial period was transformed into a medium
all-weather draft port with dockside cargo facilities ac-
commodating four vessels of about 10,000 tons.   Its
main function is to service the banana export industry.
Kismayu is also the site of a newly-installed meat-
processing plant (q.v.).

                        - L -

LAND TENURE.   The 1960 constitution declared that all
    land belongs to the state.   Traditionally much of the
    cultivated and unoccupied land was under the control of
    certain lineage groups.   These groups often alloted
    plots of land to arifa, who inherited rights of use, but
    not land ownership.   A 1960 law upheld the right of
    every citizen to live and farm where he wished and
    abolished the arifa system.   Implementation of the law
    has, however, been hindered by the rigid traditional
    land tenure system.   See ABBAAN; HABASHO.
        Among the nomadic population, it is said that
    the land "belongs to God" and should be open to com-
    mon usage.   But many clan groups have their tradi-
    tional grazing areas, which they fiercely defend against
    intruders, especially during the seasons when pasturage
    is limited.   Thus, there is no individual land tenure
    system, no system of demarcating and registering land
    holdings, and no general land tax.   Some clans have
    sold land to Italian and Somali plantation owners, and

these individual holdings are recognized by the government as valid.

LANGUAGE. All Somalis speak the Somali language, with slight dialect differences from region to region. Until late 1972, disagreements based largely on religious inclinations or preferences for certain clan-related scripts prevented the government from adopting Somali as a written national language. Several scripts existed, but there was disagreement over whether the language should be written in an Arabic- or Latin-based alphabet. In 1972, a Latin-based script (with a 31-letter alphabet) was adopted, and Somali became the only official national language. Prior to that, the official written languages were Arabic, English, and Italian. Somali is a Cushitic language. Among the thirty or so Cushitic languages and dialects spoken in northeast Africa, Somali is most closely related to Galla.

Arabic is the language of Islam, and all Somalis have some knowledge of Arabic. It is not readily adaptable to written Somali, however, because the phonetic structures of the two are quite different. Arabic, for example, has six vowels, three long and three short, whereas Somali has five long vowels and five short. In the Latin script, long Somali vowels are usually shown by doubling the letter. Somalia is the only Muslim country that does not employ the Arabic alphabet, with the exception of those Muslim territories which now lie within the USSR. See LITERACY; SHIRREH JAMA AHMED.

LAS. A cistern dug for the purpose of collecting and conserving rain water.

LEATHERWORK. Traditionally workers in leather come primarily from the Madarrala, Yibir, and Midgan sab groups. Their products include prayer mats, shields, amulets, and sandals.

Small tanneries and leatherworking factories are found throughout Somalia. The Catholic Mission opened a leather factory in Mogadishu in 1955, where handbags, sandals and similar leather objects were produced. Other leather factories are in operation in Mogadishu as well as in Brava, Merca, and Hargeisa. A large state tannery is being developed at Kismayu in connection with the meat-processing plant.

LEGAL SYSTEM.   Prior to independence and union, the le-
     gal system of the Northern Region was based on a
     British pattern superimposed on Somali customary law
     (heer; testur), while that of the Southern Region com-
     bined Italian law and Somali customary law.   Also
     throughout the country, Islamic law (the Sharia) was
     observed in some areas of marriage, inheritance, and
     contract arrangements.   In 1960, the Republic appointed
     a Consultative Commission for Integration (later for
     Legislation).   When the Commission finished its work
     in 1964, a unified system of law, embracing Islamic
     and customary law, as well as modern law, and apply-
     ing to the nation as a whole, was well developed, al-
     though some remnants of the British and Italian sys-
     tems remained.   After the 1969 coup, the Supreme
     Revolutionary Council (SRC) assumed all judicial as
     well as legislative and executive power.   The SRC
     suspended the 1960 constitution, and announced that a
     new one would be written.   No steps had been taken in
     this direction, however, to 1974.   See COURTS.

LEGISLATIVE ASSEMBLY.   Before independence, both Bri-
     tish Somaliland and the Trust Territory had legislative
     assemblies.   Upon unification, the two legislatures
     combined to form the Republic's National Assembly, or
     Parliament.   The Legislative Assembly in British So-
     maliland was established in February 1960.   It was
     composed of 33 elected members.   The leader of the
     four-member cabinet was Mohamed Haji Ibrahim Egal.
     (He was Prime Minister of the Republic from 1967 un-
     til the October 1969 coup.)   See also LEGISLATIVE   .
     COUNCIL.
          The Legislative Assembly in the Trust Terri-
     tory was formed in 1956, and was composed of 70
     elected members: 60 Somali members and ten repre-
     sentatives of the Italian, Arab, Pakistani, and Indian
     minorities.   The assembly was a unicameral body,
     with complete legislative power in domestic affairs,
     although the trusteeship administration retained a veto
     power.   The assembly assumed control over foreign
     and financial affairs and defense and public order in
     1957 and 1958.   In 1959, the assembly was enlarged
     to 90 elected members.   In 1957, the assembly of the
     Trust Territory began writing the constitution, which
     became the constitution of the Republic in 1960.   From
     1956 to 1960, Aden Abdulla Osman was president of
     the Trust Territory's Legislative Assembly.   (He was

President of the Republic from 1960 to 1967.) See
NATIONAL ASSEMBLY.

LEGISLATIVE COUNCIL.   The forerunner of the Legislative
Assembly in British Somaliland.   It was established in
1957, and initially had six appointed members representing the various clan groups.   In 1959, it was expanded to include 12 elected members, along with 17
appointed members.

LIJ YASU.   Emperor of Ethiopia from 1913 to 1916; the
grandson of Menelik II.   It is said that Lij Yasu converted to Islam in 1915 and that he was friendly toward
Sayyid Mohamed Abdullah Hassan.   He was deposed in
1916, at which time Ras Tafari (later Emperor Haile
Selassie) became regent.   In the conflict following the
coup in which Lij Yasu was deposed, his Somali followers were annihilated.

LINEAGE.   A descent group whose members can trace their
ancestry directly to a common ancestor.   Each Somali
clan is divided into lineages with a genealogical depth
of six to 12 or 14 generations.   The lineages are further divided into dia-paying groups and rers.
        Among the Saab clans, lineage groups are nor-
mally more directly associated with particular territories than is true among the Samaal clans, and the
lineage group may even have a name that reflects its
association with a specific place.   Among the nomadic
Samaal clan families, lineage is not related directly to
land possession, but to genealogy per se, and lineage
groups bear the name of their ancestral founders.
        In the traditional society, kinship did not en-
sure friendship or unity among clan segments.   Therefore within clan families, lineages would unite under
formal heer arrangements for collective military or
political purposes, such as the payment and receipt of
blood compensation, defense against livestock raids,
and protection of watering places and grazing areas.
See SAAB; SAMAAL; TRIBALISM.

LITERACY.   The literacy rate was estimated at about five
per cent in 1970.   A number of factors have played a
part in keeping the rate so low: lack of a written
Somali language until 1972; the reluctance of many
Somalis to attend European-language schools, which
were considered anti-Islam, especially during the

colonial period; the nomadic way of life of a majority
of the population, which makes regular school attend-
ance almost impossible; and the policy of the colonial
governments to interfere as little as possible in the
traditional mode of life.   Until the adoption of Somali
as a written language in 1972, literacy required the
learning of at least one foreign language, and usually
two--Arabic plus a European language.

A literacy campaign was initiated in 1973, and
in 1974 high school students were sent to all parts of
the country to teach reading and writing.   In some
places, it is reported, the literacy rate has already
risen dramatically.

LITERATURE.   Poetry (q. v.) is the chief form of individu-
ally created literary works, and, indeed, the chief
form of individual artistry.   A rich oral or folk literature embraces legends, myths, tales, riddles, and
proverbs.   The first modern Somali novel, From a
Crooked Rib, by Nuruddin Farah, was published in
1971.   Short stories were sometimes published in
newspapers and periodicals before the 1969 coup.   A
number of Somali poets, including Sayyid Mohamed Abdullah Hassan, wrote in Arabic or in a Somali script
based on the Arabic alphabet.   Some poets invented
their own systems of writing Somali.   See, e.g.,
GADABURSI SCRIPT; OSMANIYA.   See also THEATER.

LIVESTOCK DEVELOPMENT.   Programs dealing with livestock improvement and management come under the
Ministry of Livestock and Rural Development.   They
include the study, treatment, and control of animal
diseases, the dissemination of information regarding
animal husbandry, the construction of wells and other
watering places.   The Livestock Development Agency,
which is concerned primarily with livestock marketing,
has several holding grounds.   The largest, at Kismayu,
can hold up to 10, 000 head of cattle; its main function
is to supply the Kismayu meat-processing plant.   The
agency also runs a hides, skins, and leather development center.

LIVESTOCK RAIDING.   Livestock raiding was much more
common in the past than it is today.   Traditionally,
livestock raids were carried out only after consultation
in a general assembly, or shir, unanimous approval by
the assembled members, selection of a raid leader,

and a decision about the division of the loot.   Such
raids almost inevitably led to intergroup warfare (q. v.).

LOCUST CONTROL.   The Northern Region is one of the locust breeding grounds of northeast Africa.   Efforts by
the British to control locusts by putting out poison
were often misunderstood by the Somalis, who thought
that the poison was intended for their camels and other
livestock.   Such a misunderstanding culminated in riots
in the Burao district in 1944-1945.   The most recent
locust plague came in 1967-1968.   The Republic cooper-
ates with the Desert Locust Control Organization of
East Africa, an international group which carries out
surveillance and control operations.

LUGH   see   GANANE.   Sometimes spelled Luk or Lugh Ferrandi.

- M -

MA'ALIN JAMA BILAAL   see   JAMA BILAL MOHAMED

MACAIAD.   A "coffeehouse" where men gather to drink tea
(shah) and to chat and talk politics.

MAGAALA.   The Somali word for "town. "

MAIT.   An ancient port on the Gulf of Aden in the Sanaag
Region.   Mait was one of the dispersal centers of
early Somali expansion.

MAIZE.   The principal traditional crop in the wet-farming,
irrigated, areas of the river basins; a staple in the
diet.

MALARIA.   A common disease in Somalia.   Extensive efforts have been made to bring it under control.   In
their traditional medical practice, the Somalis' chief
means of controlling malaria was avoidance of mosquitoes.   In 1855, Richard F. Burton recorded, with
some amusement, that the Somalis attributed malaria
to mosquito bites.   He wrote that this "superstition"
arose from the fact that mosquitoes and fevers became
most troublesome at about the same time.

MANSO.   A poetic form traditionally used in the southern

part of the Republic. <u>Mansos</u> are generally love songs,
often light and joking. They contain two to eight lines,
and are alliterated in one letter. See POETRY; SONGS.

MARIANO, MICHAEL. A leader of the National United Front,
an amalgamation of several politically concerned groups,
organized in British Somaliland to protest the Anglo-
Ethiopian Agreement of 1954, under which the Haud and
"reserved" area were transferred to Ethiopia. He was
a government employee in the protectorate and a member of the Legislative Council, which was established
in 1957. He was also a member of the Somaliland
Legislative Assembly, and later of the Republic's National Assembly. In 1964 he was named Chairman of
the Consultative Commission for Legislation, and in
1969 was Minister for Planning and Coordination. After the coup of October 1969, he was detained for about
four years, along with others, at the presidential palace at Afgoy. He is now (1974) a "roving ambassador, " especially for African affairs. As a Catholic,
Michael Mariano belongs to that small percentage of
Somalis who are non-Muslim.

MARKET CENTERS. Markets develop around towns that
are government centers. The markets deal largely in
products that are consumed locally, and many of the
traders are women, who sell mats, rope, charcoal,
eggs, fruit, and water. Markets for export goods--
aromatic gums, hides and skins, and livestock--are
located primarily in the largest cities. Market
centers established at wells and other watering places
are often seasonal. In the Southern Region, small
permanent market centers grew up in areas of dryland
farming and along the rivers.

MARRIAGE. Among the nomadic Samaal clans, marriage is
traditionally within the clan family, but outside the
primary lineage segment, which traces ancestry back
six to ten generations. Marriage is thus exogamous,
and is viewed as an alliance of two dia-paying groups.
The woman remains a member of her father's dia
group, rather than becoming a member of her husband's. Marriage may heal hostilities between groups
and lead to a sharing of watering or grazing rights.
Cousin-marriage is not prohibited, but is normally disapproved because it carries with it none of the advantages of intergroup marriage.

Among the sedentary village-oriented Saab clan families, marriage is endogamous, often taking place within the dia-paying group. Patrilateral parallel-cousin marriage or matrilateral cross-cousin marriage is preferred. Since kinship ties are weaker among the genealogically heterogeneous sedentary Saab clan families than among the Samaal, endogamous marriage helps to strengthen kinship ties among the Saab.

Marriage rules are traditionally Somali, but do not conflict with Islam, under which a man may at one time have four wives. The woman's virginity at the time of her first marriage is regarded as extremely important, and the intact-status of her infibulation is regarded as proof of her virginity. Lack of virginity is grounds for annulment. Marriage may be contracted by family arrangement, by elopement if the couple wish to marry and the families do not consent, or by capture, which is today rare. After elopement, the man brings the woman back to her family, pays a compensation if requested, and asks her family's blessing. In the case of capture, enmity may develop between the two clan groups and the bride's group may demand compensation. Normally, a marriage is not legal unless the woman consents, even though her parents may be strongly in favor of it.

Marriage payments, sometimes referred to as bride wealth, are an indication of the groom's economic situation, a safeguard of the bride's security, and an assurance that she is esteemed and will be welcome and well treated in her new family. They are made directly by the groom and his kinsmen to the bride and her family. They may be used to set up the new household. That part of the marriage payment which is given to the bride herself is called mahar. The marriage is binding when the mahar is promised in the presence of a wadad. Among the poor this may be the only payment. The bride's family may provide a dowry if it is well-off and if this is part of the marriage contract arranged between the two families.

Somali society is patrilocal; thus, families ordinarily live with the clan of the husband, and children belong to the clan of their father. Somalis usually marry in the mid or late teens. An unmarried girl of twenty is rare, except among the well educated. See also DIVORCE.

MEAT PROCESSING. One of the new industries in Somalia

is meat processing. A plant, with about 400 employees, was opened in Kismayu in 1968. It produces not only canned and smoked beef, but such by-products as bone-meal and dressed hides. The plant was built with aid from the USSR, its technicians were trained in the USSR, and in its early years a considerable part of its output was purchased by that country.

MEDICINE. In October 1972 the Supreme Revolutionary Council nationalized all medical facilities; all medical personnel, including physicians, are now employed by the government and have no private practice.

Modern medical practices and modern hospital facilities were introduced by the colonial powers, but in the traditional society, medicine was practiced by the Midgan and by wadads. Traditional medicine involves the use of herbs, myrrh, and other vegetable products for treating hemorrhage, tuberculosis (one of the most common diseases in Somalia), rheumatism, headache, sores, and other ailments. Animal products, such as ghee (butter), broths of milk and myrrh or water and meat, are used to treat constipation, asthma, eye ailments, headache, tuberculosis, impotence. Traditionally cauterization was used to treat headache, pneumonia, tapeworm, rheumatism.

Vaccination against smallpox was performed by taking the lymph from a calf suffering from pox and vaccinating the individual on the wrist. Persons who contracted smallpox were isolated, and their huts and other belongings burned. Aromatic plants were burned under their beds, and sometimes the patients were treated by being buried for a while in the sun-heated sand, with only the head exposed.

Long before Europeans recognized that malaria (q.v.) was carried by the mosquito, the Somalis knew this and tried to protect themselves against mosquito bites. Malaria is a common disease throughout the country, even among the nomads.

Other traditional modes of treatment were primarily psychological in approach. Considerable attention was paid to diet and rest during convalescence, and sexual relations were avoided. Use was also made of bloodletting, which was generally believed to be conducive to good health. Amulets, magic, and the recitation of special formulas were also employed to ward off or cure illness. Epilepsy, insanity, and paralysis were thought to be caused by evil spirits.

MENELIK II (1844-1913).   Emperor of Ethiopia from 1889
to 1913.   During the European scramble for Africa,
Menelik II felt threatened by European encroachments
in the Horn of Africa, and he began an expansionist
policy to protect his country and to extend Ethiopian
control over areas that, according to Ethiopian traditions, had been under Ethiopian sovereignty in the 16th
century and earlier.   See ANGLO-ETHIOPIAN DIPLO-
MACY; FRANCO-ETHIOPIAN AGREEMENTS OF 1897;
ITALO-ETHIOPIAN AGREEMENTS OF 1897 AND 1908.

MERCA.   The chief town and administrative center of the
Lower Shebelle Region.   Like the other coastal cities
of the Benadir Coast, Merca, which lies south of Mogadishu, was founded in the 10th century or earlier by
immigrants from Arabia or Persia.   It was an important port and center of trade, lying only ten miles
from one of the most fertile stretches of the Shebelle
River valley.   It appears that the Jiddu clan of the
Hawiye clan family were the first Somalis to settle
near Merca, in the 13th century, although there may
have been earlier migrations of Digil groups.
        As the southwestward migrations continued,
various Somali groups probably paused in the Merca
area before being pushed out by newcomers.   By the
late 1600s, it is believed that the Bimal, who live in
the area today, were in effective control of Merca, its
hinterland, and the caravan trade from the interior.
Trade in slaves, ivory, spices, aromatic gums, cattle,
and hides was carried on in exchange for such imported
goods as textiles, metal, pepper, tobacco, coffee,
sugar, and manufactured products.
        The coral reefs at Merca seem to rule out
any great expansion of the port.   In the colonial period,
the Italians reconstructed the port to facilitate the
handling of the banana exports, but it is necessary to
use lighters to carry goods from the port to ocean-
going ships.

MERICANI.   From the mid-1850s, mericani, a cotton cloth
from the US was sold at the southern Somali ports.
By 1880, it was widely preferred to some of the other
imported cottons.   This trade died out as Somali trade
with Italy increased.

MIDGAN.   The use of this term is now prohibited by law.

The Midgan are the most numerous sab (q.v.) group.
They hunt (the ostrich, especially), and also act as
medical practitioners, barbers, and hairdressers.
Traditionally, Midgan women perform the infibulation
operation and Midgan men perform the circumcision.
They are believed to be descendants of hunting peoples
who lived in the Somali peninsula before the arrival of
the Somalis.

MIGRATIONS. Migrations are a major phenomenon in the
    Horn of Africa and have played a significant part in
    the history of many Somali clans. The migrations of
    the Somalis are traditionally traced back to Saab and
    Samaal, the sons of a Muslim Arab who came to the
    northern Somali coast, perhaps in the mid-700s, and
    married a Galla woman. According to one legend, the
    two sons left their home village with their families;
    Saab moved inland and Samaal journeyed along the
    coast. It is believed that all the later Somali migra-
    tions took one or the other of these routes, one follow-
    ing the river valleys and the other the line of coastal
    wells. The migrations were not great waves of entire
    clans, but movements of smaller groups, perhaps of
    younger sons who moved out with their families to seek
    better pasturelands, to ease the pressure of population
    growth, or to preach and propagate Islam.
        As the Somalis advanced, they displaced the
    Gallas and, in the riverine areas, ousted, conquered,
    or assimilated the Bantu-speakers who preceded them
    in the area. The Digil reached the Shebelle River
    area and the Hawiye reached Merca by the 13th century.
    The Ajuran, a Hawiye-related clan arrived in the
    southern region at this time, and had by the late 14th
    century moved into the interriverine area, established
    a hereditary dynasty, and gained control of the interior
    trade routes to Mogadishu and other coastal cities.
    From the 14th to 16th centuries, the holy wars in the
    north led by Haq ad-Din, Sa'ad ad-Din, and Ahmad
    Guray pushed the Galla in the northern area westward
    and permitted Somali expansion in that direction. The
    westward movement of the Somalis was effectively
    halted by their defeat by the Ethiopians, however, in
    the 16th century. The Rahanweyn had moved into the
    interriver Doi area and crossed the Juba by the 17th
    century. By that time, also, Hawiye groups had de-
    feated the Ajuran and taken over their territory in the
    mid and lower Shebelle valley. The Darod moved into

the trans-Juba about 1840 and by 1909 had moved as
far south as the Tana River in Kenya.   See SOMALI
LINE.

The migrations were not always peaceful, although the first Somali arrivals in an area may have
entered into arifa, or client, agreements with earlier
Negroid or Galla occupants.   Eventually, with more
migrants over a long period, the new arrivals might
gain a numerical superiority.   They would then take
over the territory militarily, or if unable to do that,
move on into a new area.   Over the course of almost
a thousand years, the Somalis moved from their foot-
hold on the northern shore to the areas they now occupy.

While Somali oral traditions generally support
this picture of a millennium-long north-to-south migration, linguistic evidence places the homeland of the
Somali language in south Ethiopia.   From this, one
might tentatively conclude that Somali-speakers have
occupied the Horn of Africa from a very early (unknown) date; that they fanned out from southern Ethiopia in small numbers in the first millennium AD; and
that north-south migrations are a relatively recent
phenomenon prompted at different times by population
growth, desiccation of northern pastures, wars with
Ethiopia, and the zeal of converts to Islam.   See
PREHISTORY.

MIJERTEYN.   It is not known when the sultanate of the Mijerteyn was established, though it was perhaps as early
as the 15th or 16th century.   It was powerful in the
17th century, headed by a leader with the title of bogor,
whose headquarters were at Alula, on the Gulf of Aden
coast.   The sultanate controlled the sea commerce of
the area and profited from salvaging ships that over-
turned on the rocky coast.   In 1866, the British paid
the sultan to permit them to rescue disabled ships and
take them to Aden.   About 1870, a dispute between the
Mijerteyn sultan Bogor Osman Mahmoud, and his relative and father-in-law, Yusuf Ali, led to a war and split
in the sultanate.   Yusuf Ali and his followers migrated
to Obbia, on the Indian Ocean coast, where he established a new sultanate.   See YUSUF ALI "KENADID."

In 1889 both sultans signed treaties of protection with the Italian consul at Zanzibar, V. Filonardi.
Under these treaties, Italy paid the sultans an annual
subsidy.   The two sultanates were often at war, and the

land between them, a distance of about 500 miles, was
occupied by nomadic pastoralists. Until 1908, the
sultanates were under the nominal protection of the
Italian consul at Aden.   Thereafter, they were under
the administration of the governor of Italian Somaliland,
but were left much to themselves. In 1904, the Italians
established a third protectorate in the Nugal Valley, between the Mijerteyn and Obbia sultanates--that of Sayyid
Mohamed Abdullah Hassan.   This proved to be another
source of intergroup warfare in the area.

Under Bogor Osman Mahmoud, the Mijerteyn
Somalis and their chiefs tried to remain independent
and resisted Italian efforts to control them.   In 1909,
after the sultan refused to allow the Italian flag to fly
at Alula, the Italians suspended his annual subsidy and
bombarded the coastal villages.   Interclan rivalries in
1910, however, forced the Mijerteyn to accept the establishment of Italian Residents in the coastal towns.
When Sayyid Mohamed Abdullah Hassan moved his headquarters to Taleh in 1913, the area became more peaceful, but after 1920, and the defeat of the Sayyid, the
sultans of Obbia and the Mijerteyn resumed their competition over the region between their seats.

With the ascendancy of Mussolini in Italy and
a new period of Italian expansionism, the Somalis in
the Mijerteyn were dis-armed, and their region was
brought under closer Italian administration in 1927.
The sultan submitted only after a series of battles in
which there were many losses among the Mijerteyn
forces as well as among the Corpo Zaptié.

MIJERTEYN MOUNTAINS.   Part of the maritime range of
hills and mountains along the Gulf of Aden in the
northern Bari Region.

MILK PROCESSING.   A state-owned milk plant was established in Mogadishu in 1965 with USSR aid.   Output
varies seasonally, according to milk production, which
is lowest during the dry months.

MILLET.   Holcus sorghum.   Also called durra, jowari, and
in Somali, hirad.   It is the chief grain crop in the
rain-fed dry-farming areas, especially in the interior
between the two rivers, but also in any area where
there is enough rain.   Millet is pounded and crushed
in a mortar.   The meal is used to make cakes and
porridge, and the milky liquid may be used for cooking
or as a nutritious drink for children.

MINING. Mineral resources are still being explored. Large
    reserves of gypsum have been found near Berbera and
    in the Nugal Valley. Recent discoveries of iron and
    bauxite have been made in the Precambrian granite
    area between Bur Acaba and Dinsor. In 1968, urani-
    um deposits were discovered in the Bai Region, near
    Bur Acaba. Sea salt is found at Ras Hafun, on the
    northern Indian Ocean coast, at Gezira on the Benadir
    coast, and at Zeila in the north. Although a consider-
    able amount of petroleum exploration has been carried
    out, no reserves have been found.

MIRIFLE CONFEDERACY. The most numerous group of the
    Saab, consisting of a cluster of clans. The term is
    sometimes used to refer to the Rahanweyn.

MISSION SCHOOLS. The French Catholic mission established
    a school in Berbera in 1891, primarily for orphans.
    It is said that Sayyid Mohamed Abdullah Hassan de-
    nounced the school vehemently, regarding it as an at-
    tempt to Christianize the British protectorate. The
    school was closed in 1910. Twelve elementary schools
    established in the towns of the Italian colony were also
    mission-run. They were attended by Italian children,
    Somali orphans, and other Somalis. Swedish Lutherans
    (1896-1935), the (American) Sudan Interior Mission
    (1954-1963), and American Mennonites (beginning in
    1953) are the only Protestant missionary groups to
    have operated schools in the Southern Region--all large-
    ly among former Bantu-speaking groups. No non-Mus-
    lim missionaries have been permitted to proselytize in
    Somalia since 1963.

MOGADISHU. The Republic's capital, located on the Bena-
    dir coast. In the reorganization of regions in 1973,
    Mogadishu, the "union city, " was made a separate
    governmental entity. The capital area consists of
    about 100 square miles and contains thirteen villages,
    or quarters, each with its own governmental bodies.
        Mogadishu, sometimes called Hamar, is the
    largest Somali city, its population having grown from
    about 75, 000 in 1958 to about 200, 000 in 1975. It is
    believed that the population was about 5, 000 in the
    mid-1800s. The construction of deep-water port fa-
    cilities at Mogadishu was initiated with US aid in the
    mid-1960s, and the port was further improved in the
    early 1970s. Mogadishu has the only airport capable

of handling large aircraft, although there are smaller
airports around the country.

It is believed that Mogadishu was founded by
pre-Islamic Arabs and Persians. From the 9th or 10th
century, it was an Islamic trading colony, ruled by
Arab and Persian families. The Fakhr ad-Din dynasty
ruled the city from about the 13th century. It flour-
ished as a center of trade and religious instruction
until the 15th century when it began to decline. Ibn
Battuta, a Moroccan who visited Mogadishu in 1331,
described the city as the capital of a prosperous sultanate which exported colored cotton cloth, skins, and
other products. It is believed that Chinese ships
visited Mogadishu, as well as Zeila, Brava, and perhaps other Somali ports in 1416 and 1421. In 1499
the Portuguese Vasco da Gama bombarded the city,
but did not enter it. Portuguese activity in the area
temporarily interrupted the city's traditional trade with
Arabia, Persia, and India.

In the 16th century, Mogadishu was ruled by
the Muzaffar dynasty and was connected with the Ajuran
sultanate of the interior. Other Somali settlers, probably Hawiye (Darandolla, Abgal) pushed the Ajuran out,
and gained control of Mogadishu in the early 17th century. Mogadishu at this time had grown into two rival
walled quarters, Hamarweyn and Shangani, composed
largely of representatives of the two great Somali
groups, the Samaal and Saab, respectively. By the
late 17th century, Mogadishu was under the rule of the
Sultanate of Oman. In the early 1800s, the Omani sultanate headquarters were moved to Zanzibar, and Mogadishu was then nominally controlled by the Sultan of
Zanzibar. In 1843, a Somali was named governor of
Mogadishu by the sultan, but he remained in office only
a few years. The sultan's control, in any event, was
minimal; in actuality, the Geledi (q.v.) controlled Mogadishu and Brava via their control of the hinterland
and its trade.

When the Italians arrived in Mogadishu in the
late 1880s, they established their post on the boundary
between the two old walled towns and over the next
forty years built up an Italian quarter.

Today representatives of all the Somali clan
families are found in Mogadishu. A number of resi-
dential quarters surround the old city, whose buildings
range in age and type from the Mosque of Sheikh Abdul Aziz built in 1238 to the modern multistory hotels

and new Parliament building constructed in the late
1960s.

MOHAMED ABDULLAH HASSAN   see   SAYYID MOHAMED
ABDULLAH HASSAN

MOHAMED ABSHIR MUSA.   Commander of the Somali National Police from 1959 until his resignation early in
1969.   After the October 1969 coup, he was placed
under house arrest.   He was released in 1972, but was
soon rearrested after a spontaneous popular demonstra-
tion on his behalf in Mogadishu.
        Mohamed Abshir Musa was born in the British
protectorate but has spent most of his life in the
Southern Region.   During the British Military Administration, from 1941 to 1950, he was a member of the
police force, attaining the position of police inspector.
He joined the police in the Southern Region during the
trusteeship administration and was made commandant
in 1959.   He attended Princeton University in 1962-63.

MOHAMED HAJI IBRAHIM EGAL (b. 1928).   In 1960, he
was selected Prime Minister of the state of Somaliland
when the British protectorate became independent.   In
the first governments of the Republic, he held ministerial posts (Defense, and later Public Education), and
in 1967, became Prime Minister of the Republic.   He
held that post at the time of the coup d'état in October
1969.   After the coup he and other former government
leaders and private citizens critical of the coup were
detained at the presidential palace at Afgoy.   In April
1973, the Supreme Revolutionary Council announced that
he and five other detainees would be charged and tried
by the National Security Court for conspiracy and mis-
appropriation of funds.   No further public announcement
concerning the trial had been made by late 1974.
        Although Mohamed Haji Ibrahim Egal, like the
earlier prime ministers of the Republic, favored a
Greater Somalia, it was his policy to give first priority
to economic and social development and to improved re
lations with other African countries, especially Ethiopia
and Kenya.   The 1969 coup was not specifically a revolt against Egal, but a move to relieve the chaotic
political situation that followed the assassination of
President Abdirashid Ali Shermarke.   See SUPREME
REVOLUTIONARY COUNCIL.
        Mohamed Haji Ibrahim Egal was born in the

district of Berbera in the Northern Region. His father
was a wealthy Berbera merchant. He received his
formal education in the Northern Region and in England.
From 1958 to 1960, he was a nominated member of the
British protectorate's Legislative Council, representing
the mercantile interests of the protectorate. He was a
leader of the Somaliland National League, and was
elected to the Legislative Council in the protectorate's
first general election in February 1960.

MOHAMED HUSSEIN (HAJI). A religious leader and early
member and president of the Somali Youth League,
which he represented before the Four Power Commission (q.v.) in 1948. See GREATER SOMALIA LEAGUE.

MOHAMED SIAD BARRE (b. 1919). President of the Somali
Democratic Republic and Major General in the Army.
Mohamed Siad Barre was born at Lugh; his parents,
who were pastoralists, died when he was ten years old.
He attended school in Lugh and in Mogadishu. During
the British Military Administration (1941-1950) he
joined the police force and rose to the highest rank
possible for a Somali. In the 1950s he attended the
Carabinieri police school in Italy for two years, and
took courses at the School of Politics and Administration in Mogadishu. During the trusteeship period, he
was the first Somali officer to be assigned a police
post, and in 1960 was a brigadier general in the police.
When the Somali National Army was created in 1960,
he went into the army, and in 1965 became its commander.

Mohamed Siad Barre was the leader of the
bloodless coup that took over the government in October 1969 and placed the state under a military regime,
the Supreme Revolutionary Council. Before the coup,
Mohamed Siad Barre had long stressed the importance
of civilian government; he has stated that the military
coup was a last resort in the struggle to eliminate
government corruption, extirpate tribalism, and ensure
the Republic's economic, social, and political progress.

MOHAMED SHEIKH GABIOU. A member of the Legislative
Assembly in the trust territory in the late 1950s. He
was the first Somali lawyer, and in 1959 was appointed
Minister for the Constitution. Mohamed Sheikh Gabiou
and his assistants revised the draft constitution that
had been in preparation since 1957 and presented it to

the Political Committee, which was in charge of completing the final draft that was approved by the Legislative Assembly in 1960.

MOHAMOUD JAMA ORDOH (d. 1969). A journalist and nationalist, founder of one of the first political parties in British Somaliland, the Somaliland National Society, and regarded by the protectorate government as a "dangerous" individual. He spent time in and out of jail, organized the prisoners, and called the Mandera prison in the protectorate "the free people's hotel." In 1946 he led a delegation to London, calling for the protectorate's independence. He was later a leader in the Somaliland National League (q.v.). After independence, he published several newspapers in which he accused the Republic's governments of corruption. His publications were banned, and he died in exile in Beirut, Lebanon.

MONSOONS. The monsoons determine the seasons and are felt mainly along the coast. The hot, dry, and dusty northeast monsoon blows from late December or early January to March or April, during the harsh season of jilal. The southwest monsoon is rain-bearing, and blows from April to September. The southwest winds are very erosive, especially in the north and northeast. The effect is greatest from June to August. Shipping, particularly that carried on by dhow, is greatly affected by the monsoons. See DHOW TRADE.

MOSQUES. A number of mosques in the coastal cities are of great historic interest; some date back to the 13th century. At Zeila, in the Hargeisa Region, there are the ruins of a mosque that is believed to date to the 12th century. The mosque of Abasa, whose remains show that it had twelve pillars of different shapes, probably dates to the 15th or 16th century. Abasa, in the Hargeisa Region, is one of the "ruined towns" of Somaliland, about which little is known.

In Mogadishu, the Jamma'a mosque (sometimes called Masjid-i-jami) is the oldest, and is believed by some to have been converted from a temple into a mosque. It has a tower several stories high; an inscription at the base records that it was built in 1238. The Arba'-rukun mosque has an inscription containing references to the Persian city of Shiraz, and recording that the mosque was built in 1268. The Fakhr ad-din

Mosque, according to an inscription on the mihrab,
which is decorated with colored marble, was constructed
in 1269.   The mosque of Sheikh Abdul Aziz, in a Persian style, is also believed to date to the 13th century.
Other ancient mosques in Mogadishu are the Sheikh
Ibrahim Haji Omar Rathai, the Mohamed I, and the
Faqi Omar.
      At Brava is the Mnara tower, an ancient mina-
ret, whose date is unknown.   The Jamma'a mosque contains an inscription dated 1398.   Another inscription on
a tomb in Brava is dated 1104 (the oldest inscription
noted in Somalia).   The Abukar Sayyid mosque is also
a medieval structure.   In Merca the Jamma'a mosque
contains an inscription recording its construction in
1609.   A second mosque in Merca contains an inscription dated 1771, but the mosque itself is believed to be
older than this.   The ruins of an ancient mosque of an
unknown date are found on the Bajuni island of Rasini.

MOUNT SURUD.   The highest mountain (7,900 feet above sea
      level) in Somalia.   It is in the maritime mountain range,
      in the north, about 50 miles inland and just northwest
      of Erigavo.

MUKTAL DAHIR.   One of the leaders of the Somali irreden-
      tist movement in the Ogaden during the 1960s.   See
      OGADENIA.

MUNDUL.   A fixed one-room hut, with cylindrical walls and
      a round or conical roof.   The mundul is found chiefly
      in the settled interior villages.   The walls are built of
      upright posts or poles, filled in with mud, cinders,
      and dung.   The central pole supporting the roof is
      about 9 feet high.   The roof is constructed from
      branches, then fitted over the central post and covered
      with grass or straw.   The door is often of wood.

MUNICIPAL COUNCIL.   Municipal councils were established
      in the trust territory in 48 population centers between
      1950 and 1956.   They came under the authority of the
      regional prefects.   At first the councils were appointed,
      but beginning in 1954, they were elected.   They were
      largely concerned with agriculture and stock breeding,
      public works, taxes, and public instruction.   The mu-
      nicipal councils were more effective units of local gov-
      ernment than the district councils (q.v.) in the rural
      areas because they served a more stable population.

MUSA BOGOR (HAJI) (b. 1911). Joined the Somali Youth
League in 1947 and helped to present the Somali view
to the Four-Power Commission in 1948. In the pre-
independence government in the Trust Territory, he
served as Minister of the Interior. He was a member
of Parliament, and it is reported that he was the chief
candidate for the presidency after the assassination of
President Abdirashid Ali Shermarke in October 1969.

MUSA GALAAL. An authority on Somali customs, language,
and literature. He served in the army during the
British Military Administration in the early 1940s, and
attained the highest rank possible for a Somali at the
time. After 1946 he served in the protectorate's ministry of education, and spent four years at the London
School of Oriental and African Studies. In 1960 he
headed a government-appointed committee to investigate
the best means of writing Somali. The committee
recommended a Latin-based system, but implementation
of the system had to await the decision taken by the
Supreme Revolutionary Council in October 1972. In
1974 he was with the Ministry of Higher Education.
See LANGUAGE.
        Musa Galaal has written a number of important
works on Somali literature, language, traditional medicine, weather lore, and other facets of Somali history.

MUSIC. The nomadic culture is not conducive to the development of instrumental music, but the nomads have a
great variety of songs. Wooden tubes, antelope or
kudu horns, and large triton shells are used by shep-
herds, mainly to communicate or send signals rather
than to make music. Among the sedentary population,
drums (skin-covered wooden bowls) and wooden trum-
pets, with reeds made of palm leaves, are used to ac-
company dances. A six-string lutelike instrument,
called a shirara, often decorated at the top with ostrich plumes, is also used. In the urban areas, music is more diverse, and such instruments as the lute,
tambourine, and flute have long been used. Modern
Somali music, developed largely since the Second
World War, is influenced by Arabic and Indian sources,
as well as by American music and African rhythms.
One of the most popular modern musicians is Abdillahi
Karshe, a singer and composer. See also DANCES;
POETRY; SONGS.

MUZAFFAR DYNASTY.   Rulers of Mogadishu from about
    1500 to 1625.   Believed to have been of Arab origin,
    but related to the Ajuran of the interior.   The last
    Muzaffar ruler was killed when Mogadishu was invaded
    by the Darandolla, probably a subclan of the Abgal, of
    the Hawiye clan family.

- N -

NABADDON.   Peacekeeper.   The title given to sultans,
    bogors, etc. when chiefly titles were abolished in 1970
    by the Supreme Revolutionary Council.   The establish-
    ment of the new title was apparently one move in the
    attempt to eliminate tribal distinctions and nongovern-
    mental sources of authority.   See CHIEFS.

NASSIB BUNDE (d. 1906).   A former slave who in the 1880s
    founded and governed a federation of agricultural vil-
    lages near Gosha on the lower Juba River.   All the
    people in the villages were freed slaves or fugitives.
    On his death, there was a struggle for succession to
    leadership; the Italians intervened and placed the vil-
    lages under Italian control.

NATIONAL ASSEMBLY.   The Parliament of the Somali Re-
    public, a 123-member unicameral body.   It was dis-
    solved by the Supreme Revolutionary Council in October
    1969.

NATIONAL BANANA BOARD.   Established in 1970 to regu-
    late and control the banana industry, and primarily
    concerned with marketing.   The Supreme Revolutionary
    Council has expressed no intention of nationalizing the
    industry, although some state-owned plantations have
    been initiated.

NATIONAL COMPANY FOR AGRICULTURE AND INDUSTRY
    (SNAI).   In 1963, the government purchased half of the
    Societâ Agricola Italo-Somala (SAIS), primarily involved
    in the growing of sugarcane and the production of sugar,
    and formed the National Company for Agriculture and
    Industry (SNAI).   In 1970, SNAI was nationalized.

NATIONAL SECURITY COURT.   This court was established
    in 1970 to try persons accused of acting against the
    state.   In 1972 the court found two former members of

the Supreme Revolutionary Council and a third army
officer guilty of such acts and sentenced them to death.
A number of other people have been executed or sentenced to prison terms for crimes against the state.

NATIONAL TEACHERS' EDUCATION CENTER. A training
center for teachers established at Afgoy in 1963 with
US aid. Now reorganized as the College of Education,
it is one of the branches of the National University.
See also EDUCATION.

NATIONAL THEATER. Built in Mogadishu in 1966 as a gift
from the People's Republic of China. The building
seats 1,500; it is used for national and international
conferences as well as for various kinds of artistic
presentations. The aim of the National Theater is to
promote and develop Somalia's cultural heritage.

NATIONAL UNITED FRONT (NUF). A political group organized in the British protectorate in 1954. It acted
as a liaison between the Somaliland National League,
the Somali Youth League, and other organizations, on
the one hand, and traditional and religious leaders, on
the other, to coordinate efforts to effect the return of
the Haud and "reserved" area to the protectorate.
Being unsuccessful in these efforts, the NUF lost some
of its influence, but it remained as a political party
until 1962. See ANGLO-ETHIOPIAN DIPLOMACY;
MARIANO, MICHAEL.

NATIONALISM. History shows that the Somalis have always
possessed a sense of Somali identification and have
resisted foreign interference in their territory, even
though they were often at war among themselves and
were never united under a single Somali government.
After the scramble for Africa began, the Somalis residing in various areas were governed by the French,
the British, the Italians, and the Ethiopians. The
Italians and the British--perhaps for their own national
interests--spoke of a "Greater Somalia" and propagan-
dized the Somalis on the advantages of having one
governing (European) power.
        In the immediate post-World War II period,
the scramble for the Somali areas continued, but now
the Somalis were able to express their own desires.
With a new sense of nationalism, they saw, for the
first time, the possibility of uniting all Somalis in a

modern nation-state.   They organized political parties
and presented petitions to the Four-Power Commission
(q.v.) and to the United Nations.   In British Somaliland, the Anglo-Ethiopian Agreement of 1954 regarding
the Haud and "reserved" area was a strong impetus
toward nationalistic expressions, as was the preparation for independence in the trust territory.
        It is said that of all the African states south
of the Sahara, Somalia alone has a nationwide sense
of cultural-ethnic loyalty underlying its nationalism.
Somalia has often been called the most homogeneous
state in sub-Saharan Africa.   It has a single religion
and a single language, and its people by and large
constitute a single ethnic group.   The clan-family gen-
ealogies--though they distinguish one Somali group from
another--are also a potent means of identifying Somalis
as Somalis and of maintaining their distinction from
other peoples.

NATIONALIZATION.   In May 1970 the Supreme Revolutionary
        Council (SRC) nationalized a number of industries and
        companies, some already partially owned by the govern-
        ment.   These included the National Company for Agri-
        culture and Industry (SNAI), the Italo-Somalo Electric
        Company, all oil distributors, and all foreign banks.
        The government committed itself to a satisfactory com-
        pensation for the nationalized companies.   In 1972
        health services, private schools, and printing presses,
        were nationalized.
                The SRC also announced in 1970-1972 the for-
        mation of a national insurance company with exclusive
        rights to operate in Somalia; a National Agency for
        Trade to be the sole importer and distributor of cer-
        tain consumer goods, such as medicines, dry cell
        radio batteries, tea, and coffee; a national organiza-
        tion for the distribution of grains; a national transport
        cooperative; an office to control the showing of foreign
        films.
                The nationalization of schools and printing
        presses and the takeover of film distribution were as-
        pects of the government's cultural and political revolu-
        tion.   The other moves were aimed at eliminating
        middlemen, stabilizing prices, improving distribution,
        eliminating corruption and nepotism in hiring, and im-
        proving working conditions and wages.

NAVY.   Somalia has a small navy, which is a unit of the

army. In the early 1970s, it had two destroyers and
six patrol boats and a few hundred personnel.

NEGROID PEOPLES. About 90,000 Somali citizens are the
    descendants of freed slaves or of the Bantu-speaking
    people who inhabited the area before the Somali migra-
    tions. The latter were called Zengi by medieval Arab
    writers. It is believed that these early inhabitants
    never lived north of the Webi Shebelle; today the Ne-
    groid peoples live primarily in the riverine areas.
    Most are agriculturalists, although some are hunters
    and fishermen as well. See, e.g., GOBAWEYN; SHA-
    BELLE; SHIDLE; WA-GOSHA.

NEWSPAPERS. In the early 1970s, three newspapers were
    published: Dawn, an English weekly; Stella d'Ottobre,
    an Italian-language daily; and Najmat October, an Ara-
    bic daily. All were government publications. Their
    chief purpose was to inform and educate the masses
    and to maintain contact between the people and the
    government. These newspapers have been discontinued,
    and a Somali-language daily has been published since
    January 1973, the Xiddigta Oktobar (October Star).
    The periodical New Era is published monthly by the
    Ministry of Education and National Guidance, in English,
    Italian, and Arabic editions.
        Since the 1950s, Somalia has had a variety of
    newspapers and other publications, but only those pub-
    lished by the government--both before and after inde-
    pendence--were long-lived. Privately published news-
    papers and journals, often critical of government poli-
    cies, always faced censorship problems and were soon-
    er or later forced to close, either voluntarily or through
    government action.

NOMADIC PASTORALISM see HERDING

NORTH-EASTERN REGION OF KENYA. A Somali-inhabited
    region formerly a part of the Kenyan Northern Fron-
    tier District. See KENYA.

NORTHERN REGION. The part of the Republic formerly
    known as British Somaliland. It makes up about one-
    fourth of the Republic in area and in population. The
    administrative regions of Hargeisa, Tug Dheer, Sanaag,
    and part of the Nugal form the Northern Region. See
    also SOUTHERN REGION.

NUGAL VALLEY.   This valley in the present Nugal Region
lies beyond the maritime range of the north.   It is important historically as the area in which the Italians in
1904 established the protectorate of Sayyid Mohamed
Abdullah Hassan.

NULLA.   A dry watercourse.   After a heavy rain, a nulla
may become a fast-moving stream for a few hours.
Same as douh, tug.

NURO.   A nutrient believed to exist in certain grazing areas
at certain times.   The Somali weather lore expert can
tell the herders where nuro can be found.   It is not a
physical or concrete property, but an abstract inherent
quality.   The Haud area is believed to be one of the
chief places where nuro exists, and for this reason,
the return of that area to Ethiopia in 1954 was seen as
depriving Somalis of nuro--and therefore involved much
more than political considerations.

- O -

OBBIA.   A town on the Indian Ocean coast, in the Mudugh
Region, about 300 miles north of Mogadishu.   Obbia is
historically important as the headquarters of the sultanate of Obbia, created in 1878 by Yusuf Ali "Kenadid. "   The word obbia (ho-bio) is said to mean "here
is water. "   The word water is used often as a metaphor for prosperity or good fortune.   It is said that
when Yusuf Ali broke away from the sultanate of the
Mijerteyn (q.v.) and moved to Obbia, he carried with
him masons who, immediately upon landing, began to
build a garesa--a stone building symbolic of dominion
over the area.   See also ALI YUSUF.

Obbia became an Italian protectorate in 1889,
but was not finally brought under complete Italian control until 1925.

OCTOBER REVOLUTION see COUPS D'ETAT

OGADEN.   1) The eastern area of Ethiopia, contiguous with
the Southern Region of Somalia.   It lies south of the
Haud, is inhabited by Somalis, and is also used as a
grazing ground by herders living in the Republic.   The
area has been the major subject of the boundary dispute between Ethiopia and Somalia in the Southern Region.

2) A large clan of the Darod clan family, with segments in the Ogaden area and in the trans-Juba.

OGADENIA.   In the early 1960s, a provisional revolutionary government of Ogadenia (Western Somalia) was formed by Somalis living in the Ogaden region of Ethiopia. Its aim was to secure unification with the Republic, and a number of battles were fought between Somalis and Ethiopian forces in 1963 and 1964.   There was some indication that the Ogadenia group was supported by the government of the Republic, but this was denied. One of the leaders of the group was Hassan Sheikh Abdullah, a brother of Sayyid Mohamed Abdullah Hassan.

OGO MOUNTAINS.   The maritime range, lying behind the guban coastal plain and stretching from the Ethiopian border in the Northern Region eastward toward Cape Guardafui.   Some of the cliffs in the coastal area have an altitude of 200 feet.   Further inland the mountains rise to 7, 900 feet above sea level (Mount Surud).   At about 2, 000 feet, vegetation is fairly dense.   Above 5, 000 feet, cedars of Lebanon are found in some spots.

OIL EXPLORATION.   Somalia has attracted the interest of more oil companies than any other country in East Africa, but no reserves have been found.

OMAN SULTANATE.   An independent state on the Arabian Sea which ruled all the southern Somali ports in the late 17th century.   When the headquarters of the sultanate was moved to Zanzibar in the 1830s, Mogadishu and the other southern ports came under the nominal control of the Sultan of Zanzibar.

OMAR HUSSEIN GORSE (c. 1882-1970).   A renowned poet, nationalist, and historian.   He was born in Berbera and traveled widely throughout Somalia and East Africa. He is described as having a phenomenal memory and as being an outstanding authority on Somali literature and traditional customs.

OMAR SAMANTAR (c. 1870-1945).   A Somali chief in the Ogaden (originally from the Mijerteyn area) who, with Ethiopian support, in 1925 led an army against the Italians and seized the fort at El Bur in the Galguduud Region.   He was overcome by the Corpo Zaptié and fled to Ethiopia.   In 1934, after the Wal Wal incident,

the Italians demanded that the Ethiopians turn Omar
Samantar over to them. The Ethiopians refused, and
during the Italo-Ethiopian war of 1935-1936, he fought
on the Ethiopian side as leader of a force of Somali
irregulars.

ORCHELLA WEED.   A lichen (archil) from which red and
purple dyes are obtained.   The orchella weed grows
wild in the Shebelle River area and was an article of
export in the last half of the 19th century.   It was purchased by British, French, and German merchants.

ORGANIZATION OF AFRICAN UNITY (OAU).   Somalia has
been a member of the OAU since its inception in 1963.
During the mid-1960s, the negative response of other
African states to Somalia's irredentist movement tended
to reduce Somalia's identification with the OAU and Pan-
Africanism.   Several attempts were made to place the
Somali-Ethiopian boundary controversy and the problem
of Somali refugees before the OAU, but the organization took no effective action, and urged the parties to
enter into direct negotiations.
        After 1967, the Republic's policy under Presi-
dent Abdirashid Ali Shermarke and Prime Minister Mohamed Haji Ibrahim Egal became less aggressive on
the irredentist issue, and Somalia's position in the OAU
became somewhat eased.   Under the Supreme Revolutionary Council, Somalia has become an increasingly
active member of the OAU, with President Mohamed
Siad Barre playing an important mediatory role in the
Tanzania-Uganda crisis following Idi Amin's coup in
Uganda.   See GHANA; PAN-AFRICANISM.
        In 1970, Somalia hosted the OAU Cultural
Council and a workshop on African music, dance, and
folklore.   In 1974, the conference of the heads of state
of the OAU was held in Mogadishu, and President Mohamed Siad Barre was chosen chairman of the organization in that year.

OSMAN YUSUF ALI BAH YAQUD.   More widely known as
Osman Yusuf Kenadid.   A poet and a brother of Ali
Yusuf, the last sultan of Obbia.   About 1920 he in-
vented a Somali alphabet and script, called Osmania.
He was a founding member of the Somali Youth League.
See also YASIN HAJI OSMAN SHERMARKE.

OSMANIA.   This script, invented by Osman Yusuf Kenadid,

was used briefly in some schools in the Southern Region during the colonial period.   It is said that the Italians considered the script nationalistic and subversive of Italian rule.   Its use was abandoned, and its inventor imprisoned for a while.   Although the Somali Youth League, the leading political party, favored the use of Osmania in the late 1940s, the script came to be regarded as "a Darod script," and it was never adopted for nationwide use.   Osmania was little known in British Somaliland and was less widely used in the Southern Region than various kinds of wadads' writing (q.v.).   A newspaper column in Osmania was published during the late 1950s, but was discontinued after criticism was voiced by traditional leaders.

OVERGRAZING.   Concentrations of livestock in the areas surrounding permanent watering places cause trampling and overgrazing and result in long-lasting damage to the vegetation.   This factor has been a major impetus to the well-drilling projects that preoccupied the Trusteeship Administration as well as all the Somali governments.   See RANGE MANAGEMENT.

- P -

PALEOLOGY.   Objects found on the surface seem to belong to the second Stone Age, the upper paleolithic.   They consist of rough, thin bifacial blades (some retouched and beaten back and others unretouched), thick bifacial blades, large splinters, disks, and chips.   Masses of stone, said to be the burial places of fallen warriors or famous persons, are found in the Northern Region and in the region of Bari.   Some are said to be the tombs of "foreigners," probably built by pre-Islamic inhabitants of the Horn.   The tombs occur in several shapes, perhaps made by different peoples at different times.   All are made of dry masonry.   See ARCHAEOLOGY; PREHISTORIC RUINS; ROCK PAINTINGS.

PAN-AFRICANISM.   Somalia has been a member of the Organization of African Unity (OAU) since its formation in 1963.   The Republic's Pan-Somali policy, the effort to unite all the Somali-inhabited areas within the Republic, was seen by some African states, particularly Ethiopia and Kenya, as disruptive of the Pan-African ideal. The Somalis, however, viewed Pan-Somalism as com-

patible with Pan-Africanism. They saw it as an attempt
to right--through self-determination--some of the wrongs
dealt the African people by the European colonialists,
who established boundaries that divided kinsmen and
tribal groups and placed them under different colonial
rules--and ultimately in different nation-states. Until
1967, when the Somali government adopted a less aggressive Pan-Somali policy, the Republic, though at-
tending OAU meetings, generally played a very minor
role in Pan-African activities.

Historically, the Somali people have identified
themselves more closely with the Arab-Muslim world
than with the Christian-pagan African world. This atti-
tude is probably changing, though the Republic has recently (1974) joined the Arab League.

PAN-ARABISM. Somalis were in contact with the Arab
world perhaps as early as the 7th century. Most trace
their ancestries back to immigrants from Arabia, and
their religion, Islam, was introduced by Arab refugees
and proselytizers. They thus have a strong pro-Arab
tradition (though it is said that some Somalis express
disdain for the Arabs now living in Somalia). Pan-
Arabism has played an important part in the Republic's
politics. In the Arab-Israeli controversy, for example,
Somalia has stood staunchly behind the Arabs and in
1974 joined the League of Arab States.

PAN-SOMALISM. The issue of a Greater Somalia dominated
the international policies of the Republic until 1967.
Before independence and unification, the political parties
in the Southern Region directed their Pan-Somali aims
toward the inclusion of the Ogaden and the North-
Eastern Region of Kenya in the Republic; the pre-
independence Northern Region parties were more directly concerned with the Haud and "reserved" area of
Ethiopia. The issue is still very much alive, and most
likely the Somali governments will continue to pursue
it peacefully. See IRREDENTISM.

PERIPLUS OF THE ERYTHRAEAN SEA. A guide to the
Indian Ocean written about 60 AD by an anonymous
Greek mariner and trader. It contains the earliest
known written record of the Somali area, and shows
that the Benadir ports were already controlled by Arabs
in the 1st century. The book states that frankincense
and myrrh were exported from the Cape of Spices

(Cape Guardafui) to Egypt, Rome, and Byzantium.
Tortoise shells, ivory, and slaves are also mentioned
as exports. Graeco-Roman and Indian ships traded at
the ports, selling cloth, grain, oil, sugar, and metals.

PERSIANS. Persian navigators are believed to have visited
the coastal towns of the Horn of Africa in the 7th
century. Oral tradition as well as inscriptions on
tombs show that Persians from Shiraz inhabited Mogadishu in the mid-1200s, and the Arabic inscriptions
show that the persons buried there were Muslim. The
southern coastal towns were dominated by Arab and
Persian dynasties until about 1625.

POETRY. Poetry is a traditional means of transmitting information, folklore, customs, and historical events.
It is used in entertainment, political speeches, religious ceremonies, and litigation. It is also used to
teach children their clan's history and to instruct them
in proper behavior. Children are taught riddles and
tongue twisters, and their intelligence is measured by
their verbal skills.
         The art of composing and reciting poetry is
highly cultivated throughout Somali society. In the
traditional society, poets were often the spokesmen for
their clans; they engaged in poetic duels and excited
their kinsmen's battle ardor. Some poems stress interclan hostility and detail the violence of clan warfare.
Poems of this kind, whatever their poetic merit, are
today regarded as tribalistic and are banned from
radio presentation.
         Alliteration in a particular initial letter through-
out a poem is a rigid requirement in classical Somali
poetry. To meet this requirement, the poet must be
a master of the Somali language, in both its archaic
and current forms. See BURAAMBUR; GABAY;
GEERAAR; JIIFTO; MANSO. See also LITERATURE;
SONGS.

POLICE. The Somali National Police (SNP) was formed in
1960 and placed under the authority of the Ministry of
the Interior. In the SNP were integrated about 1,000
men from the Northern Region's force, and about
3,500 from the Southern Region.
         In 1884, the British organized an armed con-
stabulary; in 1910, they formed the Somaliland Coastal
Police; and in 1926, the Somaliland Police Force, with

British officers and Somali inspectors, noncommissioned
officers, and constables.   Law enforcement was largely
the responsibility of British district commissioners, assisted by uniformed and armed illalos.

    A similar development took place in the Italian
area: first a small coastal police; then in 1911, a
Somali Police Force; in 1914, a rural armed force, the
gogle, to assist the Italian Residents; and in 1924, the
Corpo Zaptié, with Somali, Eritrean, and Arab noncommissioned officers and police led by an Italian Carabinieri command.   In the Italo-Ethiopian war, the
Corpo Zaptié, with about 6,000 Somali members, fought
alongside the Italian army.

    In 1941, when the British Military Administra-
tion assumed control of the Horn, the police were placed
under the British Colonial Police in both areas; then,
with the trusteeship administration, the police of the
Southern Region were again placed under Italian Carabinieri officers.   In 1958, the Somali Police Force,
with a Somali commandant and all-Somali personnel,
took over all law-enforcement responsibilities in the
South.   In 1960, British officers were withdrawn from
the police in the Northern Region, and at independence,
the forces of the two regions were united.

    The coup d'état in October 1969 was carried
out by the Army, with Police participation.   The police
are a part of the armed forces.   The Army, which was
formed in 1960, has been financed and trained largely
by the USSR; whereas the Police received financial and
technical aid from the US from 1958 until 1969.

    The SNP has a mobile unit (Darawishta Polis-
ka), which operates in remote areas and along the
frontier; a riot unit (Birmadka Poliska), which maintains order in urban areas; a Criminal Investigation Division, which handles investigations, fingerprinting,
criminal records, immigration, and passports, and
operates in both rural and urban areas; and other units.
A women's unit was formed in 1962 to deal with women and children and to curb social evils.   The entire
police force numbers about 6,000.

POLITICAL PARTIES.   Between 1945 and October 1969, when
    political parties were banned by the Supreme Revolu-
    tionary Council, about 80 political parties were formed
    and took part in one election or another.   In the last
    elections, in March 1969, over 60 parties supporting
    some 1,000 candidates participated in the competition

for the 123 seats in the National Assembly.

Except for the Somali Youth League (SYL), none of the parties gained nationwide appeal, and the SYL itself was largely composed of persons from Samaal clan families. The Hizbia Dastur Mustaquil Somali, the second largest party, appealed primarily to the Digil and Rahanweyn of the river areas. In the Northern Region, the major parties, such as the Somaliland National League and the National United Front (both mostly Isaaq) and the United Somali Party (Darod and Dir), were on the whole composed of persons from particular clan families. In the south, some parties represented only one dia-paying group and ran only one candidate in the national elections.

Ideologically, all the parties based their nationalist aims on a Muslim orientation; all favored the Pan-Somali movement; all claimed to be anti-tribalistic and opposed to traditional customs which stressed lineage identification; eventually all came to favor a policy of "positive" neutralism in dealing with the East-West power blocs.

The Somali Youth League of the Southern Region and the Somaliland National League and United Somali Party, both of the Northern Region, formed the first Republic government. Although party names and party affiliations changed, the reins of government remained in the hands of a relatively small group of men representing all clan families, both Samaal and Saab. The main function of opposition parties came to be that of securing the interests of their own clan groups. One way in which the governments sought to allay the fears and mistrusts of small parties and groups was the policy of ethnic balance (q. v.).

In October 1973, President Mohamed Siad Barre announced a forthcoming "congress of the working masses" to decide on the form, structure, and content of a "true socialist party" in Somalia. No such congress had been held, however, by early 1975.

POPULATION.   Although government estimates of population in 1971 were set at 4. 5 million, other estimates were as low as three million. The annual rate of population growth is about 2. 9 per cent. The population is sparse and unevenly distributed between the fertile riverine areas and the semidesert regions of the rest of the country. Aside from the concentration of people in the urban centers on the Benadir Coast, population density

is greatest in the river areas, where it is perhaps 16
persons per square mile. It is estimated that males
outnumber females by as much as four per cent, and
that 84 per cent of the population is under 45 years of
age.

In the pastoral regions, the population of a
village built up around a permanent watering place will
double, or even quadruple, during the dry seasons
when the nomads concentrate at the wells. Historically,
the same dramatic change in population density also occurred in the coastal trading centers when shipping was
more dependent on the monsoon winds than it is today.

An estimated 60 per cent of the population is
engaged in pastoralism; the percentage was estimated
at 80 per cent a few decades ago, but has decreased
as the country has modernized. About 15 to 20 per
cent are agriculturalists. The remainder are town
dwellers, engaged in trade, commerce, and government services (schools, hospitals, police, civil service,
etc.). The estimated 30,000 Arabs and 1,000 Indians
and Pakistanis in Somalia are mostly traders and re-
tailers; the 3,000 Europeans, predominantly Italian, are
engaged in commercial and transportation operations,
banana production, and government service.

PORTUGAL. During the 15th and 16th centuries, the Portuguese were at war with the sultans of the Arabian
coast. They interrupted the Arab trade with the coast
of Africa, and temporarily took over some of the Somali coastal towns. Their interest in the Somali area
was not great, however, because of the poor anchorage
of the ports and the hostility of the Somali people. In
1499 Vasco da Gama bombarded Mogadishu; in 1507
Tristao da Cunha sacked Brava; and in 1518, the Portuguese sacked Berbera. Their activities hastened the
decline of the coastal cities as centers of trade. In
the 1540s, the Portuguese supported the Ethiopians in
securing the defeat of Ahmad Guray and the Muslim
sultanate of Adal.

POTTERY. Ceramic or meerschaum articles are produced
primarily at Merca and the Bur Acaba area. They are
mainly items for practical use, such as vessels and
bottles for coffee and tea, charcoal burners, incense
burners, and lamps. Some are decorated with geometric designs. Both men and women engage in pottery production.

PRE-HAWIYE. A group of clans believed to be closely related to and genealogically anterior to the Hawiye.
Though a small group numerically, the Pre-Hawiye are
sometimes regarded as a clan family. They live mainly in the riverine areas of the Southern Region.

PREHISTORIC RUINS. Two monuments said to be of Phoeni-
cian origin are found in the Northern Region, but there
is no known written record to authenticate this belief.
In the Elayo coastal area (Sanaag Region) are ruins of
an ancient town believed to belong to an earlier culture.
Ruins at Mudun in the area of Skushuban in the northeast (Bari Region) appear to be the remains of three
mosques, surrounded by about 2,000 tombs with cone-
shaped towers. At the end of the Baladi valley near
Bosaso on the Gulf of Aden coast (Bari Region) lies a
grave said to be two miles long--the largest reported
in eastern Africa. In the Arie valley between Skushuban and Gardo (Bari Region) is the ruin of an ancient
town of large buildings with thick walls. At Goan
Bogame in the inland Las Anod area (Nugal Region) is
found the ruin of an ancient city with about 200 buildings; the architecture is said to be similar to that of
the old sections of Mogadishu. Also in the Las Anod
district, at Gubyaley is a well where camel brands are
drawn on the walls, with inscriptions below the brand
marks. Similar brands are still used by the Somalis
to distinguish ownership of camels. In the Hargeisa
Region, at Abasa, near the Ethiopian border, the ruins
of several towns can be seen. These are believed to
date back to the 16th century. Little archaeological
work has been done in Somalia, and many prehistoric
ruins have not been dated or conclusively identified.
See ARCHAEOLOGY.

PREHISTORY. A number of theories exist about the prehistory of the Horn of Africa and its settlement and early
inhabitants. All seem to agree that the present inhabitants resulted from a mixture of migrants from south-
western Asia and people already living in the area.
    One theory suggests that migrants from the
Caucasus Mountains passed through the Middle East to
Egypt; after centuries of conflict they intermarried with
Bantu-speaking people from the central African lake
region; some moved westward and others southward
along the Nile to the Ethiopian plateaus; thereafter some
moved back toward the Gulf of Aden and Indian Ocean

coast. A second theory suggests that immigrants from southern Arabia came directly to the Red Sea area, with some moving northward to Egypt and others southward to the Land of Punt. A third hypothesizes that peoples from Mesopotamia and the Persian Gulf invaded Arabia, which at the time was inhabited by African Negroes. The people intermixed, and later these mixed groups invaded the coastal regions of Africa, where they intermarried with the local inhabitants.

It is believed that the Somali area has been inhabited for at least 100, 000 years. Some writers suggest that the area was once the home of bushmanoid peoples, who were absorbed over the centuries by Bantu-speakers moving up from the south. The Bantu-speaking groups were then largely displaced by pastoral peoples--first the Galla, then the Afar, and lastly the Somali--beginning perhaps before the 1st century AD. See MIGRATIONS.

PRE-ISLAMIC CUSTOMS. Certain pre-Islamic practices, often with a heavy overlay of Islam, are still carried on in Somalia. The roobdoon, or rainmaking, ceremony; celebrations marking the death and rebirth of the land at seed and harvest time; rites to protect crops against evil and to ensure a good harvest; the kindling of the fire, or dabshid, at the time of the seasonal new year; the celebration of the istunka festival; the taking of oaths on a stone; the belief in the evil eye; the reverence of holy trees--all these and other practices may be observed. Some may be equivalent to such practices as lighting the Christmas tree or knocking on wood for good luck.

PROTECTORATE ADVISORY COUNCIL. Established in the British protectorate in 1947. It was composed of appointed delegates from the various districts and represented both modernist and traditional views. Known as the Council of Elders after the establishment of the Legislative Council in 1957 and the Legislative Assembly in 1960, it met every two years. Its chief purpose was to encourage interest in government and to facilitate the collection and expenditure of public funds.

PROVERBS. Proverbs play an important role in communication. In the traditional clan assemblies, or shirs, and in debates, the speaker with a broad knowledge of proverbial sayings carried considerable weight and was

regarded as an able orator.   Special proverbs about
women usually describe them as inferior to men, jeal-
ous, untrustworthy.   One proverb says: Either give
up women or accept their defects.   But another says:
The woman is the builder of the nation.

PTOLEMY'S GEOGRAPHY.   This book, much of it by
Claudium Ptolemaus of Alexandria, Egypt, was originally written in the 2nd century A.D., and was edited
and added to by geographers in the 5th century.   The
Geography does not mention Negroid peoples along the
northeast African coast.   This seems to substantiate
the belief that a population change did occur in the
area, as some of the theories of prehistory suggest.
In fact, it is now generally believed that the Bantu-
speaking peoples expanded into East Africa in the second half of the first millennium A D and did not reside north of the Shebelle River.   See PREHISTORY.

PUNT.   The Land of Punt, which is mentioned in the Bible
and in ancient historical works, was probably the area
reaching from Eritrea eastward to perhaps the Bari Region of Somalia.   Somalis often refer to the Horn of
Africa as the Land of Punt.

- Q -

QADI.   Also spelled kadi.   Traditional as well as modern
Islamic judge.   Until the late 1880s, qadis were primarily an institution of the coastal cities.   The qadi
courts deal with family and personal matters under Islamic and customary law.   Under the colonial adminis-
trations, their power was extended to deal with many
questions formerly handled by clan elders.

QADIRIYA.   One of the major Sufi orders in Somalia.   It is
the oldest Islamic order, and was the first to be introduced into Somalia, perhaps by Arab traders in the
15th century.   By 1900 it was widespread in the country.   The spread of the Qadiriya in the Northern Region is associated with Sheikh Abdarahman Zeilawi (d.
1883), while the order's success in the Southern Region
is often attributed to Sheikh Awes Muhammad Barawi
(d. 1909).   The order concentrates on teaching, and
its followers have congregations among both the nomads
and the riverine agriculturalists.   See AHMADIYA;

DANDARAWIYA; RIFAIYA; SALIHIYA. See also
SHEIKH MADDER; SHEIKH SUFI; SHERIF ABUBAKR BIN
'ABDALLAH AL-' EIDARUS.

QAMAN BULHAN (c. 1860-1925). A Somali poet and philosopher.

QASIM MUHYID DIN (d. 1929). A poet and member of the
Qadiriya from Brava. He was a student of Sheikh
Awes Muhammad Barawi, and left many short poems
in Arabic on mystical subjects.

QAUDHAN DUALEH (c. 1860-1959). A Somali poet and leader.

- R -

RAAGE UGAS (c. 1811-1881). One of the greatest Somali
poets; his work is considered illustrative of pure,
classic Somali poetry, presenting the traditional view
of life. He was the son of a sultan of the Ogaden clan
(Darod) and was distinguished as a skillful negotiator
in clan disputes.

RADIO. Owing to the low literacy rate in Somalia, the radio
stations at Mogadishu and Hargeisa are extremely important as means of mass communication. The station
in Hargeisa was installed in 1943. In 1969, it had a
10, 000-watt transmitter and a 5, 000-watt transmitter.
The Mogadishu station was opened in 1951, and in 1969
had a 50, 000-watt transmitter (largely for overseas
broadcasts) and a 5, 000-watt transmitter. They oper-
ate under the auspices of the Ministry of Information
and National Guidance. It is estimated that at least
half the population has daily access to radio broadcasts.

RAHANWEYN. One of the two clan families derived from
the eponymous ancestor Saab. The Rahanweyn (literally,
"large crowd") are often referred to as the Mirifle confederacy. Together with the Digil, they number over
600, 000. They live primarily between the Shebelle and
Juba Rivers and on both sides of the Juba. Many are
agriculturalists; some have large herds of cattle. By
the early 19th century, the Geledi (q.v.) were the dominant Rahanweyn group and the source of the chiefly
family.

RANGE MANAGEMENT. Overgrazing and erosion are special
    problems where large herds of camels and goats con-
    gregate around permanent wells and other watering
    places.   Earlier governments made little effort to en-
    force range-management practices because of the fear
    of clashes with the nomadic pastoralists, but, following
    a program of education and public relations, the Su-
    preme Revolutionary Council initiated a range-manage-
    ment program in 1971.

REGIONAL AND LOCAL GOVERNMENT.   Until 1973 the na-
    tion was divided into eight administrative regions; a
    reorganization of regions in 1973 raised the number to
    fourteen--plus the capital area of Mogadishu.

Old Regions	New Regions (and administrative center)
Hargeisa	Hargeisa (Hargeisa)
Burao	Tug Dheer (Burao) Sanaag (Erigavo)
Mijerteyn	Nugal (includes also the district of Las Anod, formerly in the Burao Region) (Garowe) Bari (Bosaso, or Bender Kassim)
Mudugh	Mudugh (Galcaio) Galguduud (Dusa Mareb)
Hiran	Hiran (Beled Weyn)
Upper Juba	Bakool (Hoddur) Gado (Garbaharrey) Bai (Baidoa)
Lower Juba	Lower Juba (Kismayu)
Benadir	Central Shebelle (Jowhar) Lower Shebelle (Merca)

        The regions are divided into districts, each
headed by an official appointed by the central government, under the Ministry of the Interior.   Municipal
governments formerly had elected officials and an appointed administrative officer.   Under the Supreme
Revolutionary Council, all regional and district officials

are chosen by the central government. Village councils,
however, may have some elected members. See
DISTRICT COUNCIL.

RELIGION. Almost all Somalis are Muslim; there are a few
Christians. The constitution of 1960 established Islam
as the state religion, but guaranteed religious freedom.
No proselytizing by Christian missions is permitted.

RER. A nomadic hamlet. A rer may have from five to 50
families; 20 to 30 rers from one lineage group may
camp near one another while the herders are dispersed
during the wet season. The rer is the smallest unit
of government in the traditional political system. The
word means "people of" or "descendants of, " or in
some cases "persons engaged in" a certain occupation.
Examples: Rer Au is a lineage composed of wadads
and their families. Au is a traditional wadad title.
Rer Hamar is the primary lineage group in the Hamarweyn quarter of Mogadishu.

RER MANYO. Literally, "hunters of the sea. " Rer Manyo
village in Mogadishu is situated near the Mosque Sheikh
Abdul Aziz. Traditionally, the care of the mosque was
the responsibility of the Rer Manyo.

RER SHEIKH MUMIN see SHEIKH MUMIN ABDULLAHI

"RESERVED" AREA see ANGLO-ETHIOPIAN DIPLOMACY

RESIDENT. Title of the chief Italian colonial officer in the
districts. Provincial heads were called Prefects. The
Resident was equivalent to the District Commissioner
in the British protectorate. The title of Resident was
used by both the British and the Italians in the early
days to designate the officer in charge of a post.

RICE. Rice is a popular food; much of it is imported.
Several rice-growing experiments have been undertaken
including one by a University of Wyoming group and
another by the People's Republic of China.

RIFAIYA. One of the Sufi orders in Somalia. The Rifaiya
is found largely among Arabs in Mogadishu and Merca.
See also AHMADIYA; DANDARAWIYA; QADIRIYA;
SALIHIYA.

RIVER TRANSPORTATION. The Juba River is navigable by
shallow draft boats to a few miles beyond Bardera.
River transportation is to some extent important for
the movement of bananas to Kismayu and for the trans-
port of manufactured goods to the interior. The Webi
Shebelle is navigable by raft for short stretches in the
flood season; it has never been used as a major artery
of transportation.

ROCK PAINTINGS. Paintings are found in a number of
caves, especially in the Northern Region. Paintings
of animal and other figures are found in a cave at Gaan-
libah (about 45 miles from Hargeisa). The oldest paintings are black; later ones are red and white. At Gel-
weita, about 25 miles from Las Koray (Sanaag Region)
are rock paintings and evidence of a stone-age culture.
At Golharfo, about 20 miles east of Hudun (Sanaag Region), there are caves with rock paintings of animals,
human figures, weapons, and household articles. In a
cave at Karinhegane, between Las Koray and Elayo,
are rock paintings of animals, each having beneath it
an as-yet untranslated inscription. Some of the animals shown in the paintings are found in Somalia today,
while others are extinct. No archaeological surveys
have been made to determine the date or origin of the
paintings. See also PREHISTORIC RUINS.

ROOBDOON. A rainmaking ritual held by groups of southern
cultivators. Prayers and animal offerings are made
for rain and prosperity. Roobdoon is celebrated dif-
ferently in various localities; it takes place only when
the elders foresee a delay in the rains or when it does
not rain during the regular rainy seasons of gu and dair.

ROYAL BANANA MONOPOLY. In 1931 the Italian government prohibited the import of bananas into Italy from
any source other than Somalia, and in 1935 the Royal
Banana Monopoly was established. It became inopera-
tive during World War II. During the trusteeship administration, the Italians organized a new agency to
protect the Somali banana industry. See BANANA MO-
NOPOLY.

ROYAL ITALIAN EAST AFRICA COMPANY. No such company ever existed. The name was invented by a representative of the Imperial British East Africa Company (IBEAC) in 1890. He was signing treaties of

protection with Somali chiefs on the west bank of the
Juba River (the British area of influence), and when
some chiefs from the east bank (the Italian area) appeared to sign treaties also, the IBEAC representative
substituted the name "Royal Italian East Africa Company" for IBEAC and allowed the chiefs from the east
bank to sign. Sometimes the Filonardi Company is
referred to as the Royal Italian East Africa Company.

- S -

SAAB. The eponymous ancestor of two major clan families,
the Digil and its more numerous offshoot, the Rahanweyn. It is estimated that the Digil and Rahanweyn
make up about 15 to 20 per cent of the total population
of Somalia. The Saab clans are lineage confederations,
and probably contain representatives of every major
Somali lineage. They live primarily in the riverine
and interriverine areas.
    Political and territorial boundaries among the
sedentary and semisedentary Saab coincide to a far
greater extent than among nomadic groups. That is,
the political structure is centered on a particular village, or group of villages, rather than being deter-
mined solely by lineage affiliation. Villages are, traditionally, ruled by councils of elders, and the village
itself, or a group of villages, constitutes the dia-paying
group. Descendants of the original Somali inhabitants
of an area hold a special place in the society, and usually have the task of slaughtering animals used in
sacrifice and performing other services. These men
are the dalad (q.v.), urad, or mindihay.
    The Saab are agriculturalists, but they also
have large numbers of cattle, sheep, and goats, and
some camels. The villages are often centered on
wells or ponds, and strict regulations govern the use
of the wells and the surrounding land, both of which
normally belong to the clan. The headman of the village is traditionally known as gob; some clans also
have a titular head who represents them in dealing with
other clans. Groups of religious leaders bless new
villages and wells, perform rites to protect the crops,
officiate at marriages and deaths, etc.
    Traditionally, newcomers to an area could be
adopted into a clan, and this practice is largely the
source of the Saab heterogeneity. Such clan clients

(arifa) gave up their original lineage association, were allocated land for cultivation, and agreed to abide by the customs of the clan that adopted them (abbaan). The status of client was abolished, however, in 1960. Thus a man who had been a client might, if he wished, revert to his original lineage but still retain the land he had been granted under the client relationship. See MIGRATIONS; SAMAAL.

The designation Saab is falling into disuse; it seems to imply that the individual is not a Somali, which, of course, is not the case.

SAAR.   An ancient dance or ceremony of exorcism still sometimes performed despite government disapproval. Possession by the spirit Saar is said to cause madness or sickness.   Such possession is often related to (or perhaps caused by) irregular or troublesome male-female relationships, depression, and insecurity--situations for which normal life patterns supply no solution.   Symptoms of possession include fainting, vomiting, unhappiness, and physical pain.   Exorcism involves a ceremony in which certain formulas are repeated and in which dancing, drumming, handclapping, and singing are used.

SAB.   This term is falling into disuse; it is seen as pejorative.   Traditionally, the sab were regarded as lower-caste groups; they usually were held in a client relationship with a patron group near whom they lived and for whom they worked as blacksmiths, barbers, medicine men, leatherworkers, etc.   Since the traditional occupations of the sab are of great value in a modern economy, their skills have been important in bringing about their social and economic advancement.   The aim of the government to eliminate the caste system has to a large degree been achieved.

The sab themselves believe that their groups inhabited the Horn of Africa before the Somalis arrived and that their more immediate ancestors intermarried with the younger sons--and therefore less powerful offspring--of the Somali eponymous ancestors, Saab and Samaal.   They make up about one per cent of the total population; they look like other Somalis and speak Somali, though some also have their own languages.   See, for example, MIDGAN; TUMAL; YIBIR.   See also ABBAAN.

SA'D AD-DIN. Muslim ruler of Adal (Ifat) in the 14th century. He was killed in a holy war against the Ethiopians. Arab historians refer to Adal as the land of
Sa'd ad-Din; an island off the coast of Zeila is today
referred to by this name. See also HAQ AD-DIN.

SAID KHALID BIN BARGASH. Sultan of Zanzibar in the
latter part of the 19th century with whom the British
and Italians dealt in gaining control of the Benadir
Coast.

SAID SULEIMAN. Viceroy of the Sultan of Zanzibar in 1905;
the last representative of the Zanzibari sultanate in Somalia.

SAINTS. The title "saint" is applied to hundreds of outstanding religious leaders, both living and dead. Saints are
venerated as intercessors between the people and the
Prophet Mohamed, who is "in the doorway of God."
Saints include the founders of tariqas, local religious
leaders whose piety has influenced Somali Islam, and
founders of lineages who have been incorporated into
Somali Islam. Tombs of Islamic saints, as well as
tombs of some pre-Islamic figures, are places of pilgrimage and gift offering.
        The tomb of Sheikh Jabarti ibn Ismail, an an-
cestor of the Darod, near Erigavo (Sanaag Region), and
that of Sheikh Isaaq ibn Ahmed, an ancestor of the
Isaaq, at Mait (Sanaag Region), for example, are places
of annual pilgrimage. Further examples: Sheikh Mumin, whose tomb is at Bur Acaba (Bai Region), is regarded as a protector of crops; Au Hiltir, a legendary
protector against crocodiles, is honored especially in
the riverine areas; Au Mad is the protector of crops
against predatory birds; Au Barkhadle, whose tomb is
near Hargeisa, is honored in the north.

SALAAN ARRABEY (c. 1841-1943). A poet and philosopher
of the Isaaq clan family who composed many poems
criticizing the Darod. He traveled and worked in Aden
and Kenya as a trader, interpreter, and guide. A
talented linguist, he used many foreign words in his
poems, and coined new Somali words. Many of his
sayings have entered Somali literature and are now regarded as proverbs.

SALIHIYA. One of the major Sufi orders in Somalia. The

Salihiya is a puritanical order, introduced into Somalia
in the late 19th century by Sheikh Muhammad Guled.
Salihiya jamaha are collective farms along the two
rivers and in the interriverine area, but the order is
also active in the Northern Region. Sayyid Mohamed
Abdullah Hassan was a member of this order. See
AHMADIYA; DANDARAWIYA; RIFAIYA; QADIRIYA.

SALT. Ras Hafun, a town in the Bari Region, on the Indian
Ocean, was the site of an Italian-operated salt plant in
the 1920s and 1930s. In 1933, it produced 260,000 tons
of salt, most of it exported to East Africa, India, and
Japan. Today, salt for domestic use is produced at
Gezira, south of Mogadishu, and at Zeila, in the Hargeisa Region. Restoration of the mine at Hafun is being planned.

SAMAAL. The eponymous ancestor of four major clan families: the Darod, Dir, Hawiye, Isaaq. The four clan
families are traditionally associated with rather specific
expanses of grazing territory, but sometimes the territories of the groups overlap. The clan family's territory describes the circuit of nomadic migration, but
there is no land ownership per se. Land is believed
to belong to God, but the wells on the land belong to
the men or clan groups who constructed them. Some
Samaal groups have in the past few decades begun to
practice agriculture in addition to livestock-keeping.
These groups are located chiefly in the northwestern
sections of the Northern Region. It is estimated that
the Samaal make up about 80 to 85 per cent of the
total population of Somalia. See HERDING; MIGRA-
TIONS; SAAB.

SAYYID MOHAMED ABDULLAH HASSAN (1864-1920). A religious leader (sayyid) of the puritanical Salihiya order;
a poet who devised a Somali script in Arabic characters
and composed many celebrated classical poems; and a
political leader who led a 20-year jihad, or holy war,
against European and Ethiopian intrusion into Somali-
inhabited territory. Mohamed ibn Abdullah Hassan, as
he is popularly known, is today regarded by many as a
great national hero, but during his lifetime he was
feared and hated by members of the large Qadiriya
Sufi order and by victims of the chaos caused by his
guerrilla wars.
         By the age of 20, Sayyid Mohamed was a

religious teacher and sheikh. In 1894, he visited
Mecca and joined the Salihiya order. The next year
he returned to Somalia and spoke out most vehemently
against the French Roman Catholic mission at Berbera.
In 1897, he returned to his birthplace in the eastern
part of the protectorate where he taught and built a
mosque. His first political acts were against the Ethiopians in the Haud, where his people, the Dolbahanta
of the Darod clan family, took their animals for grazing, and his first adherents came from the Ogaden Ahmadiya tariqa settlements which had been ousted by the
Ethiopians.

His anti-British activities began in 1899. His
followers at this time were estimated to be 6,000
strong. To secure weapons, his followers, called
darwish (dervish) to indicate their non-tribal affiliation,
began to attack caravans and engage in camel raids.
The British, supported by Ethiopian forces to some extent, led four expeditions against Sayyid Mohamed from
1900 to 1910, but were unable to defeat him. In 1904,
the Italians, hoping to pacify him and concentrate his
activities in one area, granted him a protectorate in
the Nugal Valley. After a 4-year lull, however, he
began raiding the Mijerteyn and Obbia protectorates to
the north and south of the Nugal, and carried out activities against the Rahanweyn and Hawiye in the south
and southwest. Raids were again extended into the
British protectorate.

One of his followers, Abdullah Sharari, de-
fected and, perhaps with Italian and British encouragement, obtained a letter from the Salihiya founder in
Mecca denouncing the Sayyid's religious teachings as
unorthodox. Some of his followers in the south then
abandoned him, but he remained strong in the north.

In 1910, the British, unable to defeat the dervishes or maintain order, retreated to their coastal
outposts. From that year, fighting between the dervishes and other clan groups led to widespread devas-
tation, uncontrolled intergroup warfare, and terror in
the interior of the British protectorate. In 1912, some
of the Sayyid's followers attacked the British at Berbera, and in 1914, they attacked places in the southern
area. The need to secure more arms led the Sayyid
to seek an alliance with Lij Yasu, the Muslim-oriented
Emperor of Ethiopia, who was soon deposed (1916) by
the Ethiopians.

Sayyid Mohamed also began to build military

fortresses, the largest of which at Taleh had towers
60 feet high and walls 14 feet thick.   After World War
I was over in Europe, the British organized further
expeditions against the dervishes, and in 1920 employed
an air force unit to bomb the dervish strongholds.   The
British captured Taleh, but Sayyid Mohamed escaped
into Ethiopia where he died within the year.

Some historians say that Sayyid Mohamed established a true Muslim "state" to reclaim his land
from the Christian invaders--British, Italian, and Ethiopian.   The "state" had flexible boundaries, depending
upon the territory controlled by Sayyid Mohamed's
forces at any one time, and it had only military control, since Sayyid Mohamed established no civil administrative institutions.   Some strategists claim that the
building of fortresses, such as that at Taleh, led to
Sayyid Mohamed's defeat.   Unlike the earlier guerrilla
bases, the fortresses concentrated the dervish forces
and supplies and provided easy targets for attack.

The British called Sayyid Mohamed "the Mad
Mullah, " a somewhat derogatory name which, however,
described not only his political fervor but also his religious fanaticism (opposition to the narcotic khat, to
veneration of saints, to consorting with Christians,
etc.).   Sayyid Mohamed called himself "the Poor Man
of God, " a name often used in Somalia for religious
teachers who have no worldly goods and who live off
the good graces of the people among whom they teach
or perform religious services.   See AHMAD SHIRWA
BIN MUHAMMAD.

SCIENTIFIC SOCIALISM.   The Supreme Revolutionary Council declared Somalia a socialist state in 1969, with a
policy of "scientific socialism. "   The policy is regarded by the SRC as fully compatible with Islam and
adaptable to national needs, commending hard work and
public service.   Although a number of industries and
large firms have been nationalized under the policy,
private ownership of homes, farms, herds, and flocks
is encouraged.   The policy has been described as
Maoist-tinged.

SELF-HELP PROJECTS.   Many self-help projects were organized after independence, and some were successful.
The Somali Police and the American Peace Corps were
active in initiating some of the projects.   Since 1970,
the Supreme Revolutionary Council has organized and

promoted such projects as cleaning the towns and villages, constructing roads and sidewalks, digging and
maintaining wells and irrigation canals, building in-
firmaries and schools, and stabilizing sand dunes.

SHABELLE.   A Negroid group living along the Shebelle River.

SHAMBA.   Farm or garden plot.

SHANGANI.   An old quarter of Mogadishu.   Tomb inscriptions in Arabic show that the Shangani quarter was inhabited at least from the 13th century.   The location
of tombs shows that the quarter was much larger at
that time than in the late 19th century.   See HAMAR-
WEYN.

SHARIA.   The Islamic rules governing social, political,
economic, domestic, and other affairs, laid down in
the Koran.   See QADI.

SHEBELLE RIVER   see   WEBI SHEBELLE

SHEEGAT.   A Somali word meaning "client."   The majority
of client (arifa) arrangements were in the Bai, Bakool,
Gado, and Lower Juba Regions.   Several important
Saab political leaders in the Somali Youth League were
members of clans that were clients.   Clients were
considered only slightly "inferior" to the hosts, or
abbaan.

SHEEP.   Somali sheep are white, black-headed, and fat-
tailed, of the Persian variety.   The sheep are short-
haired and unshorn.   Sheep supply meat, milk, and
ghee (butter).   They are usually herded by women and
girls.   The skin of the sheep is a major export item
in the Northern Region, and many sheep are exported
on hoof.

SHEIKH.   1) An inland town in the Tug Dheer Region, about
40 miles southeast of Berbera; Sheikh is the educational center of the Northern Region.
        2) A religious title sometimes used for a
wadad or religious teacher.   The sheikh is not usually
a political figure among the nomads.   Among the agriculturalists, sheikhs are often involved in political life;
their mystical powers were traditionally important in
clan warfare.

SHEIKH 'ABD ALLAH IBN YUSIF AL-QALANQULI. The
chief propagator of the Qadiriya order among the Mijerteyn. He wrote a number of pamphlets (1919-1920)
on Sufism, one of which is a violent attack on the
Salihiya order.

SHEIKH ABDARAHMAN AL-ZEILAWI (d. 1883). Leader of
a Qadiriya settlement in the Ogaden region which was
sacked by the Ethiopians in the 1880s. It is said that
he could raise men from the dead or halt a smallpox
epidemic by the wave of a hand. It is believed that
the Qadiriya was introduced into Somalia by Sheikh
Abdarahman, although this is not certain. Besides the
settlement in the Ogaden, the Qadiriya had another important center at Brava and one at Hargeisa.

SHEIKH ABDARANMAN IBN ABD ALLAH ASH-SHASHI see
SHEIKH SUFI

SHEIKH ABDULLAHI YUSUF. A student of Sheikh Awes Muhammad Barawi (d. 1909) who spread the mystical teachings of the Qadiriya tariqa in the northeast.

SHEIKH ALI MAYE DUROGBA (d. 1917). He introduced the
Ahmadiya order into Somalia and is today venerated as
a saint. His tomb at Merca is the site of an annual
festival. He was an opponent of Sayyid Mohamed Abdullah Hassan and the dervishes and is remembered as
a performer of miracles.

SHEIKH AWES MUHAMMAD BARAWI (1847-1909). Born at
Brava, Sheikh Awes was a freedman whose family was
associated with the Tunni confederation. Between about
1870 and 1880, he studied in Baghdad, and made several pilgrimages to Mecca and Medina. Upon his return
to Brava, he was recognized as head of the local
Qadiriya groups and was largely responsible for the
spread of the Qadiriya order in the interior. He wrote
religious poetry in Arabic and translated hymns from
Arabic into Somali. He was opposed to Sayyid Mohamed
Abdullah Hassan, and some of his poems express his
dislike of the dervish movement. He was assassinated
by the dervishes, and his tomb at Biolay, about 150
miles north of Brava, is a pilgrimage site. He is also
called Sheikh Awes (or Ueiz) Ahmed. It is said that
when Sheikh Awes' village was burned by the dervishes, his body remained intact, with neither his

hair nor his clothing being scorched.   See also AWES
CADRIA.

SHEIKH BASHIR.   A religious leader who in 1945 organized
an armed attack on British installations in the Northern
Region.   It is believed that Sheikh Bashir was related
to Sayyid Mohamed Abdullah Hassan and that, possibly,
he was attempting to carry on the Sayyid's movement.

SHEIKH IBRAHIM HASSAN JEBRO.   Born in Dafet, in the
Bai Region, he established the first Somali jamaha in
Bardera in 1819.   See BARDERA.

SHEIKH ISAAQ IBN AHMED.   According to tradition, Sheikh
Isaaq migrated from Arabia to Somalia in the 12th or
13th century.   He settled at Mait, a coastal town in
the Sanaag Region, where his tomb is located.   Sheikh
Isaaq is probably the founder of the Isaaq clan family.

SHEIKH JABARTI IBN ISMAIL.   According to one tradition,
Sheikh Jabarti is the founder of the Darod clan family.
It is believed that he arrived in Somalia from Arabia
in the 10th or 11th century.   His tomb at Erigavo, in
the Sanaag Region, is the site of an annual pilgrimage.

SHEIKH MADDAR (1825-1917).   Leader of an important
Qadiriya settlement at Hargeisa.   His tomb at Hargeisa
is the site of an annual ziara, or pilgrimage.

SHEIKH MUHAMMAD GULED (d. 1918).   Introduced the
Salihiya order into Somalia and fostered the formation
of collective farms along the banks of the rivers.

SHEIKH MUMIN ABDULLAHI.   Regarded by the Rahanweyn
agriculturalists as a protector of the crops against
birds and other pests.   His tomb at Bur Acaba (Bai
Region) is the scene of an annual celebration.   Active,
probably in the early 18th century, Sheikh Mumin was
a missionary and the ancestor of the Rer Sheikh Mumin
in Mogadishu, which provided the ruling family to the
Baidoa Helai, a Rahanweyn group which forced the Galla out of Bur Acaba (q.v.) in the 17th century.

SHEIKH SUFI (d. 1913).   The popular name of Sheikh Abdaranman ibn Abd Allah Ash-Shashi.   Sheikh Sufi
founded a Qadiriya congregation at Mogadishu, where
his tomb-mosque is located.   He was an astrologer who

stressed mysticism in religion. The sheikh's popular
name is derived from the mystical nature of his religion and the fact that he led a pious life. Sheikh Sufi
wrote a number of books on religious subjects and performed many miracles. It is said that he extracted
water from wells for his daily ablutions without using
a rope or bucket.

SHEIKH YUSUF KAWNEYN. It is believed that Sheikh Yusuf,
also known as Au Barkhadle, came to the Northern Region from Arabia as a teacher of Islam in the 13th
century. He devised a Somali nomenclature for Arabic
letters which enabled his students to learn to read and
write Arabic with great facility. The system is still
used even today. It is said that Sheikh Yusuf introduced
the black-headed sheep into Somalia. The Sheikh is
regarded as a saint, and his tomb, near Hargeisa, is
the scene of an annual pilgrimage.

SHERIF ABU BAKR BIN 'ABDALLAH AL-'EIDARUS (d. 1503).
It is believed by some authorities that he introduced the
Qadiriya order into Somalia. The order did not be-
come widespread, however, until the 19th century. See
QADIRIYA.

SHERIF EIDARUS SHERIF ALI EIDARUS (1892-1958). A
learned religious leader who wrote not only on religious
matters, but on Somali history. In 1931 he founded the
Islamic Assembly in Mogadishu, representing all the
Somali tariqas, and having as its chief function the celebration of the birth of the Prophet Mohamed.

SHIDLE. A Negroid group living along the Shebelle River.
Freed slaves joined the Shidle and other Negroid groups
who remained in Somalia after the Galla and Somali migrations. The Shidle were traditionally federated in
villages and aligned with the Mobilen clan of the Hawiye
clan family.

SHIR. Clan or lineage councils of groups formally associated by contract (heer) to carry on political and economic affairs. Their decisions were binding on all involved. Within a shir, all adult male members of the
clan group had a right to speak out on an issue. A
member's status in the assembly was affected to some
extent, however, by his age and the seniority of his
lineage.

SHIRREH JAMA AHMED. A writer and language expert.
Shirreh Jama Ahmed developed the script for the Somali language which was adopted for nation-wide use
in 1972. See LANGUAGE.

SILO. Underground storage pits (diyehiin) for grain hold up
to 20,000 pounds. The rectangular pits are lined with
corn stalks or other fibers; then the grain is put in
and covered with fiber mats and several feet of soil.
Grain can be stored in the silos for years, but there
is spoilage and damage by insects and rodents once the
pits have been opened. Small conical pits (gut) are
also used. Some modern grain storage facilities have
been constructed by the government, and this program
is expected to be expanded.

SIRAAD HAAD. A woman poet, a composer of buraambur
(q.v.).

SLAVERY. Before 1890 slave markets existed in the coastal
cities in both the Northern and Southern Regions, as
well as in some inland cities. The importation of
slaves from countries to the south in the 1830s and
1840s permitted the stock-raising groups in the southern
Somali areas to take up farming on a large scale in
the riverine areas, and attempts to abolish slavery by
the colonialists in the late 1800s were most stiffly resisted by these groups.
        The slave trade was prohibited by the Italian
administration in 1903, but domestic servitude was permitted for a number of years thereafter. Somewhat the
same situation existed in the British protectorate,
though slavery may have been far less common there
than in the south because of the scarcity of cultivable
land. As slaves were freed or as they escaped, they
usually joined the Bantu-speaking cultivators in the
riverine areas. Some set up their own villages. See,
e.g., NASSIB BUNDE; SONGOLLO AVIVA.

SOCIETÀ AGRICOLA ITALO-SOMALA (SAIS). A company developed on the Shebelle River in 1920 by the Duke of
the Abruzzi, to produce bananas, sugar, and cotton.
The plantation had about 75,000 acres of land, which
was bought from the local inhabitants, the Shidle; it
was located at Jowhar (also called Villagio duca degli
Abruzzi or Villabruzzi). After an outbreak of bubonic
plague, the company used forced labor, but in the mid-

1920s, a system of cooperative cultivation was worked out which was later used on other plantations. The chief product of SAIS was sugar, and the company produced almost enough sugar to satisfy the nation's needs. In 1963, the Somali government purchased one-half of SAIS and renamed it the National Company for Agriculture and Industry (SNAI). After the military coup of 1969, the Supreme Revolutionary Council nationalized the company.

SOCIETÀ NAZIONALE PER L'AGRICOLTURA E L'INDUSTRIA (SNAI) see NATIONAL COMPANY FOR AGRICULTURE AND INDUSTRY

SOMALI AIRLINES. A government-owned company which provides passenger and cargo service within Somalia. The company was initially (1964) a joint venture with Alitalia, with planes provided by the US. The airline has international routes to Rome, Aden, Dar es Salaam, and Nairobi; plans for a Mogadishu-London route, using a Boeing 720 B jet, were announced in 1974. The pilots and crew are Somali.

SOMALI COMMERCIAL BANK. This government-owned bank incorporated the nationalized branches of British and Italian banks in Somalia. It was established by the Supreme Revolutionary Council in 1970 and has branches in several cities around the country.

SOMALI CREDIT BANK. Established in 1954 in the trusteeship territory, the Somali Credit Bank was a special bank from which farmers could borrow at low interest rates and avoid the usurious rates charged by merchants who traditionally furnished credit for seed and other necessities. The bank also purchased surplus crops for storage and rented out farm machinery. See BANKING.

SOMALI DEMOCRATIC REPUBLIC. In October 1969, the Somali Republic became the Somali Democratic Republic. The government was taken over in a bloodless coup by a 24-man military junta, the Supreme Revolutionary Council, and this group effected the name change.

SOMALI DEMOCRATIC UNION see GREATER SOMALIA LEAGUE

SOMALI INDEPENDENT CONSTITUTIONAL PARTY   see
HIZBIA DASTUR MUSTAQUIL SOMALI (HDMS)

SOMALI INSTITUTE OF PUBLIC ADMINISTRATION (SIPA).
Founded in 1965 under a UN development program,
SIPA has as its chief aim the training of government
officials in public administration, financial management,
and planning.   SIPA aids in the organization of government departments and carries out research to solve
public administration problems.   The institute now
forms a part of the National University.

SOMALI LINE.   The British established the so-called Somali
Line, at the Tana River in northern Kenya, in 1910
and forbade Somali migration beyond it.

SOMALI NATIONAL ARMY.   An army of about 5,000 men
was created in the trust territory in 1960, a few months
before independence.   Upon independence and unification, this army and the 5,000 men of the Somaliland
Scouts in the former British protectorate joined to form
the Somali National Army.   It was led by Col. Daud
Abdullah Hersi, who had served with the British Gendarmerie during the British Military Administration
from 1942 to 1950.   Daud Abdullah Hersi died in 1965,
and was succeeded by Col. Mohamed Siad Barre, the
present chief of state.
        In 1969, the army had about 10,000 members,
including a small women's division, a 1,500-man air
force, and a navy of about 180 men.   In 1964, the
USSR provided the army about $30 million in arms, and
has provided training and other assistance.   Aid from
the USSR was accepted after an offer from the US and
other Western nations was rejected as inadequate.   The
army has grown in size since the military coup of 1969,
the number of USSR military advisers has reportedly
increased from several hundred to over 2,000, and in
1974, it was reported that Somalia had received a
squadron of MiG-21 fighter bombers from the USSR.
See SUPREME REVOLUTIONARY COUNCIL.

SOMALI NATIONAL BANK.   The country's central bank; it
issues currency and regulates the volume of money and
credit.   It is headed (1974) by Abdurhaman Nur Hersi,
an American-educated economist.   See BANKING.

SOMALI NATIONAL LEAGUE-UNITED SOMALI PARTY.   The

joint name assumed by the two political parties in the Northern Region after independence and unification in 1960. The parties were known as the Somaliland National League and the United Somali Party before they united; they split again in 1963.

SOMALI NATIONAL NEWS AGENCY (SONNA). This government agency gathers news and supplies it to radio and press. It does not transmit news to other countries, but supplies information to foreign correspondents in Somalia.

SOMALI NATIONAL UNIVERSITY. The university was established in 1970, placing under a single administration several already-existing institutes. A number of new faculties have since been added. The university offers instruction in law, economics, liberal arts, general science, medicine, veterinary science, agriculture, mathematics, geology, engineering, and teacher training. It was announced in 1974 that new university facilities to accommodate 2,000 students would be constructed with the assistance of the European Economic Community and would be operational by 1976. See EDUCATION.

SOMALI RED CRESCENT SOCIETY. An affiliate of the International Red Cross. It was founded in 1963.

SOMALI REPUBLIC. The nation's name from 1960 to October 1969, when the Supreme Revolutionary Council adopted the name Somali Democratic Republic. See SOMALIA; NORTHERN REGION; SOUTHERN REGION.

SOMALI YOUTH CLUB see SOMALI YOUTH LEAGUE

SOMALI YOUTH LEAGUE (SYL). This was the first modern Somali political group. It was formed in the Southern Region in 1943 as the Somali Youth Club, changing its name in 1947 to the Somali Youth League. By 1947, the SYL had about 25,000 followers, mostly from the Samaal clan families, with branches in all the Somali-inhabited areas. One of its chief aims was to unite all Somalis in one independent state. It played a large role in building up nationalistic fervor; encouraged education among the youth, in particular; favored the adoption of a written Somali language (initially urging the adoption of the Osmaniya script); favored the elimination

of tribalism; and at the time of the Four Power Commission, 1948, asked for a United Nations trusteeship
for the former Italian colony.

  The SYL was the leading political party in the
trusteeship territory--and in the Republic from 1960 to
1969.   The party was abolished, along with all other
political parties, by the Supreme Revolutionary Council
in October 1969.   But it is often mentioned by SRC
speakers as a revolutionary organization--at least in its
early years--and as a continuation of the "anti-imperi-
alist" jihad of Sayyid Mohamed Abdullah Hassan.

SOMALIA.   The name commonly used to refer to the Republic.   Prior to independence, Somalia referred to the
  Southern Region only.   Names probably used for the
  Somali area in ancient times include Land of Punt,
  Land of Spices, Aromata, and Market of Spices.   Ras
  Filuch, near Alula, at the tip of the Horn, was called
  the Cape of the Elephant and was described by early
  writers as the best source of frankincense and myrrh
  in the ancient world.

SOMALIA CONFERENCE.   In the pre-trusteeship period in
  the south, the Somalia Conference (or Conferenza) was
  a political group composed of anti-Somali Youth League
  parties, and organized to present petitions to the Four
  Power Commission (1948).   It was supported by politically active Italians then living in the area, and asked
  the Four Power Commission for a 30-year Italian
  trusteeship.   It is estimated that the Conference had
  about 20,000 members, though it claimed many more.

SOMALILAND NATIONAL LEAGUE (SNL).   A political party
  in the Northern Region.   Along with other groups, it
  supported the National United Front in the mid-1950s
  effort to regain the Haud.   The SNL (formed in 1951)
  grew out of the Somaliland National Society, which had
  existed intermittently since 1935.   After independence,
  the SNL merged with the United Somali Party to become the Somali National League-United Somali Party
  (SNL-USP), which, along with the Somali Youth League,
  formed the first government of the Republic.

  The SNL leader, prior to independence, was
Mohamed Haji Ibrahim Egal.   He became the Leader of
Government Business in the Legislative Assembly of independent Somaliland (the former British protectorate),
and was Prime Minister of the Somali Republic from

1967 to the time of the military coup in October 1969.

SOMALILAND SCOUTS. A paramilitary force of about 5,000 men maintained in the British protectorate from 1950 to 1960, at which time it became part of the Somali National Army.

SOMALILAND, STATE OF. The name of the independent state which was the former British protectorate. Somaliland became independent on June 26, 1960, and united with the trust territory when it became independent five days later, on July 1, 1960. The area is now known as the Northern Region of the Republic.

SOMALTEX. A textile factory established in Balad, on the Shebelle River, northwest of Mogadishu, in 1969. Built by West German and Somali principals, the factory is today largely owned by the government. It is expected to satisfy about 40 per cent of domestic cotton cloth needs.

SONGOLLO AVIVA. Head of a small republic at Avai, founded on the bank of the Shebelle River in the 1880s. The first head of the republic was named Macrani, and the second Dao. The republic was a federation of several agricultural villages established by runaway or freed serfs or slaves. Songollo Aviva's successors negotiated with the Italian Resident at Brava, and Avai was placed under Italian control in the mid-1890s. See also NASSIB BUNDE.

SONGS. The Somalis have specific songs for all their daily activities. There are songs for watering the camels the first time, and other songs for watering them the second time (camels must be watered twice); songs for loading the camels, and others for leading them; songs for watering the sheep, and others for watering goats, cows, and horses; songs for sowing, for harvesting, for crushing millet; songs for building boats, and others for repairing them; songs for building the nomadic hut; lullabies (kol-sha arrur-ta; literally, praise of the baby), etc., etc. See BALOLEY; BALWO; HEES; HEELLO; POETRY.

SORGHUM see MILLET

SOUTHERN REGION. The part of the Republic formerly

known as Italian Somaliland or the Trust Territory. It
makes up about three-fourths of the Republic in size
and population. The administrative regions of Bai,
Bakool, Bari, Gado, Galguduud, Hiran, Lower Juba,
Mudugh, Central Shebelle, Lower Shebelle, and most
of Nugal make up the Southern Region.

SUBORDINATE COURTS. These courts were established in
1945 to replace the akil courts in the British protectorate. Proceedings were recorded in English or Arabic.

SUFI. Those belonging to the Islamic mystical movement of
Sufism. The great majority of Somalis belong to one
of the Sufi orders. See AHMIDIYA; DANDARAWIYA;
QADIRIYA; RIFAIYAH; SALIHIYA.

SUGAR. Some sugar is imported, but most of the country's
needs are supplied domestically. See NATIONAL COM-
PANY FOR AGRICULTURE AND INDUSTRY.

SULTAN. In Somalia, the title (soldaan, in Somali) was
usually hereditary and largely honorific, the sultan often being no more powerful than any other clan elder.
It is not known when the Arabic title was introduced
into Somalia. In some clans, the title passed to the
eldest son and in others to the deceased sultan's
brother. Other chiefly titles were also used. See
CHIEFS.

SUNNI SHAFI'ITE. The Somali practice the Sunni Shafi'ite
rite of Islam.

SUPREME REVOLUTIONARY COUNCIL (SRC). A 20-man
military junta which has governed Somalia, with some
changes in size and membership, since October 1969.
The SRC is headed by a president, Maj. Gen. Mohamed
Siad Barre, the leader of the 1969 coup. It is aided by
a council of (mainly) civilian secretaries with ministerial functions. The SRC established a socialist state,
following a policy of "scientific socialism," and changed
the name of the Somali Republic to Somali Democratic
Republic. The stated aim of the SRC is to achieve social and economic equality for all the people.
        The SRC inaugurated a widespread "crash pro-
gram" involving self-help schemes and cooperatives to
fight poverty, disease, and ignorance. All government
employees and many segments of the general population

(schoolteachers, former chiefs, students returning from abroad) are required to attend three- to six-month workshops in which they are instructed in the aims of the revolution. See, e.g., NABADDON. One of the chief accomplishments of the SRC has been the installation of Somali as the official written language of the nation. See LANGUAGE.

By 1975, many of the former government leaders and others detained by the SRC in October 1969 had been released; some had been assigned to important government posts.

SUR. A well, ordinarily used to supply water for livestock.

- T -

TANA RIVER   see   SOMALI LINE

TARIQA. Literally, "the Way." A religious order or brotherhood within Sufism. Each tariqa has its own distinctive liturgy. The tariqas differ not only in this respect, but also in their degree of religious conservatism. Rivalry among the orders centers on this latter factor. Most Somalis are followers of one of the Sufi orders, even if they are not tariqa menbers. The members often live in agricultural settlements or religious communities, and the tariqa hierarchy substitutes for the kin group from which the members have separated themselves. Previous heads of the order, rather than ancestors, are the basis of members' genealogy. Followers who are not actually members regard the tariqa founder as a saint. See JAMAHA; ZAWIYA.

TAXES. During colonial times, the governments often announced taxes, but would be unable to collect them on a systematic basis. Taxes on business profits, on income, on houses, on shambas (gardens), on animals slaughtered, on private caravans, on market stalls, on ferries and automobiles, etc. were at one time or another attempted.

In the late 1960s, about seven per cent of central government revenue was provided by direct taxes on income. About 75 per cent came from indirect taxes on international transactions (import and export duties; purchase, exchange, and administrative taxes) and indirect taxes on domestic transactions (sugar and tobacco taxes, primarily). About six per cent was provided by a variety of other indirect taxes. The remainder came from nontax sources.

TERRITORIAL COUNCIL. Established in the trust territory in 1950, the council was a 35-member body, appointed by the Italian trusteeship administration to represent traditional interests as well as political parties. The trusteeship administration was required, under the UN agreement, to consult this body on all important matters. The council was competent in all areas except foreign policy and national defense. The Territorial Council provided the first opportunity for Somalis in the entire Southern Region to gather in a central organ of government to confront national issues. After territorial elections were held in 1956, the Territorial Council was replaced by the Legislative Assembly.

TESTUR. The canons of clan custom. See HEER.

THEATER. Although drama is inherent in such celebrations as the istunka festival, dabshid, and roobdoon, as well as in the shir, religious celebrations, the recitation of stories, and the chanting of poetry, staged representations are a recent innovation. The earliest performances were probably put on in the schools during the 1940s. A short-lived acting company formed in the British protectorate in 1954 staged a drama that was a call to arms at the time of the return of the Haud to Ethiopia. Other early dramas dealt with nationalism and civic pride. The Police were active in presenting such dramas. Today, groups of actors, mostly in Mogadishu, write and perform their own works. They often tour the country, putting on performances at various centers, where they draw audiences from all segments of the population. Plays dealing with personal problems and the theme of love are not very popular and are not encouraged by the Supreme Revolutionary Council.

Leopard among the Women, a play by Hassan Sheikh Mumin, was published in 1974 by Oxford University with Press. The play was translated into English by B. W. Andrzejewski, who also wrote an introduction outlining the history of Somali drama. See NATIONAL THEATER.

TOBACCO. During the 1960s, efforts to produce a good to-

bacco in Somalia were unfruitful. More recently, Chinese experiments in Somalia have developed a good-
quality tobacco which is now being produced on a small
scale. Some of the religious orders forbid the smok-
ing of tobacco, while others are more lenient.

TOURISM. Tourism is not an important factor in the Somali
economy, although efforts have been made to attract
visitors. The National Agency for Tourism stresses
big game hunting and deep sea fishing.

TRADE UNIONS. The incipient trade unions of the 1960s
were on the whole linked with the International Confederation of Free Trade Unions. The Supreme Revolutionary Council dissolved existing unions in 1969 and
took action to reorganize the workers along lines more
suitable for a socialist state.

TRADITIONALISM. The traditional society of the Somalis
was quite homogeneous as far as social and political
organization, language, religion, and culture were concerned. This homogeneity formed a solid base for the
development of the modern state. Tribalism, on the
other hand, the assertion of clan-family loyalty, is
seen as a deterrent to nationalism. See TRIBALISM.

TRANSHUMANT PASTORALISM. Transhumance implies a
more strict adherence to specific grazing areas than
the Somalis on the whole practice. See HERDING.

TRANS-JUBA. The area from the Juba River to the Kenya
border, known as the trans-Juba or Jubaland, was
ceded to Italy by Great Britain in 1925. It is now en-
compassed in the Lower Juba and Gado Regions of the
Republic. See ANGLO-ITALIAN AGREEMENT OF 1925.

TRIBALISM. The Somalis are regarded as one "tribe," divided into six clan families. Traditionally, the most
binding ties among Somalis were based on clan-family
relationships. Also the strongest source of animosity
and divisiveness was intergroup, inter-clan-family antagonism and feud. Clan loyalties are today diluted
somewhat by education, urbanization, and nationalism,
but they are still strong, and are regarded as antina-
tionalistic. The Supreme Revolutionary Council has
made an all-out effort to eradicate clan antagonisms,
or "tribalism": chiefs have been redesignated peace-

keepers (nabaddon); symbolic burials and burnings of
tribalism have been held; and circulars, speeches,
plays, religious sermons, and posters have been used
to condemn tribalism. These moves of the SRC go
far beyond the efforts made by earlier Somali governments. See also TRADITIONALISM.

TRUST TERRITORY see ITALIAN TRUSTEESHIP ADMIN-
    ISTRATION (AFIS)

TSETSE FLY. The tsetse is found in the riverine areas.
    The cultivators keep little if any livestock, and the
    pastoralists avoid those areas where the tsetse is found.

TUG. A dry watercourse which may become a swift stream
    after a heavy rain. Also called douh and nulla.

TUG WAJALE. A community in the Hargeisa Region on the
    northwestern border. A mechanized farm was installed
    at Tug Wajale in 1960, with USSR aid, to produce wheat
    and millet. The farm showed some progress, but did
    not flourish. Under the Supreme Revolutionary Council,
    since 1970 a crash program using volunteer workers
    has been carried out at the farm, and significant in-
    creases in production are reported.

TUMAL. A sab blacksmith group.

TUNNI. A confederation of clans, believed by some authori-
    ties to belong to the Digil clan family. They are a
    cattle-herding, mixed-farming group. In the Somali mi-
    grations, the Tunni established themselves in the region
    inland from Brava. They absorbed or pushed out the
    Galla and Negroid groups living in the area, and by the
    17th century probably made up the majority of the in-
    habitants of Brava (q.v.).

TUR. Wells six to 12 feet deep, usually dug in the sand in
    the river and interriver areas and along the coast.
    Some are collectively owned and some individually;
    their use is governed by the same rules that apply to
    the el.

TURKEY. The Ottoman Empire long laid claims to the Red
    Sea Coast. In 1866, Turkey transferred its African
    Red Sea ports to the Egyptian Khedive Isma'el, who
    claimed that the area also included the Somali Gulf of

Aden coast. See EGYPT.
     In the 16th century, Ahmad Guray received
support from the Turks in his war with Ethiopia. See
also AHMAD SHIRWA BIN MUHAMMAD.

- U -

UAR. A man-made pool or catchment area for the collec-
     tion of rain water, constructed largely by the Rahanweyn
     who live far from wells or rivers. It is used mainly
     for irrigation, but also for drinking water for people
     and animals. The uar is kept in condition by the vil-
     lagers; it is owned by the group or individual that built
     it; and strict rules govern its use. The uar is sur-
     rounded by a dike or cactus hedge; the clayey nature
     of the soil holds the water for a long time. A uar
     may contain sufficient water for ten to 20 families.
     Some of the existing uars were dug centuries ago.

UCCIALI. The treaty of Ucciali between Italy and Ethiopia
     was signed in 1889. Italy regarded it as establishing
     an Italian protectorate over Ethiopia, whereas Ethiopia
     merely regarded it as an agreement by which Italy
     would aid Ethiopia in dealing with other European coun-
     tries. In the year the treaty was concluded, Italy also
     began to establish claims to the Benadir coastal cities.
     The British accepted the Italian interpretation of the
     Treaty of Ucciali, and in their 1894 agreement with
     Italy outlined the spheres of influence of Britain and
     Italy in the Horn of Africa. The treaty is important
     in Somali history mainly because it was a forerunner
     of the 1897 treaties which form the basis of the present
     Somali-Ethiopia boundary dispute. See ANGLO-ETHI-
     OPIAN DIPLOMACY; BOUNDARIES; ITALO-ETHIOPIAN
     AGREEMENTS OF 1897 AND 1908.

UNITED NATIONS. Somalia is sometimes referred to as a
     "child" of the UN because the Southern Region was a
     UN trust territory from 1950 to 1960 and came to inde-
     pendence under UN auspices. See ITALIAN TRUSTEE-
     SHIP ADMINISTRATION.
          The Republic became a member of the UN in
     1960 soon after attaining independence, and has re-
     ceived substantial aid from the UN and its specialized
     agencies. A Somali delegate to the UN (Abdurahim
     Abby Farah) was for four years (1969-1973) chairman

of the Special Committee on Apartheid. In 1972, Somalia was elected to the UN Security Council, and
when the Security Council met in Addis Ababa, Ethiopia,
in 1972, the Somali delegate presided over the meeting.

UNITED NATIONS ADVISORY COUNCIL. Headquartered in
Mogadishu, the Advisory Council served as a liaison
between the Italian Trusteeship Administration (AFIS)
and the people of the trust territory from 1950 to 1960.
The council was composed of members of UN delegations
from the Philippines, Egypt, and Colombia. The council made recommendations and reports on Somali development, and was sometimes called the UN "watch-
dog" in Somalia.

UNITED NATIONS TRUSTEESHIP TERRITORY see ITALIAN
TRUSTEESHIP ADMINISTRATION (AFIS)

UNITED SOMALI PARTY (USP). Founded in the Northern
Region early in 1960, the USP played a large role in
pre-independence politics. After independence, it amalgamated with the Somaliland National League to become
the Somali National League-United Somali Party (SNL-
USP), which formed a coalition government in the Republic with the Somali Youth League. By 1963, the
SNL-USP split, and its members established or joined
with other parties.

UNITED STATES. The US contributed heavily to the trust
territory's Seven-Year Development Plans (1954-1960),
and continued its support to the Republic until late
1969. It is estimated that from 1954 to 1970, Somalia
received from the US over $49 million in grants and
over $19 million in loans, a total of $69.8 million.
The US aid program was largely disbanded in 1969-
1970 when Somali flag ships were found to be trading
with North Vietnam. The Peace Corps was ousted by
the Supreme Revolutionary Council in December 1969.
Offers of US and other Western aid for Somali Army
development in 1963 were turned down by the Somalis
as inadequate, and aid for this purpose was accepted
from the USSR. The Somali police, however, were
largely financed by the US from 1958 to 1969. The US
contributed significantly to the development of the ports
of Kismayu and Mogadishu, and to other projects in the
fields of education, water resources, agriculture, and
infrastructure. The US maintains an embassy in Mogadishu.

UNITED STATES AGENCY FOR INTERNATIONAL DEVELOP-
MENT (AID). Funds and other assistance for a variety
of projects--school construction, support of the Somali
Credit Bank, agricultural experimentation and training,
well digging, livestock development, police training,
etc.--were provided by this agency from the mid-1950s
to 1969.

UNIVERSITY INSTITUTE. Established in 1954 as the Higher
Institute of Law and Economics, the name of the institute was changed in 1960. It began to offer college-
level courses in 1968 and ultimately provided instruction in law, economics, social studies, Islamic studies,
and statistics. Its graduates were given two years'
credit toward a university degree at Italian universities.
It formed the nucleus of the Somali National University,
established in 1970.

URANIUM. In 1968, a United Nations survey team reported
uranium deposits in the Bai Region in the area of Alio
Gelleh, near Bur Acaba. The team reported iron ore
and bauxite deposits also. There has been no commercial exploitation of the deposits.

URBANIZATION. The trend is toward urbanization, but not
at a very fast rate, and the Supreme Revolutionary
Council has urged a return to the land, emphasizing
agricultural development and crash programs in rural
communities. The effects of urbanization were felt as
early as 1930, with overcrowding and unemployment in
the coastal towns of the Southern Region. Mogadishu
grew from about 30,000 population in 1930 to about
200,000 in 1974. No other Somali city has a population above 100,000.
    Much of the trend toward urbanization is a re-
sult of the growth of the sense of nationalism, although
natural population growth is also higher in the urban
areas because of better medical care and lower disease
rates. The tendency to migrate to the southern cities
increased during the trusteeship administration because
of the Somalization of all kinds of government services
previously performed by Italians (or British, during the
British Military Administration). In the north, too, the
establishment of government centers, as at Hargeisa,
encouraged urbanization.
    After independence, the policy of ethnic bal-
ance (q.v.) encouraged the influx into Mogadishu of

many individuals who hoped for political and financial
favors from their kinsmen in government service. This
practice was supposedly ended, or at least discouraged,
by the October 1969 Revolution, and it appears that the
growth rate of Mogadishu has declined since 1969.

USSR.   After World War II, Russia took part in the Council
of Foreign Ministers, which discussed the disposition
of Italian colonies, and in the Four Power Commission,
which visited Somalia in 1948 (along with France, Great
Britain, and the US).
          USSR financial and technical aid to Somalia from
1959 to 1968 amounted to $65.7 million in grants and
loans.   Aid from the USSR continues to be significant.
Projects include a cotton gin, a dairy, a meat-processing plant, a fish cannery, a flour mill and grain eleva-
tor, construction of a major seaport at Berbera, a hospital, and a secondary school.   The Somali Army has
received most of its equipment and technical assistance
from the USSR.

- V -

VETERINARY MEDICINE.   Modern veterinary practices were
introduced during the colonial period and are widely
used today, but traditional veterinary medicine is still
relied upon by many pastoralists.   A few examples of
such treatment: An infusion of myrrh in water mixed
with salt is given to an animal with stomach trouble.
Ground millet is boiled and given to weak animals.   Ap-
plications of tar prepared from certain woods protect
camels against scabies and itch.   A system of vaccinating animals against rinderpest consists of making
the healthy cow swallow a mixture of urine and dung
from an infested animal.

VILLAGIO DUCCA DEGLI ABRUZZI   see   JOWHAR; SOCIETÀ
AGRICOLA ITALO-SOMALA

- W -

WA-BONI.   A group of hunters and fishermen, the Wa-Boni
live in the southern coastal areas near the major towns
and in the Gado Region.   Some also practice agriculture.   Traditionally, the Wa-Boni supplied the Somalis

with giraffe, antelope, and rhino hides for making sandals and shields. They also supplied hides and elephant, hippo, and rhino ivory for export. The Wa-
Boni are a small group of unknown ethnic origin, probably descendants of pre-Cushitic inhabitants of Somalia.

WADAD. A religious devotee who may be a student of the
Koran or a notable or sheikh. Wadads preside at weddings, burials, group prayers, and other ceremonies.
They may serve as scribes or as traditional judges.
They belong to the Sufi orders, are tariqa members,
and consider the tariqa founders and saints their ancestors. Part of the traditional learning of the wadad
includes folk astronomy or astrology (q.v.).
     It is believed that, in the pre-Islamic period,
a group similar to the wadads performed marriage and
other rites, led rainmaking and sacrificial celebrations,
and served as religious leaders in clan politics and
war. As Islamic leaders, wadads on the whole oppose
tribalism and blood compensation. Many serve as
teachers, going from one village to another to teach
the Koran. See HER SCHOOLS; WARANLE.

WADADS' WRITING. A number of nonstandardized systems
of writing devised by various wadads, usually a mixture of Somali and Arabic. Such writing was traditionally widely used in business transactions, in letter
writing, and in preparing petitions to the colonial governments. No particular system gained widespread
use.

WA-GOSHA. Gosha means forest, and wa-gosha means
people of the forest. The Wa-Gosha are Negroid or
ethnically mixed groups living in a number of communities on the Juba River banks. It is said that the Wa-
Gosha, unique among the Somali, use animal masks in
their ritual ceremonies. Most are farmers.

WAL WAL. By November 1934, the Italian policy of advanc-
ing into the interior brought the Italian forces to Wal
Wal, a village and watering place in the Ogaden, where
they battled with Ethiopian forces. The League of Nations attempted to mediate the situation, but the Italian
Fascist government used the incident as an excuse to
invade Ethiopia and, in effect, to begin the Italo-
Ethiopian war. Ethiopia was defeated in 1936 and
claimed by Italy as part of her colonial empire. See
ITALO-ETHIOPIAN WAR; OMAR SAMANTAR.

WAR.   1) A Somali word meaning "news." In spite of an
inadequate system of mass communication, news is
rapidly communicated by word of mouth. Among the
nomads, who might appear to be isolated, news passes
quickly from gatherings at watering places.
     2) See INTERGROUP WARFARE.

WARABAY.   A sab blacksmith group.

WARANLE.   A spear carrier, a warrior, an adult male.
Among the nomads, the main distinction between men,
in general, is between the wadad, or religious man,
and the waranle, or secular man. Among the agriculturalists this distinction is not so pronounced, since
religious leaders may also be secular or political
leaders.

WA-RIBI.   A small hunting group of unknown ethnic origin
living between Bardera and Lugh; they are probably descendants of pre-Cushitic inhabitants of Somalia.

WEATHER LORE.   The expert in weather lore assists the
nomadic pastoralists by advising them on grazing and
livestock care, use of water, changes in the weather,
and other matters. He assists the agriculturalists by
advising them on future weather conditions. The
weather lore expert is said to be an astronomer, astrologer, meteorologist, geographer, and soothsayer.
He gives advice on the timing of marriage, travel,
etc.; interprets personality traits; and serves as a
calendar-keeper, calculating the dates of religious holi-
days and other seasonal events. See DABSHID; NURO.

WEAVING   see   BENADIR COTTON; FIBER PRODUCTS

WEBI SHEBELLE.   One of Somalia's two major rivers.
Webi (or Uebi) means "river," and shebelle, "leopard."
The Shebelle rises in the Ethiopian highlands and dries
up in the sandy coastal area of Gelib, a short distance
from the Juba River. Flood periods are from March
to May (the gu, or heavy rain season) and from October to December (dair, the light rain season). From
May to October, the Shebelle often becomes brackish.
It is not navigable, save by locally built rafts.

WELLS.   The large number of Somali words for "well" is
some indication of the preoccupation with water in this

semi-arid land.   Drinking water is almost always available only along the Juba and Shebelle Rivers.   In the coastal areas, as in the capital city of Mogadishu, wells often contain only salty or brackish water and drinking water must be brought into the cities from some distance.   Regulation of the use of wells is an important part of the traditional legal system.   The various kinds of wells and watering places are called ag, baali, berked, el, las, sur, tur, uar, etc.

WEST GERMANY.   The West German aid program for Somalia, which began in the 1960s, was discontinued in 1970 when the Supreme Revolutionary Council recognized East Germany.

WIIL WAAL.   A poet and national hero who is said to have led the Somalis against the Galla in the Ogaden area of Ethiopia.   A large number of folk tales have grown up around Wiil Waal, describing him as a shrewd but wise leader.   Wiil Waal (literally, crazy boy or mad youth) composed geeraar, poems which deal largely with war and battle.   His dates are uncertain, but it is believed that he was active during the early 1800s.

WOMEN.   A woman is considered a member of her father's dia-paying group, not her husband's.   Under traditional Somali law, a woman is under the protection of her father, her husband, and if her husband dies, his father or brother.   Traditionally, a widow, if she consented, might become the wife of her husband's eldest brother.   Under Islamic law, in the payment and receipt of blood compensation, a woman's injury or death is valued at half that of a man's (50 camels rather than 100).   New laws have been proclaimed in Somalia to ensure that women are not treated as inferior to men.
        Women in Somalia do not wear veils unless they are religious devotees or the wives of religious men.   It is said that in the past women accompanied their husbands on the battlefield, performing intelligence work, caring for the wounded, and encouraging the fighters.   Women are also poets, their traditional poetic form being the buraambur (q. v.).
        Women in the Southern Region first voted in the municipal elections of 1958; in the Northern Region, they first voted in the national referendum on the constitution in June 1961.   Women's committees were established in all the political parties.   Under the Supreme

Revolutionary Council, women are urged to take an active part in self-help and crash programs, in athletics, in the theater, and in government. Both the army and the police have women's units. In the urban centers, most of the employed women work as domestics, clerks, telephone operators, teachers, and nurses. It should be mentioned that men also work in all these occupations. See DIVORCE; MARRIAGE.

WOODEN OBJECTS. Spoons, combs, boxes, plates, vases and larger receptacles for milk, water jugs, inkstands, stools, headrests, and camel bells are the chief objects made of wood. Many are decorated with carved geometric designs.

- Y -

YASIN HAJI OSMAN SHERMARKE. One of the founders of the Somali Youth League, established in Mogadishu in 1943. He was the son of Osman Yusuf Kenadid, the inventor of the Osmaniya script. He founded the Society for the Somali Language and Literature, and in the 1940s taught Osmaniya in Mogadishu.

YIBIR. Called Yahhar in the south. The Yibir are a sab group of medicine men. They make amulets for the newborn among the Somali, and bless the Somali weddings. Traditionally, the first Yibir who arrives after the birth of a male child is given a gift of cloth, a sheep, or a goat. In exchange, the Yibir leaves an amulet. The Yibir are nominally Muslim; they are few in number.

YOUNG PIONEERS. A wing of the army; its primary purpose is to aid in local self-help schemes. The Young Pioneers was organized by the Supreme Revolutionary Council.

YUSUF ALI "KENADID" (c. 1845-1911). Founder of the sultanate of Obbia, about 300 miles north of Mogadishu on the Indian Ocean (Mudugh Region). Until 1878, Yusuf Ali, who was a member of the chiefly family of the Mijerteyn, was a follower of Bogor Osman Mahmoud, sultan of the Mijerteyn. After several years of dispute, he broke with Bogor Osman Mahmoud, moved to Obbia, and founded his own sultanate. The Obbia sultanate,

like that of the Mijerteyn, signed a treaty of protection
with Italy in 1889, receiving an annual payment of
1,800 thalers; until 1908, when both protectorates were
placed under the administration of the governor of the
Benadir colony, they were overseen by the Italian consul at Aden. Yusuf Ali was succeeded as sultan of
Obbia by his son, Ali Yusuf.

Yusuf Ali was given the name "Kenadid" at the
time of his rebellion against the Mijerteyn sultan. The
name indicates that, like the camel, he refused to accept the saddle (or bridle). During the years 1904-
1908, when Sayyid Mohamed Abdullah Hassan occupied
the Nugal Valley, between Obbia and the Mijerteyn sultanate, Yusuf Ali was on the whole hostile to the dervishes. He was, however, in 1903 arrested by the
British and accused of cooperating with the dervish
forces.

Yusuf Ali established an effective civil administration over the Obbia sultanate. He divided the territory into four zones, with himself in charge of the
one centered on Obbia and with each of the others under an administrator known as a naib. He also had a
military chief, his cousin, Osman Shermarke. A major part of the commerce--trade in hides and skins,
which were exchanged on the coast for cotton and other
goods--was controlled by the sultan and his sons.

YUSUF MOHAMED IBRAHIM (SHEIKH) (c. 1800-1848). Probably the most renowned of the sultans of Geledi, a
group which dominated the hinterlands of Mogadishu and
Brava through most of the 19th century. Sheikh Yusuf
Mohamed Ibrahim is remembered as a great religious
and political leader. His most famous military expedition occurred in 1843, when he led an army of (some
say) 40,000 warriors against the religious reformers
of Bardera. In 1848, Sheikh Yusuf died in a battle
with the Bimal, the traditional enemies of the Geledi.

- Z -

ZANZIBAR. In 1840, Zanzibar became the permanent capi-
tal of the Omani sultanate, and all the Somali Indian
Ocean ports, including Mogadishu, Brava, and Kismayu,
came under nominal Zanzibari control. The Sultan of
Zanzibar acted as middleman in the trade between the
Somali area and Arabia, India, Europe, and America.

The Zanzibar Sultan Said Khalid bin Bargash was recognized internationally as the governor of the coast,
and it was with him that Italy and Great Britain dealt
in establishing their Benadir and Jubaland colonies in
the late 1880s.   The last representative of the sultan
in Mogadishu left in 1905 when the Italian government
purchased the Benadir coast from Warsheikh to Brava.

ZARIBA.   A thornbush enclosure which the men of the nomadic groups, the gurgi and the geelher, construct to
hold their animals at night and to protect them from
human or animal maurauders.

ZAWIYA.   Similar to jamaha (q. v.).   The zawiya is mainly
a tariqa congregation or settlement; the jamaha is mainly a tariqa agricultural community.

ZEILA.   An ancient city on the Gulf of Aden coast in the
Hargeisa Region.   Zeila was known in the classical
world long before Arabian colonization.   It is believed
that both Christians and Muslims lived there in the 9th
century.   In the 9th or 10th century, Zeila was ruled
by Somalized Arabs (or Arabized Somalis) and was inhabited by a mixture of Somalis, Afars, and Gallas.
It was the center of the Adal (Ifat) sultanate and was
an important trade center between Ethiopia and the
Arab countries in the 14th, 15th, and 16th centuries.
It began to decline after the 16th century and became
a part of the Ottoman Empire in the 17th.   Zeila,
along with the rest of the northern Somali coast, was
occupied by Egypt in the 1870s.   Egypt abandoned the
area in 1884, and British occupation began.   See
HAJI SHERMARKE ALI SALIH; HAQ AD-DIN; SA'D AD-
DIN; AHMAD GURAY.

ZENGI.   The Book of the Zengi, a medieval Arabic compila-
tion, refers to the Zengi (Black) inhabitants of the
Somali riverine areas.   The Zengi were probably the
pre-Somali Bantu-speaking inhabitants of the area,
along with the Wa-Boni and Wa-Ribi.   In The Book of
the Zengi, the Somali and the Galla of the more
northern areas are called Berberi.   Except for some
remaining enclaves in the river areas, the Zengi were
displaced or assimilated by the southern migrations
(q.v.) of the Galla and Somali.

ZIARA.   A celebration in memory of a clan ancestor or

saint. _Ziaras_ are usually held annually at the tomb of the person honored. The meetings are often quite large, sometimes attracting as many as 8,000 to 10,000 persons. They are attended by government officials as well as clan members, and prayers are said for the unity and independence of the nation.

BIBLIOGRAPHY

The most complete bibliography on the Somali areas is Bibliografia Somala, published by the Camera di Commercio, Industria ed Agricoltura della Somalia (Mogadishu) in 1958. It lists over 2,000 books, pamphlets, maps, and articles in all languages from the first decades of the 1800s through 1957.

Official Publications of Somaliland, 1941-1959, A Guide, published by the Library of Congress in 1960, is an excellent annotated source. Somalian Panorama: A Select Bibliographical Survey, 1960-1966, published by the African Bibliographic Center, Inc., Washington, D.C., is a 17-page listing covering the first six years of Somali independence. N. M. Viney's Bibliography of British Somaliland, compiled in 1947 and put out by the War Office, includes items related to the British protectorate. All the items in that publication are included in Bibliografia Somala. John William Johnson's A Bibliography of Somali Language Materials, printed in Hargeisa in 1967, and "A Bibliography of the Somali Language and Literature," African Language Review, no. 8, 1969, are quite comprehensive, listing a number of publications by Somalis in Arabic, not only on the language and literature but also on Somali genealogies and Somali saints.

Peoples of the Horn of Africa: Somali, Afar and Saho by I. M. Lewis contains an extensive bibliography of books and articles, especially those relating to anthropology and exploration. Somalia by Alphonso A. Castagno, published in 1959, contains bibliographical footnotes listing United Nations and Italian documents relating to political developments during the trusteeship period. Mark Karp's The Economics of Trusteeship in Somalia contains bibliographical footnotes referring to economic developments both before and during the trusteeship period.

165

The two chief sources of anthropological and historical information are I. M. Lewis's books and articles, most of which deal with the Northern Region of the Republic, and Enrico Cerulli's writings, most of which concern the Southern Region. Cerulli's Somalia: Scritti vari editi ed inediti, in three volumes, contains most of his articles and his translation (in Italian) of The Book of the Zengi. It also contains bibliographical footnotes.

The memoirs and official reports of the various governors of Italian Somaliland and of the British protectorate contain anthropological and cultural material as well as records of economic and social developments in the two areas.

Michele Pirone's historical studies and Nello Puccioni's and Luigi Robecchi-Brichetti's anthropological works are also of first importance. They deal largely with the Southern Region. Charles Guillain's Documents sur l'histoire, la géographie et le commerce de l'Afrique Orientale (1856) is an invaluable early source. And Ugo Ferrandi's Lugh: Seconda spedizione Bottego has been described as a classic study of one Somali subgroup, the Gasar Gudda.

"An Archaeological Reconnaissance of the Southern Somali Coast" by Neville Chittick (1969) is valuable because it points up the need for archaeological research, which would add to our knowledge of Somali history.

The Social and Diplomatic Memories of Sir James Rennel Rodd (1923) contains an account of Anglo-Ethiopian maneuvers in arriving at the controversial Ethiopian-Northern Region boundary agreement of 1897.

As to modern political developments, the articles of Alphonso A. Castagno and I. M. Lewis are the most extensive sources in English. Saadia Touval's Somali Nationalism (1963) is also of great interest. On the legal system, the chief works in English are those by Martin Ganzglass, Paolo Contini, and N. A. Noor Muhammad, and in Italian by G. A. Costanzo. Contini was chairman of the integration commission which worked on the problems arising from the union of the Northern and Southern Regions of the Republic; N. A. Noor Muhammad is an Indian jurist who served on the integration commission. Costanza was chairman of the technical committee which prepared a preliminary draft of the Somali Constitution of 1960. The Reports of the Italian Government to the UN General Assembly, the Reports of the

Visiting Missions, and other UN publications--such as the
United Nations Bulletin and United Nations Review--are all
excellent sources on events in the South from 1950 to 1960.

In economics, Mark Karp's book, noted above, deals
with the Southern Region only. Other aspects of modern
economic development are discussed in publications of the
UN and the specialized agencies, in Somali government publications and documents, and in various African and Afri-
canist periodicals.

B. W. Andrzejewski's studies of the Somali language
and literature are the most useful in English, and M. M.
Moreno's and Mario Maino's in Italian. Examples of modern
Somali music are presented by Folkways Record FD 5443:
The Freedom Songs of the Somali Republic. The record con-
tains songs by Abdillahi Karshe (Abdullah Kershi) and Ahmed
Sherif; it was copyrighted in 1962.

By far the best available English-language source for
current information is the Africa Research Bulletin, published
monthly by Africa Research Limited, London.

Few Somalis have contributed to the available scholarly English-language literature on their country. Musa H. I.
Galaal's writings on traditional culture and literature are
outstanding. They are not readily available, however; most
are published only in mimeographed form. Perspectives on
Somalia: Orientation Course for Foreign Experts Working in
Somalia, put out (in mimeographed form) by the Somali Institute of Public Administration in 1967, is a collection of articles by Somali experts in various fields. It is an excellent
source of information on historical and current topics. Mohamed Jama's History of the Somal, also mimeographed, is
sketchy and somewhat eclectic. A 1961 issue of Présence
Africaine (vol. 10, no. 38) devoted largely to articles by
Somalis is interesting, but not altogether reliable.

A Somali Historical Research Committee was established in August 1972 under the chairmanship of a member
of the Supreme Revolutionary Council. Its long-term goal is
to prepare a full and complete history of the Somali people.
Publications of this committee are in Somali and are not
easily accessible.

In the bibliography, items by Somalis are generally alphabetized under the author's first name. For example, Musa H. I. Galaal's works are under the letter M.

BOOKS

Abruzzi, Duca degli. Alle sorgenti dell'Uabi Uebi Scebele. Milan: Mondadori, 1932.

Adam, F. Handbook of Somaliland. London, 1900.

Albospeyre M. La Côte Française des Somalis: Problêmes économiques et politiques. Paris: Center des Hautes Etudes de l'Afrique et de l'Asie Modernes. Memoire No. 2873. Dec. 9, 1957.

Andrzejewski, B. W., and I. M. Lewis. Somali Poetry. London: Clarendon Press, 1964.

Angeloni, Renato. Diritto costituzionale somalo. Milan: Giuffrê, 1964.

_____. Codice penale somalo. Commentato ed annotato in base ai lavori preparatori. Milan: Giuffrê, 1967.

_____ and Mario S. Rugiu. Principi di diritto amministrativo somalo. Milan: Giuffrê, 1965.

Ansaldi, G. Il Giuba. Mogadishu: Stamp. della Colonia, 1932.

Archer, Geoffrey. Personal and Historical Memoirs of an East African Administrator. Edinburgh, 1963.

_____ and E. M. Godman. The Birds of British Somaliland and the Gulf of Aden. 2 vols. London: Gurney and Jackson, 1937.

Arkadyev, V. G. Nezavisimoye Somali (Independent Somalia). Moscow: Nauka, 1964.

Bacquart, H. Etude sur le Protectorat de la Côte Somalie. Paris, 1907.

Barile, Pietro. La colonizzazione fascista nella Somalia meridionale. Rome: Arti Grafiche, 1935.

Basset, René (trans. and ed.). Shihab ad-Din, Futuh al-habasha. Paris, 1897-1909.

_____ (trans. and ed.). Arab-Faquih, Histoire de la

Conquête de l'Abyssinie (XVe siècle). Paris, 1897.

Battersby, H. F. P. The Last Resort: A Story of Somaliland. London, 1914.

Battista, Piero. La Somalia. Rome: Signorelli, 1969.

Becker, G. H. The Disposition of the Italian Colonies:
1941-1951. Geneva: Annemasse, 1952.

Bell, C. R. V. The Somali Language. London: Longmans,
1953.

Bennett, Norman R., and George E. Brooks, Jr. (eds.).
New England Merchants in Africa: A History through
Documents: 1802 to 1865. Boston: Boston Univer-
sity Press, 1965.

Bentwich, N. Ethiopia, Eritrea and Somaliland. London:
Gollancz, 1946.

Bernasconi, J. La guerra e la politica dell'Italia nell'Africa
orientale. Milan, 1935.

Bertola, Arnoldo. Storia e politica coloniale dei territori
non autonomi. Turin, Giappichelli.

Bertucchi, C. Geografia ed esploratori italiani. Milan:
DeAgostini, 1929.

Bollati, Ambrogio. L'esplorazione del Giuba. Rome:
Loescher, 1900.

_____. Somalia italiana. Rome: Unione Editrice
d'Italia, 1938.

_____ and Ugo Ferrandi. La seconda spedizione Bottego
nella Somalia australe. Rome: Società Geografica
Italiana, 1896.

Buchholzer, John. The Horn of Africa. London, 1959.

Bulotta, A. La Somalia sotto due bandiere. Milan: Gar-
zanti, 1949.

Burton, Richard F. First Footsteps in East Africa, or An
Exploration of Harrar. London: Longmans, 1856.

Cahill, Kevin M. Health on the Horn of Africa: A Study of the Major Diseases of Somalia. London: Spottiswoode, 1969.

Cani, R. Il Jubaland. Naples: Trani, 1924.

Caniglia, Giuseppe. Genti di Somalia. Bologna: Zanichelli, 1922.

_____. I Somali dell'impero. 3 vols. Rome: Cremonese, 1940-1942.

Carletti, Tommaso. Attraverso il Benadir. Viterbo: Agnesotti, 1910.

_____. Relazione sulla Somalia italiana per l'anno 1907-1908. Rome: Tip. della Camera dei Deputati, 1910. (Official)

_____. I problemi del Benadir. Viterbo: Agnesotti, 1912.

Caroselli, Francesco S. Ferro e Fuoco in Somalia: Venti anni di lotta contro il Mullah e i dervisci. Rome: Arti Grafiche, 1931.

_____. Catalogo del Museo della Garesa a Mogadiscio. Mogadishu: Stamp. della Colonia, 1934.

_____. Relazione del governatore per l'anno 1939-1940. Mogadishu: Stamp. della Colonia, 1941. (Official)

_____. Scritti coloniale. Bologna: Zanichelli, 1941.

Cassanelli, Lee V. The Benaadir Past: Essays in Southern Somali History. Doctoral thesis, U. of Wisconsin, 1973.

Castagno, Alphonso A. The Development of the Expansionist Concepts in Italy: 1861-1896. Doctoral thesis, Columbia U., 1956.

_____. Somalia. New York: International Conciliation, No. 522, 1959.

Cecci, Antonio. Da Zeila alle frontiere del Caffra. 3 vols. Rome: Loescher, 1885-1887.

Cerrina-Ferroni, G. Benadir. Rome: Tip. Min. Affari
    Esteri, 1911. (Official)

Cerulli, Enrico. Somalia: Scritti vari editi ed inediti. 3
    vols. Rome: Istituto Poligrafico dello Stato, 1957,
    1959, 1964.

Cesari, Cesare. La Somalia italiana. Rome: Palombi,
    1935.

Chiesi, G., and E. Travelli. Le questioni del Benadir:
    Atti e relazione dei commissari della Società. Milan:
    Tip. Bellini, 1904. (Official)

Chiovenda, E. La flora somala. 2 vols. Rome: Arti
    Grafiche, 1929, 1932.

Ciamarra, G. Relazione sulla Somalia italiana. Rome:
    Camera dei Deputati, 1911. (Official)

_____. La giustizia nella Somalia. Naples: F. Giannini,
    1914.

Ciasca, Raffaele. Storia coloniale dell'Italia contemporanea.
    Milan: Hoepli, 1938.

Cimmaruta, Roberto. Ual-Ual. Milan: Mondadori, 1936.

Cipriani, L. Abitazioni indigene dell'Africa Orientale Itali-
    ana. Naples: Triennale d'Oltremare, 1940.

Clark, J. Desmond. The Prehistoric Cultures of the Horn
    of Africa. Cambridge: Cambridge University Press,
    1954.

Collins, Douglas. A Tear for Somalia. London: Adven-
    turers Club, 1961.

Colosimo, G. Relazione al Parlamento sulla situazione po-
    litica, economica ed amministrativa delle colonie ital-
    iane. Rome: Tip. del Senato, 1918. (Official)

Colucci, Massimo. Principi di diritto consuetudinario della
    Somalia italiana meridionale. Florence: La Voce,
    1914.

Contini, Paolo. The Somali Republic: An Experiment in

Legal Integration. London: Cass, 1969.

Corni, Guido. Relazione sulla Somalia italiana per l'esercizio 1928/1929. Mogadishu: Stamp. della Colonia, 1929. (Official)

_____. Relazione sulla Somalia italiana per l'esercizio 1929/1930. Mogadishu: Stamp. della Colonia, 1931. (Official)

_____ (ed.). Somalia italiana. 2 vols. Milan: Arte e Storia, 1937.

Costanzo, Giuseppe A. Problemi costituzionali della Somalia nella preparazione all'indipendenza (1957-1960). Milan: Giuffrè, 1962.

Coupland, R. East Africa and Its Invaders. London: Oxford University Press, 1938.

Cucinotta, E. Una pagina inedita della nostra storia coloniale. Rome, 1927.

D'Agostino di C. Orsini, P. Le colonie italiane. Rome, 1933.

D'Antonio, M. La costituzione somala: Precedenti storici e documenti costituzionali. Rome: Presidenza del Consiglio dei Ministri, 1962.

Defrémery, C., and B. R. Sanguinetti (trans. and eds.). Les voyages d'Ibn Batouta. 4 vols. Paris, 1862 et seq.

de la Rue, E. Aubert. Le Somalie Française. Paris, 1939.

de Marco, R. R. The Italianization of African Natives: Government Native Education in the Colonies, 1890-1937. New York: Teachers College, 1943.

DeMartino, Giacomo. Relazione sulla Somalia italiana per l'anno 1910. Rome: Tip. della Camera dei Deputati, 1911. (Official)

_____. La Somalia nei tre anni del mio governo. Rome: Tip. della Camera dei Deputati, 1912. (Official)

DeMattos, Norman. Ethiopia, Eritrea and Somaliland. London: Gollancz, 1915.

De Monfried, H. Les guerriers de l'Ogaden. Paris, 1936.

Deschamps, M., R. Decary, and A. Ménard. Côte des Somalis, Réunion-Inde. Paris: Berger-Levrault, 1948.

De Vecchi di Val Cismon, Cesare Maria. Relazione sul progetto di bilancio della Somalia italiana per l'esercizio finanziario, 1925/1926. Mogadishu: Bettini, 1924. (Official)

_____. Relazione sul progetto di bilancio della Somalia italiana per l'esercizio finanziario, 1926/1927. Mogadishu: Bettini, 1925. (Official)

_____. Relazione sul progetto di bilancio della Somalia italiana per l'esercizio finanziario, 1927/1928. Mogadishu: Stamp. della Colonia, 1926. (Official)

_____. Orizzonti d'Impero: Cinque anni in Somalia. Milan: Mondadori, 1935.

Doresse, Jean. Histoire sommaire de la Corne orientale del'Afrique. Paris: Libraire Orientale Paul Geunther, 1971.

Douin, G. Histoire du Règne du Khédive Ismail. Cairo, 1941. Vol. 3.

Dracopoli, I. N. Through Jubaland to the Lorian Swamp. London: Seeley, 1914.

Drake-Brockman, Ralph E. British Somaliland. London: Hurst and Blackett, 1912.

Drysdale, John. The Somali Dispute. New York: Praeger, 1964.

Duchenet, E. Histoires somalies. Paris, 1966.

Duyvenadak, J. J. L. Voyages de Tcheng Ho al la Côte Orientale d'Afrique. Paris, 1939.

Eby, Omar. Sense and Incense. Scottdale, Pa.: Herald Press, 1965.

_____ . A Whisper in a Dry Land. Scottdale, Pa.: Herald Press, 1968.

Eliot, Sir Charles. The East Africa Protectorate. New York: Barnes & Noble, 1966. (First published in Great Britain in 1905).

Essa Mahamud Y. Low-cost Housing in Somalia: A Study of Traditional Housing in Somalia and a Proposal for a New Housing Concept. Copenhagen, 1972. 55 pp.

Farson, Negley. Last Chance in Africa. New York: Harcourt, Brace, 1950.

Ferrand, G. Les Çomalis: Matériaux d'études sur les pays musulmanes. Paris: Leroux, 1903.

Ferrandi, Ugo. Lugh: Emporio commerciale sul Giuba. Rome: Società Geografica Italiana, 1903.

Filesi, Teobaldo. Trasformazione e fine del colonialismo. Rome: Istituto Italiano per l'Africa, 1955.

_____ . I viaggi dei Cinesi in Africa nel Medioevo. Rome: Istituto Italiano per l'Africa, 1961.

_____ . Le relazioni della Cina con l'Africa nel Medioevo. Milan: Giuffrè, 1962.

Finazzo, Giuseppina. L'Italia nel Benadir: L'azione di Vicenzo Filonardi, 1884-1896. Rome: Ateneo, 1966.

Finkelstein, Lawrence S. Somaliland under Italian Administration: A Case Study in United Nations Trusteeship. New York: Woodrow Wilson Foundation, 1955.

Fisher, G. T. Pastures of British Somaliland. Aden, 1947.

Francis, J. C. Three Months Leave in Somali Land: Being the Diaries of the Late Captain J. C. Francis. London: Porter, 1895.

Frisk, H. (ed.). Le périple de la Mer Erythrée. Göteborg: D. Göteborgs Högskolas Årsskrift, 1927.

Funaioli, Ugo. Fauna e caccia in Somalia. Mogadishu: Tip. Missione, 1957.

Gallucci, S.   La Somalia italiana.   Milan: Pavoniano Argi-
     gianelli, 1936.

Ganzglass, Martin R.   The Penal Code of the Somali Demo-
     cratic Republic: With Cases, Commentary, and Ex-
     amples.   New Brunswick, N.J.:   Rutgers University
     Press, 1971.

Gasparro, A.   La Somalia italiana nell'antichità classica.
     Palermo: Tip.   Francesco Lugaro, 1910.

Gleichen, Count A. E. W.   With the Mission to Menelik,
     1897-98.   London, 1898.

Glover, P. E.   A Provisional Check-list of British and
     Italian Somaliland: Trees, Shrubs and Herbs.   Lon-
     don: Crown Agents for the Colonies, 1947.

Graziani, Rodolfo.   Il fronte sud.   Milan: Mondadori, 1938.

Graziosi, Paolo.   L'età della pietra in Somalia.   Florence:
     Sansoni, 1940.

Grottanelli, V. L.   Pescatori dell'Oceano Indiano.   Rome:
     Cremonese, 1956.

Guillain, Charles.   Documents sur l'histoire, la géographie,
     et le commerce de l'Afrique Orientale.   3 vols.
     Paris: Bertrand, 1856.

Hamilton, Angus.   Somaliland.   Westport, Conn.:   Negro
     Universities Press, 1970.   (First published in Great
     Britain in 1911.)

Hanley, Gerald.   The Consul at Sunset.   London: Pan
     Books, 1951.

Hassan Sheikh Mumin.   Leopard among the Women: Shabeel-
     naagood.   A Somali Play.   Translated by B. W.
     Andrzejewski.   London: Oxford University Press,
     1974.

Hertiel, J. M.   Un pays ignoré: La Côte Française des
     Somalis.   Paris, 1947.

Hertslet, Sir Edward.   The Map of Africa by Treaty.   3rd
     ed.   3 vols.   London: H. M. S. O., 1909.

Hess, Robert L. Italian Colonialism in Somalia. Chicago: Chicago U. Press, 1966.

Hollis, C. Italy in Africa. London, 1941.

Hoskyns, Catherine. Case Studies in African Diplomacy. 2. The Ethiopia-Somali-Kenya Dispute, 1960-67. Dar es Salaam: Institute of Public Administration, 1969.

Hunt, John A. Genealogies of the Tribes of British Somaliland and Mijertein. Hargeisa, 1944.

_____. A General Survey of the Somaliland Protectorate: 1944-1950. London: Crown Agents for the Colonies, 1951.

Husayn Ahmad Shalabi. Agasis min al-Sumal (Stories from Somalia). Cairo, 1962.

James, F. L. The Unknown Horn of Africa: An Exploration from Berbera to the Leopard River. London: G. Phillip, 1888.

Jardine, Douglas. The Mad Mullah of Somaliland. New York: Negro Universities Press, 1969. (First published in Great Britain in 1923.)

Jaubert, P. A. (trans.). Al-Idrisi, Géographie. Paris, 1836-1840.

Jennings, J. W., and C. Addison. With the Abyssinians in Somaliland. London, 1905.

Jourdain, H., and C. Dupont. D'Obock à Djibouti. 3 vols. Paris: Corbier, 1933 et seq.

Kammerer, Albert. La Mer Rouge, l'Abyssinie et l'Arabie depuis l'antiquité. Cairo: Royal Geographical Society of Egypt, 1929-1935.

Kaplan, Irving, et al. American University Area Handbook for Somalia. Washington: Dept. of the Army, GPO, 1970.

Karp, Mark. The Economics of Trusteeship in Somalia. Boston: Boston University Press, 1960.

Kersten, O. Baron Claus von der Decken's Reisen in Ost-
     Afrika in Jahren 1859 bis 1865. 6 vols. Leipzig:
     Verlagshandluung, 1869 et seq.

Kirk, J. W. C. A Grammar of the Somali Language. Cam-
     bridge: Cambridge University Press, 1905.

Krapf, J. Lewis. Travels, Researches and Missionary La-
     bours during Eighteen Years Residence in Eastern
     Africa. London: Trübner, 1860.

LaCugna, Charles S. The UN in Somaliland. Thesis, Wash-
     ington University, 1960. Ann Arbor: University Mi-
     crofilms, 1963.

Laurence, Margaret. A Tree for Poverty: Somali Poetry
     and Prose. Nairobi: Eagle Press, 1954.

_____. New Wind in a Dry Land. New York: Knopf,
     1964.

Lee, Rev. S. Travels of Ibn Battuta. London, 1829.

Lefêvre, Renato. Politica somala. Bologna: Cappelli,
     1933.

Lewis, I. M. Peoples of the Horn of Africa: Somali, Afar,
     and Saho. London: International African Institute,
     1955. 2nd ed. 1969.

_____. A Pastoral Democracy: A Study of Pastoralism
     among the Northern Somali of the Horn of Africa.
     London: Oxford University Press, 1961.

_____. The Modern History of Somaliland: From Nation
     to State. New York: Praeger, 1965.

_____ (ed.). Islam in Tropical Africa. London: Oxford
     University Press, 1966.

Lippmann, A. Guerriers et Sorciers en Somalie. Paris:
     Hachette, 1953.

Macchioro, G. Relazione sulla Somalia italiana per l'anno
     1908-09. Rome: Tip. Camera dei Deputati, 1910.
     (Official)

Macfayden, William A.   The Geology of British Somaliland.
London: Crown Agents for the Colonies, 1933.

_____ .   Water Supply and Geology of Parts of British
Somaliland.   Hargeisa, 1952.

_____ et al.   The Mesozoic Paleontology of British Somaliland.   London, 1935.

McNeil, Malcolm.   In Pursuit of the Mad Mullah: Service
and Sport in the Somali Protectorate.   London: Pear-
son, 1902.

Mahhammed Farah Cabdullahi.   The Best Short Stories from
the Land of Punt.   Mogadishu, 1970.

Maino, C.   La Somalia e l'opera della Duca degli Abruzzi.
Rome, 1959.

Maino, Mario.   La lingua somala: Strumento d'insegnamento
professionale.   Alessandria, Italy: Ferrari, 1953.

_____ and Yasin 'Isman Kenadid.   Terminologia medica e
sue voci nella lingua somala.   Alessandria, Italy:
Ferrari, 1953.

Maitrano, Sani G.   Femmina Somala.   Naples: Dekten &
Rocholl, 1933.

Mantegazza, V.   Il Benadir.   Milan: Treves, 1908.

Manzoli, G.   Relazione sulla colonia del Benadir: Stato
attuale e lavori da compiersi.   Milan: Bellini, 1910.
(Official)

Mariam, Nesfin Wolde.   The Background of the Ethio-Somalia
Boundary Dispute.   Addis Ababa: Berhanena Selan,
1964.

Marlowe, David H.   The Galjaal Barsana of Central Somalia:
A Lineage Political System in a Changing World.
Doctoral thesis, Harvard University, 1963.

Maugini, A.   Flora ed economia agraria degli indigene delle
colonie italiane di diretto dominio.   Rome: Min.
dell'Africa Italiana, 1931.

179   Bibliography

Mellana, V.   Diritto processuale Islamico somalo.   Mogadishu: Tip. Missione, 1957.

_____.   Nozioni di diritto giudiziario somalo.   Mogadishu: Tip. Missione, 1957.

Meregazzi, Renzo.   L'amministrazione fiduciaria italiana della Somalia (AFIS).   Milan: Giuffrè, 1954.

Milesi, G.   Il diritto presso i Somali.   Mogadishu: Stamp. della Colonia, 1937.

Mocchi, L.   La Somalia italiana.   Naples, 1896.

Mohamed Jama (Habashi).   A History of the Somal.   3rd ed. rev.   Mogadishu, 1965.   (Mimeographed)

_____.   Economic Survey of Somalia.   Mogadishu, 1968. (Mimeographed)

Mohamud Ahmed Addan.   L'organizzazione giurisdizionale. Mogadishu, 1962.

Monile, Franco.   Somalia.   Bologna: Cappelli, 1932.

_____.   Africa orientale.   Bologna: Cappelli, 1933.

Moreno, Martino M.   Il somalo della Somalia: Grammatica e testi del Benadir, Darod e Dighil.   Rome: Istituto Poligrafico dello Stato, 1955.

Morgantini, A. M.   Contributo alla conoscenza demografica della Somalia sotto l'Amministrazione Fiduciaria Italiana.   Rome, 1954.

_____.   Quelques résultats préliminaires des relevés concernant les populations somalies, effectuées en 1953.   Rome, 1955.

Morison, David L. (trans.).   Teobaldo Filesi, China and Africa in the Middle Ages.   Portland, Ore., 1972.

Muhammad, N. A. Noor.   The Development of the Constitution of the Somali Republic.   Mogadishu: Ministry of Grace and Justice, 1969.

Muller, C. (ed.).   C. Ptolemaei, Geographie.   4 vols.

1883-1901.

Musa H. I. Galaal. Ḥikmad Soomalli. With an introduction
by B. W. Andrzejewski. Oxford: Oxford University
Press, 1965.

_____. The Terminology and Practice of Somali Weather
Lore, Astronomy, and Astrology. Mogadishu, 1968.
(Mimeographed)

_____. A Collection of Somali Literature Mainly from
Sayid Mohamed Abdille Hassan. Mogadishu, no date.
(Cyclostyled)

Napolitano, Gaetano. Italy in Africa: An Example of En-
lightened Colonization. Rome: Menaglia, 1950.

Nerazzini, C. La conquista musulmana dell'Ethiopia nel
XVIᵒ secolo. Rome, 1891.

Omar Au Nuh. Some General Notes on Somali Folklore.
Mogadishu, 1970. (Cyclostyled)

Onor, Romolo. La Somalia italiana: Esame critico dei
problemi di economia rurale e di politica economica
della colonia. Turin: Bocca, 1925.

Pankhurst, E. Sylvia. Ex-Italian Somaliland. London:
Watts, 1951.

Pantano, G. Nel Benadir: La citta di Merca e la regione
dei Bimal. Leghorn: Belforte, 1910.

_____. 23 anni di vita africana (Eritrea, Somalia, Libia).
Florence: Casa Editr. Mil. Ital., 1932.

Paulitschke, P. H. Ethnographie Nordost-Afrikas. Die
Materielle Kulture der Danakil, Galla und Somal. 2
vols. Berlin: Reimer, 1893, 1896.

_____ (trans.). Sahad ad-din Ahmad, Futuh el Habacha,
des conquêtes faites en Abyssinie au XVIᵉ siècle par
l'Imam Mohammed Ahmad dit Gragne. Paris: Emile
Bouillon, 1898.

Pease, A. E. Travel and Sport in Africa. 3 vols. London, 1902.

Peel, C. V. A. Somaliland. London: Robinson, 1900.

_____. Somalia: Being an Account of Two Expeditions in-
to the Far Interior. London, 1900.

Pellegrini, Lino. Nera marea: Il libro dell'Africa. Milan:
Martello, 1960.

Perham, Margery. Major Dane's Garden. New York:
Africana, 1971. (First published in Great Britain in
1926.)

Pesenti, G. Canti sacri e profani, danze e ritmi degli
Arabi, dei Somali e dei Suahili. Milan: L'Eroica,
1929.

Pestalozza, Luigi. The Somalian Revolution. Translated
from the Italian by Peter Glendening. Paris: Editions
Afrique, Asie, Amérique Latine, 1974.

Philip, Kjeld. Somalia. Copenhagen: Mellemfolkeligt Sam-
virke's Smaaskrifter, 1966.

Pia, Joseph, Paul D. Black, and M. I. Samater. Beginning
in Somali. Rev. ed. Syracuse, N. Y. , 1966.

Piazza, Giuseppe. La regione di Brava nel Benadir. Milan: Società Italiana Geografiche e Commerciale,
1908.

_____. Il Benadir. Rome: Bontempelli, 1913.

Piccioli, A. (ed.). La nuova Italia d'oltremare: L'opera del
fascismo nelle colonie italiane: Notizie, date, documenti. 2 vols. Milan: Mondadori, 1934.

Pirone, Michele. Echi di voci lontane: Immagini e figure
della storia somala. Mogadishu: Stamp. AFIS, 1956.

_____. Notes on the History of Somalia. Mogadishu,
1960.

_____. Appunti di storia dell'Africa. II. Somalia. Rome:
Edizione Ricerche, 1961.

Poinsot, J. P. Djibouti et la Côte Française des Somalis.
Paris: Hachette, 1964.

Potter, Pitman B.   The Wal Wal Arbitration.   Washington,
    D.C., 1938.

Provenzale, F.   L'allevamento del bestiame nella nostra
    Somalia.   Rome: Bertero, 1914.

Puccioni, Nello.   Antropologia ed etnografia delle genti della
    Somalia.   3 vols.   Bologna: Zanichelli, 1931-1936.

_____.   Le popolazioni indigene della Somalia italiana.
    Bologna: Cappelli, 1937.

Quadri, Rolando.   Diritto coloniale.   3rd ed.   Padua: Ce-
    dam, 1955.

Rava, M.   Parole ai coloniale.   Milan: Mondadori, 1935.

Rayne, H.   Sun, Sand and Somals: Leaves from the Note-
    Book of a District Commissioner in Somaliland.
    London, 1921.

Reece, Alys.   To My Wife: 50 Camels.   London: Flavall,
    1963.

Reinisch, Leo.   Die Somali Sprache.   3 vols.   Vienna:
    Alfred Holder, 1900, 1902, 1903.

Rennel of Rodd, Lord Francis James.   British Military Ad-
    ministration of Occupied Territories in Africa during
    the Years 1941-1947.   London: HMSO, 1948.

Révoil, G.   Voyage au Cap des Aromates (1877-1878).
    Paris: Dentu, 1880.

_____.   La Vallée du Darror: Voyage aux Pays des
    Çomalis.   Paris: Challamel Ainê, 1882.

_____.   Voyage chez les Bénadirs, les Çomalis et les
    Bayouns en 1882-83.   Paris: Hachette, 1888.

Riveri, C.   Relazione annuale sulla situazione generale della
    colonia, 1920-1921.   Mogadishu: Ufficio del Governo,
    1921.   (Official)

Rivlin, Benjamin.   The United Nations and the Italian Colo-
    nies.   New York: Carnegie Endowment for Inter-
    national Peace, 1950.

Robecchi-Brichetti, Luigi. Somalia e Benadir: Viaggio di
    esplorazione nell'Africa orientale. Milan: Aliprandi,
    1889.

_____. Prima traversata della peninsola dei Somali.
    Rome: Boll. Soc. Geografia Italiana, 1893.

_____. Lettere dal Benadir. Milan: Poligrafica, 1904.

Rodd, Sir James Rennel. Social and Diplomatic Memories,
    1894-1901. London: Edward Arnold, 1923.

Ruspoli, E. Nel paese della mirra. Rome: Tip. Coopera-
    tiva, 1892.

Santiapichi, Severino. Appunti di diritto penale della So-
    malia. Milan: Giuffrè, 1961.

_____. Il prezzo del sangue e l'omicidio nel diritto so-
    malo. Milan: Giuffrè, 1963.

Sapelli, A. Memorie d'Africa, 1883-1906. Bologna: Zani-
    chelli, 1935.

Schoff, Wilfred H. (trans.). The Periplus of the Erythraean
    Sea. New York: Longmans, 1912.

Serra Zanetti, R. Basi economiche della Somalia italiana.
    Bologna: La Rapida, 1923.

Shariif 'Aydarus ibn Shariif 'Ali. Bughyat al-amaal fii
    taariikh al-Soomaal. Mogadishu: Stamp. AFIS, 1955.

Shirreh Jama Ahmed. Gabayo, Maahmaah iyo Sheekooyin
    Yaryar. Mogadishu: National Printers, 1965.

Smith, A. Donaldson. Through Unknown African Countries:
    The First Expedition from Somaliland to Lake Lamu.
    London: Arnold, 1897.

Sorrentino, Giorgio. Ricordi del Benadir. Naples: Trani,
    1912.

Steer, George. The Abyssinian Campaigns: The Official
    Story of the Conquest of Italian East Africa. London,
    1942.

Stefanini, Giuseppe. In Somalia: Note e impressioni di viaggio. Florence: Le Monnier, 1922.

_____ . Prima risultati geologica della missione della
Reale Società Geografica in Somalia (1924). Rome,
1925.

_____ and Nello Puccioni. Notizie preliminari sui princi-
pali risultati della Missione R. Soc. Geog. Italiana in
Somalia (1924). Boll. Reale Soc. Geografica Italiana,
1926.

_____ et al. Palaeontologia della Somalia. Sienna, 1932.

Stigand, C. The Land of Zinj. London, 1913.

Strandes, J. The Portuguese in East Africa. Nairobi, 1961.

Suckert, E. Informazione e considerazione su alcune piante
coltivate nella Somalia italiana. Florence: Il Cena-
colo, 1934.

Swayne, F. A Woman's Pleasure Trip to Somaliland. Bris-
tol: J. Wright, 1907.

Swayne, H. G. C. Seventeen Trips through Somaliland: A
Record of Exploration and Big Game Shooting, 1885-
1893. London: Rowland Ward, 1895.

Thompson, Virginia, and Richard Adloff. Djibouti and the
Horn of Africa. Stanford, Calif.: Stanford University
Press, 1968.

Toussaint, A. History of the Indian Ocean. Chicago, 1966.

Touval, Saadia. Somali Nationalism: International Politics
and the Drive for Unity in the Horn of Africa. Cambridge, Mass.: Harvard University Press, 1963.

Travis, William. The Voice of the Turtle. London: Allen
and Unwin, 1967.

Trimingham, J. Spencer. The Christian Church and Missions
in Ethiopia (including Eritrea and the Somalilands).
London: World Dominion Press, 1950.

_____ . Islam in Ethiopia. London: Oxford University
Press, 1952.

_____ . The Influence of Islam upon Africa. New York: Praeger, 1968.

Vannutelli, L., and C. Citerni. La seconda spedizione Bottego: L'Omo: Viaggio nell'Africa orientale. Milan: Hoepli, 1899.

Vecchi, Bernardo V. Sotto il soffio del monsone (un anno nel'Oltregiuba). Milan: Alpes, 1927.

_____ . Vecchio Benadir. Milan: Alpes, 1930.

_____ . Somalia. Milan: Marangoni, 1935.

Villier, A. Monsoon Seas: The Story of the Indian Ocean. 1952.

Walsh, L. P. Under the Flag, and Somali Coast Stories. London, 1932.

Waterfield, Gordon. Morning Will Come. London, 1945.

_____ (ed.). First Footsteps in East Africa by Sir Richard Burton. London: Routledge & Kegan Paul, 1966.

Woronoff, Jon. Organizing African Unity. Metuchen, New Jersey: Scarecrow Press, 1970.

Zoli, E. Relazione generale dell'Alto Commissario per l'Oltre Giuba. Rome: Arti Grafiche, 1926. (Official)

_____ (ed.). Oltregiuba. Rome: Arti Grafiche, 1927.

_____ (ed.). Notizie sul territorio di riva destra del Giuba. Oltre-Giuba. Rome, 1927.

_____ (ed.). Africa Orientale. Bologna, 1935.

Zucca, Giuseppe. Il paese di madreperla: Sette mesi in Somalia. Milan: Alpes, 1936.

_____ . Somalia. Rome: Tosi, 1950.

ARTICLES, CHAPTERS, MASTERS' THESES

Abir, M.   "Caravan Trade and History in the Northern Parts of East Africa," Paideuma, vol. 14, 1968.

Afrah, Hussein Culmie.   "The Blue Berets of the Somali Republic," International Police Academy Review, vol. 1, no. 2, 1967.

Andrzejewski, B. W.   "Speech and Writing Dichotomy as the Pattern of Multilingualism in the Somali Republic." Conseil scientifique pour l'Afrique: Colloque sur le multilinguisme (Brazzaville), July 1962.

_____.   "Poetry in Somali Society," New Society, vol. 1, no. 25, Mar. 21, 1963.

_____.   "Reflections on the Nature and Social Function of Somali Proverbs," African Language Review, vol. 7, 1968.

_____.   "Recent Researches into the Somali Language and Literature," Somali News, June 27, 1969.

_____.   "The Role of Broadcasting in the Adaptation of the Somali Language to Modern Needs," in W. H. Whiteley (ed.), Language Use and Social Change. London, 1969.

_____.   "The Art of the Miniature in Somali Poetry," African Language Review, vol. 6, 1967.

_____.   "Drought as Reflected in Somali Literature," Savanna, vol. 2, December 1973.

_____.   "Somali Drama."   Introduction, in Hassan Sheikh Mumin, Leopard among the Women.   London: Oxford University Press, 1974.

_____.   and Musa H. I. Galaal.   "A Somali Poetic Combat," African Languages, vol. 2, part 1, 1963.

_____.   and _____.   "The Art of the Verbal Message in Somali Society," in J. Lukas (ed.), Neue Afrikanistische Studien.   Hamburg, 1966.

_____.   "The Roobdoon of Sheikh Aqib Abdullahi Jama: A

Somali Prayer for Rain, " African Language Studies, vol. 8, 1969.

Anene, J. C.   "The Omani Empire and Its Impact on East African Societies, " in J. C. Anene and G. N. Brown (eds.), Africa in the Nineteenth and Twentieth Centuries.   Ibadan: Ibadan University Press, 1966.

Apollonio, Sergio. "Somalia Heads toward Independence: Border Disputes, Egyptian Influence Are Thorny Problems, " Africa Special Report, vol. 3, no. 12, 1958.

Ayele, Negussay. "Rhetoric and Reality in the Making of Boundaries on the Horn of Africa in 1897, " Ethiopian Observer, vol. 8, no. 1, 1970.

_____. "The 1952-1959 Ethio-Italian Boundary Negotiations: An Exercise in Diplomatic Futility, " J. Ethiopian Studies (Addis Ababa), vol. 9, no. 2, 1970.

Baldini, A. "Somalia italiana, " Enciclopedia italiana, vol. 32, 1936.

Bayne, E. A. "Somalia on the Horn: A Counterpoint of Problems Confronting One of Africa's New Nations, " American Universities Field Staff Reports Service, March 1960.

_____. "Brinkmanship on the Horn: Somali Irredentism Remains a Perilous Factor in Eastern Africa, " American Universities Field Staff Reports Service, 1963.

_____. "From Clan to Nation, " American Universities Field Staff Reports Service, March 1963.

_____. "Somalia's Myths Are Tested, " American Universities Field Staff Reports Service, October 1969.

Beachey, R. W. "The Arms Trade in East Africa in the Late Nineteenth Century, " J. African History, vol. 3, no. 3, 1962.

_____. "The East African Ivory Trade in the Nineteenth Century, " J. African History, vol. 8, no. 2, 1967.

Beckingham, C. "Barawa, " Encyclopaedia of Islam, vol. 1, 1954.

Benardelli, Gualtiero. "Uno scavo compiuto nella zona archeologica di Hamar Gerjeb nel territorio de Meregh durante l'agosto 1932, " Somalia d'Oggi, vol. 2, no. 1, 1957.

Bernard, M. "Description de la circoncision dite 'Moha': Côte des Somalis," J. African Society, vol. 4, no. 1, 1934.

Bonanni, Camillo. "Literacy for Nomads in Somalia, " Overseas Education, vol. 33, July, 1961.

Box, Thadis W. "Nomadism and Land Use in Somalia, " Contribution No. 66, International Center for Arid and Semi-arid Land Studies. Lubbock, Tex., 1969.

Brotto, Enrico. "Le popolazioni della Somalia, " in L'Italia in Africa, Comitato per la Documentazione dell'Opera dell'Italia. Rome, 1955.

Brown, J. A. "Land Tenure in Somaliland, " Chartered Surveyor (London), October 1957.

Buonomo, Maurizio. "Banking in Somalia, " Banker's Magazine (London), May 1966.

Burkitt, M. C., and P. E. Glover. "Prehistoric Investigations in British Somaliland, " Proc. Prehistoric Society, London, 1946.

Bwana, Rhoda. "Nationalism or Land-grab? Somali Irredentism, " East Africa Journal (Nairobi), December 1964.

Caroselli, F. S. "Il Giuba e l'avvenire della Somalia, " Rivista Coloniale, vol. 16, 1921, p. 173.

_____. "Il Museo della Somalia, " Rivista delle Colonie Italiane, 1934.

Cassanelli, Lee V. "Patterns of Trade and Politics in the Somali Benadir, 1840-1885. " Master's thesis, University of Wisconsin, 1969.

Castagno, A. A. "Lo sviluppo politico in Somalia e nel Prottetorato di Somaliland, " Somalia d'Oggi, vol. 1, no. 3, 1957.

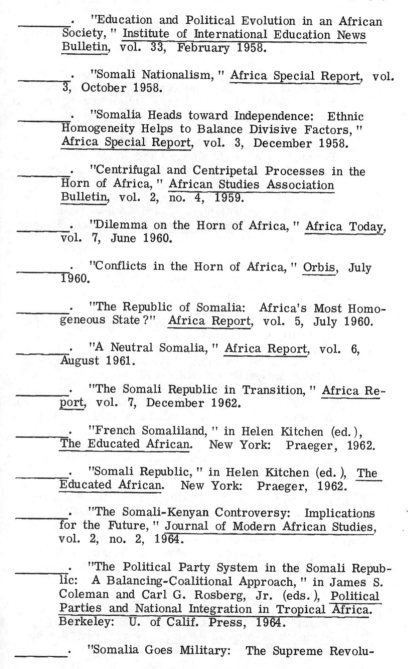

_____. "Education and Political Evolution in an African Society, " Institute of International Education News Bulletin, vol. 33, February 1958.

_____. "Somali Nationalism, " Africa Special Report, vol. 3, October 1958.

_____. "Somalia Heads toward Independence: Ethnic Homogeneity Helps to Balance Divisive Factors, " Africa Special Report, vol. 3, December 1958.

_____. "Centrifugal and Centripetal Processes in the Horn of Africa, " African Studies Association Bulletin, vol. 2, no. 4, 1959.

_____. "Dilemma on the Horn of Africa, " Africa Today, vol. 7, June 1960.

_____. "Conflicts in the Horn of Africa, " Orbis, July 1960.

_____. "The Republic of Somalia: Africa's Most Homogeneous State?" Africa Report, vol. 5, July 1960.

_____. "A Neutral Somalia, " Africa Report, vol. 6, August 1961.

_____. "The Somali Republic in Transition, " Africa Report, vol. 7, December 1962.

_____. "French Somaliland, " in Helen Kitchen (ed.), The Educated African. New York: Praeger, 1962.

_____. "Somali Republic, " in Helen Kitchen (ed.), The Educated African. New York: Praeger, 1962.

_____. "The Somali-Kenyan Controversy: Implications for the Future, " Journal of Modern African Studies, vol. 2, no. 2, 1964.

_____. "The Political Party System in the Somali Republic: A Balancing-Coalitional Approach, " in James S. Coleman and Carl G. Rosberg, Jr. (eds.), Political Parties and National Integration in Tropical Africa. Berkeley: U. of Calif. Press, 1964.

_____. "Somalia Goes Military: The Supreme Revolu-

tionary Council Follows a Pragmatic Course and Seeks
to End Corruption, " Africa Report, vol. 15, February
1970.

_____ . "Interview with General Mohamed Siad Barre,
President of the Supreme Revolutionary Council of the
Somali Democratic Republic, " Africa Report, vol. 16,
December 1971.

_____ . "The Horn of Africa and the Competition for
Power, " in Alvin J. Cottrell and R. M. Burrell (eds.),
The Indian Ocean: Its Political, Economic, and Mili-
tary Importance. New York: Praeger, 1972.

Central Asian Research Centre.   "Soviet Views on the Somali Republic, " Mizan Newsletter (London), December
1963.

Cerulli, Enrico.   "Canti e proverbi somali nel dialetto degli
Habar Auwal, " Rivista degli Studi Orientali, vol. 7,
1918, pp. 797-836.

_____ . "Nota sui dialetti somali, " Rivista degli Studi
Orientali, vol. 8, 1921, pp. 693-699.

_____ . "Tentative indigeno di formare un alfabeta somalo,
Oriente Moderno, vol. 12, 1932.

Chittick, Neville.   "An Archaeological Reconnaissance of the
Southern Somali Coast, " Azania, vol. 4, 1969, pp. 115-
130.

Clark, J. Desmond.   "Dancing Masks from Somaliland, "
Man, vol. 53, no. 72, 1953.

Clifford, H. M.   "British Somaliland-Ethiopian Boundary, "
Geographical J., vol. 97, 1936, pp. 289-307.

Colucci, M.   "La composizione per l'omicidio e l'origine
della pena nella consuetudini dei Somali meridionali,"
Rassegna Sociale dell'Africa Italiana, 1943, pp. 155-
170.

Contini, Jeanne.   "The Somalis: A Nation of Poets in
Search of an Alphabet, " in Helen Kitchen (ed.), A
Handbook of African Affairs.   New York: Praeger,
1964.

_____. "The Somali Republic: Politics with a Difference, "
Africa Report, December 1964.

Contini, Paolo.   "Integration of Legal Systems in the Somali
Republic, " International and Comparative Law Quarterly, vol. 16, 1967, p. 1088.

Costanzo, Giuseppe A.   "The Development of a Middle Class
in British Somaliland, French Somaliland, and in Somalia under Italian Trusteeship, " in Développement
d'une classe moyenne dans les pays tropicaux.   Brussels: Institut International des Civilisations Différentes,
1956.

_____. "Problêmes de la coexistence de groupements
ethniques différents dans le Territoire de la Somalia
sous tutelle italienne, " in Document de travail pour la
30° Session d'études de l'Institut International des
Civilisations Différentes.   Lisbon, Apr. 15-18, 1957.
Doc. 26.

Cotran, E.   "Legal Problems Arising out of the Formation
of the Somali Republic, " International and Comparative
Law Quarterly, vol. 12, 1963, p. 1021.

_____. "Somali Republic Supreme Court, " Journal of Af-
rican Law, vol. 8, no. 2, 1964.

Cruttenden, C. F.   "Report on the Mijjertheyn Tribe of So-
malis Inhabiting the District Forming the North East
Part of Africa, " Transactions, Bombay Geographical
Society, vol. 7, 1946, pp. 111-126.

Cucinotta, E.   "Delitto, Pena e giustizia presso i Somali del
Benadir, " Rivista Coloniale, vol. 16, 1921, pp. 15-41.

_____. "La proprietâ ed il sistema contrattuale nel
'destur' somâlo, " Rivista Coloniale, vol. 16, 1921,
pp. 243-264.

_____. "La costituzione sociale somâla, " Rivista Colo-
niale, vol. 16, 1921, pp. 389-405, 442-456, 493-502.

Cummings, B. C.   "British Stewardship of the Italian Colonies: An Account Rendered, " International Affairs
(London), vol. 29, January 1953.

Curle, A. T.   "The Ruined Towns of Somaliland, " Antiquity,
   vol. 11, 1937, pp. 315-327.

_____ .   "Carved Stones: British Somaliland, " Antiquity,
   vol. 11, 1937, pp. 352-354.

Dawson, George G.   "Education in Somalia. "   Comparative
   Education Review, vol. 8, no. 2, 1964.

des Avanchers, Leon.   "Esquisse géographique des pays
   Oromo ou Galla, des pays Soomali, et de la Côte
   orientale d'Afrique, " Bulletin Société de Géographie,
   4th ser., vol. 17, 1859.

De Villard, U. M.   "Note sulla influenza asiatiche nell'Africa
   orientale, " Rivista degli Studi Orientali, vol. 17, 1938,
   pp. 303-349.

_____ .   "I minaretti di Mogadiscio, " Rassegna di Studi
   Etiopici (Rome), vol. 21, 1943, pp. 127-130.

Diria, Ahmad.   "Note brève sur les tribus somalies, "
   Cahiers d'Etudes Africaines, vol. 2, 1962, p. 171.

Doob, L. W., and I. M. Hurreh.   "Somali Proverbs and
   Poems as Acculturation Indices, " Public Opinion
   Quarterly, vol. 23, Winter, 1970-1971.

Drysdale, J. G. S.   "Some Aspects of Somali Rural Society
   Today, " Somaliland Journal (Hargeisa), vol. 1, no. 2,
   1955.

_____ .   "Somali Frontier Problems, " World Today, January 1964.

_____ .   "The Problem of French Somaliland, " Africa Report, November 1966.

Duchenet, E.   "Le chant dans le folklore somali, " Revue de
   Folklore Français, vol. 9, no. 2, 1938.

Dundas, F. G.   "Expedition up the Juba River through Somaliland, East Africa, " Geographical Journal, vol. 1,
   1893.

Eblan, Joseph.   "Basic Data on the Economy of the Somali
   Republic, " Overseas Business Report (Washington),

February 1965.

Elliot, F. "Jubaland and Its Inhabitants, " Geographical Journal, vol. 41, 1913, p. 558.

Farer, Tom J. "Somali Democracy, " Africa Today, vol. 12, no. 5, 1965.

Filesi, Teobaldo. "Il sindicalismo in Somalia, " Africa (Rome), May-June, 1961.

_____ et al. "La Somalia al termina dell'amministrazione fiduciaria, " Africa (Rome), 1960.

Fleming, H. C. "Baiso and Rendille: Somali Outliers, " Rassegna di Studi Etiopici (Rome), vol. 20, 1964, pp. 35-96.

Francolini, B. "Arte indigena somala, " Rivista delle Colonie (L'Oltremare), vol. 11, 1933, pp. 891-894.

_____ . "Migiurtina, " Rivista delle Colonie (L'Oltremare), January 1936.

_____ . "I Somali del Harar, " Gli Annali dell'Africa Italiana (Rome), December 1938.

Freeman-Grenville, G. S. P. "East African Coin Finds and Their Historical Significance." J. African History, vol. 1, 1960, pp. 31-43.

_____ . "Note on Coins from Mogadishu c. 1300 to c. 1700, " University of Ghana Institute of African Studies Research Review, vol. 1, no. 1, 1965.

Ganzglass, Martin R. "A Common Lawyer Looks at an Uncommon Legal Experience, " American Bar Assoc. J., vol. 53, 1967, p. 815.

Gavin, Robert. "Economic and Social Conditions in Somaliland under Italian Trusteeship, " International Labour Review, vol. 46, September 1952.

Gilliland, H. B. "The Vegetation of Eastern British Somaliland, " J. Ecology, vol. 40, February 1952.

Goldsmith, K. L. G., and I. M. Lewis. "A Preliminary

Investigation of the Blood Groups of the 'Sab' Bonds-
men of Northern Somaliland, " Man, vol. 58, 1958,
pp. 188-190.

Gorini, M. P. "L'Oltregiuba: Com'ê e come potrà essere, "
Agricoltura Coloniale, vol. 20, 1926, pp. 238-259.

Graziosi, Ascanio. "L'economia somala nell'attuale processo
di sviluppo, " Il Risparmio, vol. 14, March 1967.

_____. "La banca centrale della Somalia, " Il Risparmio,
vol. 15, November 1967.

Grottanelli, Vinigi L. "Asiatic Influences on Somali Culture, "
Ethnos, vol. 4, 1947, pp. 153-181.

_____. "I Bantu del Giuba nelle tradizione dei Wazegua, "
Geografica Helvetica, vol. 7, no. 3, 1953.

_____. "Somali Wood Engraving, " African Arts, vol. 1,
no. 3, 1968.

_____. "The Peopling of the Horn of Africa, " Africa
(Rome), vol. 27, September 1972.

Gurr, Ted. "Tensions in the Horn of Africa, " in Feliks
Gross (ed.), World Politics and Tension Areas. New
York: New York University Press, 1966.

Haji Farah. "Somali Proverbs. " Ethiopian Observer, vol.
1, December 1956.

Hall, Sir Douglas. "Somaliland's Last Year as a Protectorate, " African Affairs (London), January 1961.

Hamelin, R. W. "Motoring through the Somali Republic, "
Travel, February 1972.

Hemming, C. F. "Vegetation Arcs in Somaliland, " J. Ecology, vol. 53, March 1965.

Henderson, Laton M., and Marvin M. Melton. "Somalia's
Agriculture, Animal Husbandry, Suggest Processing,
Shipping Activities, " International Commerce, vol. 71,
Dec. 20, 1965.

Hess, Robert L. "The 'Mad Mullah' and Northern Somalia, "

J. African History, vol. 5, no. 3, 1964.

_____. "The Poor Man of God: Muhammad Abdullah Has-
san," in Norman R. Bennett (ed.), Leadership in
Eastern Africa: Six Political Biographies. Boston:
Boston University Press, 1968.

Howard, Charles P. "Unity of Somalia, " Freedomways
(N. Y.), Spring, 1964.

Irvine, Keith. "Storm Clouds Over the African Horn, "
Current History, vol. 58, March 1970.

Izmailow, V. "The Somali Republic, " New Times (Moscow),
July 1960.

Jaenen, C. J. "Whither Somalia?" Middle Eastern Affairs,
vol. 8, April 1957.

_____. "The Somali Problem, " African Affairs, vol. 58,
April 1957.

James, G. L. "A Journey through the Somali Country to
the Webbe Shebeyli, " Proc. Royal Geographical Society, vol. 7, 1885.

Johnson, John William. "Research in Somali Folklore, "
Research in African Literature, vol. 4, no. 1, 1973.

Jousseaume. "Sur l'infibulation ou mutilation des organes
génitaux de la femme chez les peuples des bords de
la Mer Rouge et au Golfe d'Aden, " Revue d'Anthro-
pologie, ser. 3, vol. 4, 1889.

_____. "Reflexions anthropologiques à propos des tumules
et silex taillés des Çomalis et des Danakils, " L'Anthro-
pologie, vol. 6, 1895.

Kapil, Ravi L. "Integrating Disparate Colonial Legacies:
The Somali Experience, " Race (London), July 1966.

King, L. N. "The Work of the Jubaland Boundary Commission, " Geographical Journal, vol. 72, 1928.

Kirk, J. W. C. "Yibir, Midgan and Tumal, " J. African
Society, vol. 4, no. 13, 1904.

Kirk, John. "Visit to the Coast of Somali-land." Proc. Royal Geographical Society, vol. 27, July 1873.

Kittermaster, H. B. "British Somaliland," J. African Society, vol. 28, 1928, pp. 329-337.

_____. "The Development of the Somali," J. African Society, vol. 31, 1932, pp. 234-244.

Konstant, A. "Across Somaliland on Foot," Blackwood's Magazine, 1934, pp. 130-136.

Lamy, R. "Le destin des Somalis," Cahiers de l'Afrique et l'Asie, Mer Rouge-Afrique Orientale (Paris), 1959, pp. 163-212.

Lathan Brown, D. J. "The Ethiopia-Somaliland Frontier Dispute," International and Comparative Law Quarterly, April 1956.

_____. "Recent Developments in the Ethiopia-Somaliland Dispute," International and Comparative Law Quarterly, January 1961.

Legum, Colin. "Somali Liberation Songs," J. Modern African Studies, vol. 1, no. 4, 1963.

_____. "Kenya's 'Little' Guerrilla War Heats Up," Africa Report, April 1967.

Lessona, A. "Politica indigena ed economica in Somalia," Agricoltura Coloniale, vol. 28, 1935, p. 231.

Leva, A. Enrico. "Ibn Batūta in Somalia," Africa (Rome), May-June 1961.

Lewis, Herbert S. "The Origins of the Galla and Somali," J. African History, vol. 7, no. 1, 1966.

Lewis, I. M. "The Somali Lineage System and the Total Genealogy," Hargeisa, 1957. (Cyclostyled)

_____. "La communità (Giamia) di Bardera sulla rive del Giuba," Somalia d'Oggi, vol. 1, no. 1, 1957.

_____. "Modern Political Movements in Somaliland," Africa, vol. 28, no. 3 and no. 4, 1958.

_____ . "The Godhardunneh Cave Decorations of North-Eastern Somaliland, " Man (London), vol. 58, no. 234, 1958.

_____ . "The Gadabursi Somali Script, " Bull. School of Oriental and African Studies, vol. 21, 1958, pp. 134-156.

_____ . "Clanship and Contract in Northern Somaliland, " Africa, vol. 29, no. 3, 1959.

_____ . "The Galla in Northern Somaliland, " Rassegna di Studi Etiopici (Rome), vol. 15, January-December 1959.

_____ . "Force and Fission in Northern Somali Lineage Structure, " American Anthropologist, December 1960.

_____ . "The New East African Republic of Somalia, " World Today (London), vol. 14, no. 7, 1960.

_____ . "Problems in the Development of Modern Leadership and Loyalties in the British Somaliland Protectorate and UN Trusteeship of Somalia, " Civilisations (Brussels), vol. 10, no. 1, 1960.

_____ . "The Somali Conquest of the Horn of Africa, " J. African History, vol. 1, no. 2, 1960.

_____ . "The So-called 'Galla Graves' of Northern Somaliland, " Man (London), June 1961.

_____ . "Lineage Continuity and Modern Commerce in Northern Somaliland, " in P. Bohannan and G. Dalton (eds.), Markets in Africa. Evanston, Ill.: Northwestern University Press, 1962.

_____ . "Marriage and the Family in Northern Somaliland," East African Studies (Kampala), no. 15, 1962.

_____ . "Historical Aspects of Genealogies in Northern Somali Social Structure, " J. Modern African History, vol. 3, no. 1, 1962.

_____ . "The Somali Republic since Independence, " World Today (London), vol. 19, no. 3, 1963.

_____. "The Problem of the Northern Frontier District of Kenya, " Race, vol. 5, no. 1, 1963.

_____. "Dualism in Somali Notions of Power, " J. Royal Anthropological Institute, vol. 93, part 1, 1963.

_____. "Recent Progress in Somali Studies, " J. Semitic Studies, vol. 9, no. 1, 1964.

_____. "The Northern Pastoral Somali of the Horn, " in J. L. Gibbs, Jr. (ed.), Peoples of Africa. New York: Holt, Rinehart & Winston, 1965.

_____. "Shaikhs and Warriors in Somaliland, " in International African Institute, African Systems of Thought. London: Oxford University Press, 1965.

_____. "Integration in the Somali Republic," in Arthur Hazlewood (ed.), African Integration and Disintegration: Case Studies in Economic and Political Union. New York: Oxford University Press, 1967.

_____. "After the Referendum. I. Prospects in the Horn," Africa Report, April 1967.

_____. "Literacy in a Nomadic Society: The Somali Case, " in Jack Goody (ed.), Literacy in Traditional Societies. London: Cambridge University Press, 1968.

_____. "Nationalism and Particularism in Somalia, " in P. H. Gulliver (ed.), Tradition and Transition in East Africa: Studies of the Tribal Element in the Modern Era. Berkeley: Univ. of Calif. Press, 1969.

_____. "From Nomadism to Cultivation: The Expansion of Political Solidarity in Southern Somalia, " in Mary Douglas and Phyllis M. Kaberry (eds.), Man in Africa. London: Tavistock, 1969.

_____. "Somalia's Leaders Go Forward with Confidence, " New Middle East, no. 51, December 1972.

_____. "Politics of the 1969 Somali Coup, " J. Modern African Studies, vol. 10, October 1972.

Lusini, G. "Le saline somale, "Affrica, vol. 3, 1948.

Macfayden, W. A. "Vegetation Patterns in the Semi-Desert Plain of British Somaliland, " Geographic Journal, vol. 116, 1950.

Mahamud, M. "La medicina empirica somala, " Meridiano Somalo (Mogadishu), vol. 1, no. 5, 1952.

Mahomoud Abdi Hirad. "Somali Marriage Custom in Outline," Somaliland Journal (Hargeisa), vol. 1, no. 2, 1955.

Maino, M. "L'alfabeto 'Osmania' in Somalia, " Rassegna di Studi Etiopici (Rome), vol. 10, 1951, pp. 108-121.

Marcus, Harold G. "After the Referendum. II. A 'Danzig Solution' ?" Africa Report, April 1967.

Mariam, Mesfin N. "The Background of the Ethio-Somalian Boundary Dispute, " J. Modern African Studies, vol. 2, 1964, pp. 189-219.

Mariano, Anthony. "Somali Betrothal and Marriage Customs," Somaliland Journal, vol. 1, no. 3, 1956.

Marin, G. "Somali Games, " J. Royal Anthropological Institute, vol. 61, 1931, pp. 499-512.

Marshall, Anthony D. "Somalia: A United Nations Experiment, " Focus, vol. 6, no. 8, 1956.

Martin, Bradford G. "Muslim Politics and Resistance to Colonial Rule: Shaykh Uways b. Muhammad al-Barawi and the Qadiriya Brotherhood in East Africa, " J. African History, vol. 10, no. 3, 1969.

Martin, C. J. "The Somali Republic, " British Survey, no. 203, February 1966.

Massari, Claudia. "Maschere da danza degli Uaboni, " Archivo per L'Antropologia e la Etnologia, vol. 80-81, 1950-1951, pp. 143-148.

Mathew, A. G. "Chinese Porcelain in East Africa and on the Coast of South Arabia, " Oriental Art, N.S. 2, 1956, pp. 50-55.

Mathew, G. "Recent Discoveries in East African Archaeology, " Antiquity, no. 108, 1953.

Matveyev, V. V. "Northern Boundaries of the Eastern Ban-
     tu (Zinj) in the Tenth Century, according to Arab
     Sources, " Twenty-fifth International Congress of
     Orientalists. Moscow: Oriental Literature Publish-
     ing House, 1960.

_____. "Records of Early Arab Authors on Bantu
     Peoples, " Seventh International Congress of Anthro-
     pological and Ethnological Sciences (Moscow), August
     1964.

Mehmed, Ozay. "Effectiveness of Foreign Aid: The Case
     of Somalia, " J. Modern African Studies, vol. 9, no.
     1, 1971.

Melamid, Alexander. "The Kenya-Somalia Boundary Dispute,"
     Geographical Review, vol. 54, no. 4, 1964.

_____. "The Background of the Kenya-Somali Boundary
     Conflict, " Scope (N. Y.), December 1964.

Miles, S. B. "On the Somali Country, " Proc. Royal Geo-
     graphic Society, vol. 16, 1872, pp. 147-157.

Mohamed Farah Abdillahi and B. W. Andrzejewski. "The
     Life of 'Ilmi Boundheri, a Somali Oral Poet Who is
     Said to Have Died of Love, " J. Folklore Institute
     (Indiana University, Bloomington, Ind.), vol. 4, no.
     2-3, June-December 1967.

Mohamed Farah Siad. "Le elezioni in Somalia, " Africa
     (Rome), no. 1-2, 1956, pp. 16-17.

_____. "Somali e Occidente, " Africa (Rome), no. 3,
     1956, p. 69.

Mohamed Scek Gabiou. "La lingua somala, " Corriere della
     Somalia, May 24, 1954.

Mohamed Warsama Ali. "The 'Scir' Institution: Its Basis

Mohammed Haji Ibrahim Egal. "Somalia: Nomadic Indi-
     vidualism and the Rule of Law, " African Affairs, vol.
     67, June 1968.

Mohammed Scek Osman. "Migrazioni e urbanesimo in So-
     malia, " Africa, 1952, p. 185.

and Its Functions, " Présence Africaine, vol. 10, no. 38, 1961.

Muhammad, N. A. Noor. "The Rule of Law in the Somali Republic, " J. International Commission of Jurists, vol. 5, no. 2, 1964.

_____. "Judicial Review of Administrative Action in the Somali Republic, " J. African Law, vol. 10, no. 1, 1966.

_____. "Civil Wrongs under Customary Law in the Northern Regions of the Somali Republic, " J. African Law, vol. 11, 1967.

Musa H. I. Galaal. "Arabic Script for Somali, " Islamic Quarterly, vol. 1, no. 2, 1954.

_____. "From the Somali Story Teller's Anthology, " National Review (Mogadishu), no. 5, 1965, pp. 35-36.

_____. "Somali Poetry, " Afrika, vol. 7, no. 2, 1966.

_____. "Preservation of African Culture." Notes for the Joint Annual Meeting of the African Studies Association and the Committee on African Studies, Montreal, October 1969. (Mimeographed)

Newman, E. W. Polson. "Italian East Africa, " Nineteenth Century, June-August 1937.

Odone, Augusto. "Somalia's Economy: Prospects and Problems, " Civilisations (Brussels), vol. 11, no. 4, 1961.

Panceri. "Le operazione che nel Africa orientale si praticano sugli organi genitali, " Archivo per l'Antropologia e la Etnologia, 1873, pp. 353ff.

Pankhurst, Richard. "The Trade of the Gulf of Aden Ports of Africa in the Nineteenth and Early Twentieth Centuries, " J. Ethiopian Studies (Addis Ababa), vol. 3, no. 1, 1965.

_____. "The Trade of Southern and Western Ethiopia and the Indian Ocean Ports in the Nineteenth and Early Twentieth Centuries, " J. Ethiopian Studies (Addis Ababa), vol. 3, no. 2, 1965.

_____. "Colonialism in the Gulf of Tajurah: An Histori-
cal Perspective, " Ethiopian Herald, June 7-8, 1966.

Panza, Bruno. "Canti Somali, " Somalia d'Oggi, December
1956; January-February 1957.

_____ and Yaasiin 'Ismaan Keenadiid. "Gabai di Inna Abdille Hassan, " Somalia d'Oggi, October 1956.

Parenti, D. R. "I Bagiuni, " Rassegna di Studi Etiopici
(Rome), vol. 5, 1946, pp. 156-190.

_____. "Gli Amarani, " Atti Rivista di Antropologia, vol.
35, 1947, pp. 209-246.

_____. "Antropologia della Somalia meridionale, "
Archìvio per l'Antropologia e la Etnologia, vol. 77-79,
1947-1949, pp. 89-113.

_____. "Gli Uaboni, " Rivista Biologia Coloniale, vol. 9,
1948, pp. 66-90. (Extract)

Parkinson, J. "Customs in Western British Somaliland, " J.
Royal African Society, vol. 35, 1936, pp. 241-245.

_____. "Notes on the N. F. P. , Kenya, " Geographical
Journal (London), vol. 94, 1939.

Pease, A. E. "Some Accounts of Somaliland with Notes on
Journeys through the Gadaburse and Western Ogaden
Countries, " Scottish Geographical Magazine, vol. 14,
1898, pp. 57-73.

Peaslee, Amos J. (ed.). "Constitution of the Somali Republic, " in Constitutions of Nations. I. Africa. 3rd ed.
rev. The Hague: Martinus Nijhoff, 1965.

Perricone-viola, A. "La liberazione degli schiavi nel vecchio Benadir, " Rivista delle Colonie, vol. 10, no. 8,
1936.

Pia, J. Joseph. "Language in Somalia, " Linguistic Reporter,
vol. 8, no. 3, June, 1966.

Pirone, M. "Leggende e tradizioni storiche dei Somali Ogaden, " Archìvio per l'Antropologia e la Etnologia, vol.
84, 1954, pp. 119-128. (Extract)

———. "Le popolazioni dell'Ogaden, " Archìvio per l'An-tropologia e la Etnologia, vol. 84, 1954, pp. 129-143. (Extract)

———. "What the Ogaden Somali Say about Their Past, " Somaliland Journal (Hargeisa), vol. 1, no. 2, December 1955.

———. "La maschere di Bur Eybi, " Somalia d'Oggi, vol. 1, no. 2, 1957.

———. "Evolution sociale des Somalis, " Civilisations (Brussels), vol. 7, no. 4, 1957.

———. "Somalie sous tutelle italienne: Développement de l'éducation, de l'instruction et de la culture de la population somalie, " Civilisations (Brussels), vol. 7, no. 1, 1957.

Prins, A. H. J. "The Somaliland Bantu, " Bull. , International Committee on Urgent Anthropological Research, no. 3, 1960, pp. 28-32.

Puccioni, Nello. "Studi sui materiali antropologici ed etno-grafici raccolti della missione Stefanini-Paoli nella Somalia italiana meridionale, " Archìvio per l'Antro-pologia e la Etnologia, vol. 49, 1919, pp. 158ff.

———. "Caratteristiche antropologiche ed etnografiche delle popolazioni della Somalia, " Boll. Reale Società Geografica Italiana, vol. 7, 1936, pp. 1-18.

———. "Osservazioni sui Uaboni, " L'Universo, vol. 6, 1936, pp. 1-8.

———. "Osservazioni sui Bagiuni, " Annali dell'Africa Italiana, vol. 55, 1937, pp. 1-4.

Rayne, H. "British Somaliland, " Asiatic Review, October 1935.

Rayne, H. A. "Somali Tribal Law, " J. African Society, vol. 20, no. 78, 1921.

———. "Somali marriage, " J. African Society, vol. 21, no. 81, 1921.

Reece, Sir Gerald. "The Horn of Africa, " International Affairs, vol. 30, no. 4, 1954.

_____. "The Somalilands, " British Survey (London), no. 98, May, 1957.

Révoil, G. "Voyage au pays des Medjourtines, " Bull. Société de Géographie, 1880, pp. 254-269.

Reyner, Anthony S. "Somalia: The Problems of Independence, " Middle East Journal, vol. 14, no. 3, 1960.

Rice, Edward. "Somalia Must Rely Heavily upon the Help of the United Nations, " Vista, vol. 6, March-April 1971.

Rivlin, Benjamin. "The Italian Colonies and the General Assembly, " International Organization, vol. 3, no. 3, 1949.

Rocchetti, Giuseppe. "Gli scambi commerciali della Somalia," Rivista di Agricoltura Subtropicale e Tropicale, vol. 49, October-December, 1955.

_____. "La bananicoltura della Somalia, " Rivista di Agricoltura Subtropicale e Tropicale, vol. 50, 1956, pp. 87-89.

_____. "Produzione agraria e commercio con l'estera in Somalia nel periodo 1950-1959, " Rivista di Agricoltura Subtropicale e Tropicale, vol. 54, April-September 1960.

Roncati, Remo. "Luci e ombre sull'istruzione agraria in Somalia, " Africa (Rome), June 1966, pp. 198-204.

Rossetti, Carlo. "Nassib Bunda: Sultano di Goscia, " L'Italia Coloniale, vol. 1, no. 10, 1900.

Roucek, Joseph S. "Somalia in Geopolitics, " New Africa (London), vol. 7, May 1965.

Russo, Enrico. "La residenza di Mahaddei-wen, " Rivista Coloniale, 1919, p. 14.

_____. "Il mullah ed i suoi seguaci nella Somalia italiana, " Rivista Coloniale, vol. 17, no. 1, 1920.

Salad Abdi Mohamud. "Linea di politica agraria somala, " Rivista di Agricoltura Subtropicale e Tropicale, vol. 54, April-September 1960.

Salkeld, R. E. "Notes on the Boni Hunters of Jubaland, " Man (London), vol. 94, no. 5, 1905.

Samater. "Proverbs as a Cultural Vehicle, " Dalka (Mogadishu), vol. 2, no. 2, 1967.

Sanger, Clyde. "Somalia's Criteria of Friendship: Assessed on Merit, Not Aid, " Guardian (London), Jan. 13, 1965.

Sayre, F. B. "United States Views on Staggering Problems in Somaliland. " U.S. Dept. of State Bull., vol. 25, 1951, pp. 32-34.

Scalapino, Robert A. "Sino-Soviet Competition in Africa, " Foreign Affairs (N.Y.), July 1964.

Schmid, Peter. "Somalia's Instant Army, " Reporter (N. Y.), Sept. 24, 1964.

School and Society. "Somalia's New Educational System, " vol. 98, December 1970.

Sears, Mason. "Statement on Somaliland." U.S. Dept. of State Bull., vol. 31, 1954, p. 34.

Seton-Karr, H. "Discovery of Evidence of the Palaeolithic Stone Age in Somaliland, " J. Royal Anthropological Institute, vol. 25, 1896, pp. 271ff.

_____. "Further Discoveries of Ancient Stone Implements in Somaliland, " J. Royal Anthropological Institute, vol. 27, 1897, pp. 93-95.

_____. "Prehistoric Implements from Somaliland, " Man (London), vol. 106, 1909, pp. 182-183.

Silberman, Leo. "Somali Nomads, " International Social Science Journal, vol. 11, no. 4, 1959.

_____. "Change and Conflict in the Horn of Africa, " Foreign Affairs, vol. 37, no. 4, 1959.

_____. "The Mad Mullah: Hero of Somali Nationalism, "

History Today (London), vol. 10, no. 8, 1960.

_____ . "Why the Haud Was Ceded, " Cahiers d'Etudes Africaines, vol. 2, 1961, pp. 68-69.

Smirnov, S. R.   "State Formation in the Course of Liberation Wars, " Second International Congress of Africanists.   Papers presented by the USSR Delegation, Moscow, 1967.

Stafford, F. E.   "The ex-Italian Colonies, " International Affairs, vol. 25, January 1949.

Thomas, Benjamin E., and John B. Whittow.   "Climate and Economic Activity in the Somali Country, " Annals, Assoc. American Geographers, vol. 51, December 1961.

Thurston, Raymond.   "Détente in the Horn, " Africa Report, vol. 14, no. 2, 1969.

Touval, Saadia.   "The Somali Republic, " Current History (Philadelphia), March 1964.

_____ . "The Organization of African Unity and African Borders, " International Organization, vol. 21, 1967, pp. 111-113.

_____ . "The Sources of Status Quo and Irredentist Policies, " in the Scandinavian Institute of African Studies, African Boundary Problems (Uppsala), 1969.

Treakle, H. Charles.   "Somalia's Growth Depends on Its Farms, " Foreign Agriculture, vol. 6, no. 35, 1968.

Turton, E. R.   "The Impact of Mohammad Abdille Hassan in the East Africa Protectorate, " J. African History, vol. 10, no. 4, 1969.

_____ . "Somali Resistance to Colonial Rule and the Development of Somali Political Activity in Kenya, 1893-1960, " J. African History, vol. 13, no. 1, 1972.

_____ . "The Isaq Somali Diaspora and Poll-tax Agitation in Kenya, 1936-1941, " African Affairs (London), vol. 73, no. 292, 1974.

Vedovato, G. "La Somalia: Stato indipendente," Rivista di Studi Politici Internazionale (Florence), vol. 27, no. 5, 1960.

Vermont, M. R. "La corne de l'Afrique," Afrique Contemporaine, vol. 6, no. 30, 1967.

Vianney, John J. "La musica somala," Somalia d'Oggi, vol. 2, no. 3, 1957.

Wakefield, T. "Routes of Native Caravans from the Coast to the Interior of Eastern Africa," J. Royal Geographical Society, vol. 40, 1870, p. 322.

Ware, Gilbert. "Somalia: From Trust Territory to Nation: 1950-1960," Pylon, vol. 28, 1965, pp. 173-186.

Waterfield, Gordon. "Trouble in the Horn of Africa: The British Somali Case," International Affairs (London), vol. 32, January 1956.

Watt, W. Montgomery. "The Political Relevance of Islam in East Africa," International Affairs (London), January 1966.

Wright, A. C. A. "The Interaction of Various Systems of Law and Custom in British Somaliland and Their Relation with Social Life," J. East African Natural History Society (Nairobi), vol. 17, nos. 1-2, 1943.

Zdravkovic, R. "The Problems of Somalia," International Affairs (London), August 1960.

Zoehrer, L. G. A. "Study on the Nomads of Somalia," Arch. Volkerk, vol. 19, 1964-1965, pp. 129-165.

PUBLIC DOCUMENTS

I. Somali Republic/Somali Democratic Republic

National Assembly Records. Annually. 1960-1969. (English, Italian, and Arabic.)

Official Bulletin. 1960-1969. Annually.

The Constitution (in English) contained in The Development

of the Constitution of the Somali Republic, by N. A. Noor Muhammad, published by the Ministry of Grace and Justice, 1969.

Criminal Procedure Code, 1963.

Economics and Development:

First Five Year Plan: 1963-1967. 1963.

Progress of the First Five Year Plan: 1963-1967. June, 1965.

What Went Wrong with the Somali First Five Year Economic Plan: 1963-1967. Report of the Somali Institute of Public Administration Special Seminar.

Short Term Development Program: 1968-1970. 1968.

Development Program: 1971-1973. 1971.

Five Year Development Plan: 1974-1978. 1974.

National Bank Bulletin. The Balance of Payments of Somalia from 1964 to 1966. 1967.

_____. Semiannually. 1971-

Statistical Department. Statistical Abstract of Somalia. Annually. 1964-

_____. Quarterly Statistical Bulletin. 1965-

_____. Statistics of Foreign Commerce. Annually. 1967-

_____. Industrial Production. Annually. 1968-

_____. Index of Cost of Living and Household Expenditure Survey, 1966. 1967.

_____. Multipurpose Surveys of Berbera (1964); Boramo (1964); Burao (1964); Erigavo (1964); Gebileh (1964); Hargeisa (1964); Las Anod (1964); Las Koray (1964); Odweina (1964); Zeila (1964); Afgoy (1966); Baidoa (1968); Brava (1968); Merca (1968); Kismayu (1969).

Utilization of Manpower in the Public Service in Somalia (by
    S. B. L. Nigam and G. E. Eaton).   Presidency of
    the Council of Ministers, 1964.

The Manpower Situation in Somalia (by S. B. L. Nigam).
    Ministry of Health and Labor, 1965.

Study of the Performance of the Somali Customs Service,
    Somali Institute of Public Administration, 1967.

Development Bank.   1969.

Appraisal of Administrative Capability in Somalia: 1970-1972.
    Somali Institute of Public Administration, 1972.

Education and Language:

Committee on Higher Education in Somalia.   1968.

The Development of Broadcasting in Somalia.   1968.

Report on Educational Developments in 1967-1968.   1968.

Il problema della lingua somala.   1969.

The Writing of the Somali Language.   1974.

Foreign Affairs:

The Somali Peninsula: A New Light on Imperial Motives.
    1962.

Frontier Problem Planted by Britain between Kenya and the
    Somali Republic, 1963.

The Issue of the Northern Frontier District.   1963.

The Somali Republic and the Organization of African Unity.
    1964.

The Somali Peoples' Quest for Unity.   1965.

The Future of French Somaliland: The Somali Viewpoint.
    1966.

French Somaliland in True Perspective. 1966.

French Somaliland: A Classic Colonial Case. 1967.

The Portion of Somali Territory under Ethiopian Colonization. 1974.

Somalia and the Arab League. 1974.

General:

Perspectives on Somalia: Orientation Course for Foreign
Experts Working in Somalia. Somali Institute of Public Administration, 1967.

Beautiful Somalia. 1971.

Somalia Today: General Information. 1970.

My Country and My People: Selected Speeches of Maj. Gen.
Mohamed Siyad Barre, President, Supreme Revolutionary Council, 1969-1974. 1974.

New Era. Monthly. January 1973-   (English, Italian, Arabic.)

II.   Ex-Italian Somaliland under United Nations Trusteeship

Bollettino ufficiale dell'Amministrazione fiduciaria Italiana
della Somalia. Monthly from 1950 to June 1960.

Assemblea legislativa. Verbale di riunione. 1956-1960.

Comitato technico per studi e lavori preparatori per la Costituzione della Somalia. 1958-1959.

Consiglio territoriale. Bollettino mensile. 1951-1956.

Rapport du gouvernement italien à l'Assemblée générale des
Nations Unies sur l'administration de tutelle de la
Somalie. Rome: Ministry of Foreign Affairs. An-
nually. 1951-1959.

Piani di sviluppo economico della Somalia: 1954-1960.
Rome, 1954.

Le primi elezioni politiche in Somalia, 1956. Mogadishu,
      1957.

Economic Requirements of the Territory of Somalia on the
      Expiration of the Trusteeship Mandate.   Rome, 1958.

L'amministrazione fiduciari della Somalia. Rome: Ministry
      of Foreign Affairs, 1961.

III. Ex-British Somaliland and Northern Kenya

Somaliland Protectorate. London, HMSO. Annually until
      1950; Biannually, 1950-1960.

Somaliland Protectorate Gazette. Hargeisa. Monthly and
      weekly.

Protectorate Advisory Council. Debates. Hargeisa, 1946-
      1958.

Legislative Council. Debates. Hargeisa, 1958-1960.

Agreements and Exchanges of Letters between the Govern-
      ment of the United Kingdom of Great Britain and
      Northern Ireland and the Government of Somaliland in
      Connexion with the Attainment of Independence by So-
      maliland. London: HMSO, 1960.

British Somaliland Protectorate Development Plan. Hargeisa.
      1950.

Annual Trade Report of the Somaliland Protectorate. Ber-
      bera.

The Report of the Northern Frontier District Commission.
      London, December 1962.

IV. Council of Foreign Ministers of the Allied Powers

Four Power Commission of Investigation for the Former
      Italian Colonies. Vol. II. Report on Somaliland.
      London, 1948. (Mimeographed)

V. <u>United Nations and Related Specialized Agencies</u>

General Assembly resolution 289 (IV), Nov. 21, 1949 (Recommendation that Somalia become independent after a 10-year trusteeship under Italian administration).

Trusteeship Agreement, approved by G. A. Res. 442 (V), Dec. 2, 1950.

G. A. Res. 1418 (XIV), Dec. 5, 1959. (Recommendation that date of independence of the UN trust territory be advanced from December 1960 to July 1, 1960.)

Advisory Council for the Trust Territory of Somaliland under Italian Administration. Annual reports, 1950-51 to 1959-60.

Technical Assistance Mission to the Trust Territory of Somaliland under Italian Administration. 1952. (UN doc. ST/TAA/K Somaliland.)

Trusteeship Council Official Records. 20th Sess. Annexes, Agenda item 11. Reproduction of the report of the International Bank for Reconstruction and Development: <u>The Economy of the Trust Territory of Somaliland</u>: <u>Report of a Mission Organized at the Request of the Government of Italy.</u> January 1957, Washington, D.C.

Trusteeship Council. Visiting Mission to Trust Territories in East Africa. Report on Somaliland under Italian Administration together with Related Documents: T/1033, TCOR, 11th Sess., Suppl. No. 4 (1951); T/1200, TCOR, 16th Sess., Suppl. No. 2 (1954); T/1404, TCOR, 22nd Sess., Suppl. No. 2 (1957).

Development Programme. <u>Terms of Reference of Projects of International Assistance in the Somali Republic, 1967-1968.</u> 1967.

————. <u>Current Activities of the United Nations in Somalia</u> (by W. M. Harding). 1968.

Educational Scientific and Cultural Organization. <u>L'Instruction publique en Somalia.</u> Rapport of Technical Council. Geneva, 1953.

Food and Agricultural Organization. <u>Agricultural Development</u>

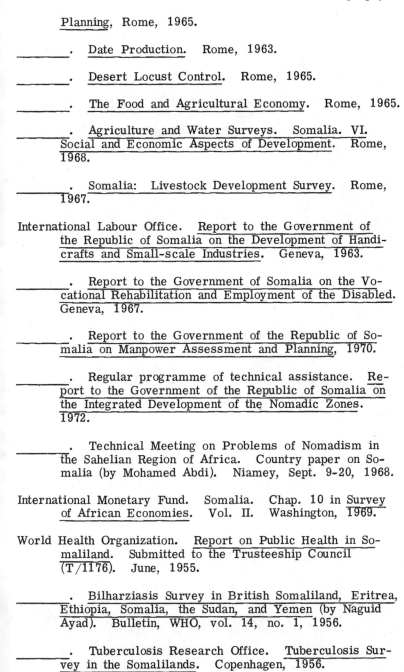

Planning, Rome, 1965.

_____ . Date Production. Rome, 1963.

_____ . Desert Locust Control. Rome, 1965.

_____ . The Food and Agricultural Economy. Rome, 1965.

_____ . Agriculture and Water Surveys. Somalia. VI.
Social and Economic Aspects of Development. Rome,
1968.

_____ . Somalia: Livestock Development Survey. Rome,
1967.

International Labour Office. Report to the Government of
the Republic of Somalia on the Development of Handicrafts and Small-scale Industries. Geneva, 1963.

_____ . Report to the Government of Somalia on the Vocational Rehabilitation and Employment of the Disabled.
Geneva, 1967.

_____ . Report to the Government of the Republic of Somalia on Manpower Assessment and Planning, 1970.

_____ . Regular programme of technical assistance. Report to the Government of the Republic of Somalia on
the Integrated Development of the Nomadic Zones.
1972.

_____ . Technical Meeting on Problems of Nomadism in
the Sahelian Region of Africa. Country paper on Somalia (by Mohamed Abdi). Niamey, Sept. 9-20, 1968.

International Monetary Fund. Somalia. Chap. 10 in Survey
of African Economies. Vol. II. Washington, 1969.

World Health Organization. Report on Public Health in Somaliland. Submitted to the Trusteeship Council
(T/1176). June, 1955.

_____ . Bilharziasis Survey in British Somaliland, Eritrea,
Ethiopia, Somalia, the Sudan, and Yemen (by Naguid
Ayad). Bulletin, WHO, vol. 14, no. 1, 1956.

_____ . Tuberculosis Research Office. Tuberculosis Survey in the Somalilands. Copenhagen, 1956.